Popular Film and Television Comedy

What is comedy? Can it easily be defined and described? Despite its immense and longstanding popularity, comedy has been relatively neglected in recent theoretical and historical work on film, television, and other popular media. This book seeks to redress the balance.

Steve Neale and Frank Krutnik take as their starting point the remarkable diversity of comedy's forms and modes – feature-length narratives, sketches and shorts, sit-com and variety, slap-stick and romance. Relating this diversity to the variety of comedy's basic conventions – from happy endings to the presence of gags and the involvement of humour and laughter – they seek both to explain the nature of these forms and conventions and to relate them to their institutional contexts. They propose that all forms and modes of the comic involve deviations from aesthetic and cultural conventions and norms, and, to demonstrate this, they discuss a wide range of programmes and films, from *Blackadder* to *Bringing Up Baby,* from *City Lights* to *Blind Date,* from the *Roadrunner* cartoons to *Bless This House* and *The Two Ronnies.* Comedies looked at in particular detail include: the classic slapstick films of Keaton, Lloyd, and Chaplin; Hollywood's 'screwball' comedies of the 1930s and 1940s; *Monty Python, Hancock,* and *Steptoe and Son.* The authors also relate their discussion to radio comedy.

This wide-ranging and comprehensive discussion will be of particular interest to students of cinema, television, the mass media, and popular culture.

Steve Neale and Frank Krutnik both lecture in Film Studies at the University of Kent at Canterbury.

POPULAR FICTIONS SERIES

Series editors:
Tony Bennett
Associate Professor
School of Humanities
Griffith University

Graham Martin
Professor of English
Literature
Open University

In the same series

Popular Fiction
Technology, ideology, production, reading
edited by Tony Bennett
Contributors to this text include: Dana Brand, Catherine
Belsey, John Ellis, Raymond Williams, Stephen Heath, Tania
Modleski, Annette Kuhn, and Jacqueline Rose.

Cover Stories
Narrative and ideology in the British spy thriller
by Michael Denning
Combining cultural history with narrative analysis, Michael
Denning tracks the spy thriller from John Buchan to Eric
Ambler, Ian Fleming, and John Le Careé, and shows how these
tales tell a history of our times, and attempt to resolve crises
and contradictions in ideologies of nation and empire, of class
and gender.

Lost Narratives
Popular fictions, politics and recent history
by Roger Bromley
Explores the ways in which certain popular cultural forms –
narrative fictions, autobiographical writings, television
productions – contribute to the social production of memory.

Forthcoming
John Caughie on **Television Drama**
Colin Mercer on **Popular Narratives**

POPULAR FICTIONS SERIES

Popular Film and Television Comedy

Steve Neale
and
Frank Krutnik

R

Routledge: LONDON AND NEW YORK

First published 1990
by Routledge
11 New Fetter Lane, London EC4P 4EE

Simultaneously published in the USA and Canada
by Routledge
a division of Routledge, Chapman and Hall, Inc.
29 West 35th Street, New York, NY 10001

Phototypeset by Input Typesetting Ltd, London
Printed in Great Britain by
Richard Clay Ltd, Bungay, Suffolk

British Library Cataloguing in Publication Data

Neale, Steve
    Popular film and television comedy. – (Popular fiction series)
    1. Cinema films. Comedies.   2. Television
    programmes comedies
    I. Title   II. Krutnik, Frank   III. Series
    791.43′09′0917

    ISBN 0–415–04691–2
          0–415–04692–0 pbk

Library of Congress Cataloging in Publication Data

Contents

Series editors' preface

There are many good reasons for studying popular fiction. The best, though, is that it matters. In the many and varied forms in which they are produced and circulated – by the cinema, broadcasting institutions, and the publishing industry – popular fictions saturate the rhythms of everyday life. In doing so, they help to define our sense of ourselves, shaping our desires, fantasies, imagined pasts, and projected futures. An understanding of such fictions – of how they are produced and circulated, organized and received – is thus central to an understanding of ourselves; of how those selves have been shaped and of how they might be changed.

This series is intended to contribute to such an understanding by providing a context in which different traditions and directions in the study of popular fiction might be brought into contact so as to interanimate one another. It will thus range across the institutions of cinema, broadcasting and publishing, seeking to illuminate their respective specificities, as well as the relations between them, with a view to identifying the ways in which popular film, television, and writing interact as parts of developed cultural technologies for the formation of subjectivities. Consideration of the generic properties of popular fictions will thus be situated within an analysis of their historical and institutional conditions of production and reception.

Similarly, the series will represent, and coordinate, a debate between the diverse political perspectives through which the study of popular fiction has been shaped and defined in recent years: feminist studies of the part popular fictions play in the production of gendered subjectivities and relations; Marxist perspectives on the relations between popular fictions and class formations; popular fiction as a site for the reproduction and contestation of subordinate racial and national identities. In encompassing contributions from these often sharply contrasting traditions of thought the series will explore the complex and intertwining web of political relations in which the production and reception of popular fictions are involved.

It should be clear, though, that in all of this our aim is not to transform popular fiction into something else – into literature, say, or art cinema. If the study of popular fiction matters it is because what is ultimately at stake in such analysis is the production of a better popular fiction as well as of better, politically more productive, ways of reading it.

Tony Bennett
Graham Martin

Acknowledgements

We would both like to thank: Tony Bennett and Graham Martin for initiating this book and for very helpful editorial assistance and advice; our colleagues at Kent, Ben Brewster, Elizabeth Cowie, and Michael Grant (Ben, in particular, provided us with important ideas and information on early cinema); the staffs of the libraries at Kent University and the British Film Institute; and Maureen Humphries and the AVA unit at Kent.

Frank Krutnik would like to express special additional thanks to the Krutnik family (Stanislaw, Sheila, Sasha, Olga, Conrad, Alex, and Vanda) for their appreciation of the value of the comic; Carl Tallintyre, for his video services; and W. DeMoncatte, Phil Kaplan, M. P. Beefster, and Steve House, for their enthusiasm and encouragement.

Steve Neale would like to express special additional thanks to Don Grieg (for *Cheers* mark 1), Bill New (for *Fawlty Towers*), Steve Pinhay (for *Richard Pryor Live In Concert*), Heather Temple (for *The Odd Couple*), Clare and Kim Slattery (for Woody Allen, the Marx brothers, and *Cheers* mark 2, and for putting up with the typing and the videos), and Kate ('Dear Friend') – for everything.

Introduction

This book is about comedy in the cinema and on television. As such it is particularly, and necessarily, diverse in its scope and concerns. Comedy is itself a varied phenomenon, both in the range of forms it encompasses – from the joke to the sit-com – and in the range of defining conventions it can involve: from the generation of laughter, to the presence of a happy ending, to the representation of everyday life. Moreover, discussion of these various forms and conventions necessitates drawing on quite distinct – and diverse – fields of study, from narrative theory to philosophy, psychology, and psychoanalysis.

Even within the more specific and restricted fields of cinema and television, the diversity of comic forms is quite considerable – from narrative features to sketches and shorts, from cartoons to stand-up performances. In addition, cinema and television are marked by their own particularities, and by their differences one from another. They each have their own histories, their own forms of institutional organization, their own aesthetic characteristics and modes of address, and their own range of genres. As a result, the forms of comedy in which they have tended to specialize have been different: the cinema has tended to concentrate on shorts of various kinds, and self-contained narrative features, television on variety and sit-com.

Rather than collapse these elements of diversity and difference together in pursuit of a single thesis (yet another 'theory of comedy'), or privilege some over others under the influence of a particular set of critical preferences, or particular historical concerns, our aim has been to identify them, and to discuss as many of them as we can. We have tried, therefore, to devote as much attention to the cinema as to television, to shorts and cartoons as to features and sit-coms, to variety forms as to narrative ones, and to happy endings as to gags, wisecracks, and jokes. In order to facilitate these aims, we have divided the book into three sections.

The first section is concerned with general aspects of comedy – basic definitions, generic criteria, and typical features, conventions, and forms. It is here that we discuss happy endings, characteristic narrative patterns, stereotypes, laughter, and the structure of gags, funny lines, and funny moments. We account for comedy's unique formal diversity by indicating the extent to which its two most fundamental conventions – a happy ending and the generation of laughter – can exist not only in combination with one another, but also independently, in separate formal contexts. While happy endings necessitate a narrative context, the forms that specifically generate laughter (gags, jokes, wisecracks, and the like) do not. On the one hand, narratives with happy endings do not always require the subsidiary presence of these forms to qualify generically as comedy (in which case narrative comedy can come close, at times, to melodrama, both in its structure and sphere of concerns, a point we explore, alongside other issues of narrative convention, in chapter 2). On the other, gags, jokes, and wisecracks can occupy narrative contexts as diverse as comic songs and stand-up solo performances. (We examine the extent to which these forms can be integrated into their narrative contexts, and the extent to which they resist such integration, making them equally suitable to contexts which lack a narrative basis, in chapter 3.)

This division in basic criteria, and in basic generic conventions, is embodied in the terminological distinction between 'the comic' and 'comedy'. While the former refers to the forms that make us laugh, the latter refers, on the one hand, specifically to narrative forms, and, on the other, to the field of comedy forms as a whole. The significance of this distinction provides the primary focus of chapter 1. The remaining chapters in this section are concerned with the topics of laughter and verisimilitude.

In discussing laughter, we draw extensively both upon psychoanalytic theory and upon Jerry Palmer's recent work on gags and jokes.[1] We examine Freud's categories of 'wit', 'humour', and 'the comic', and assess their applicability to various aspects of film and television comedy. And we suggest that laughter in comedy stems ultimately from a pleasurable losing and regaining of a position for the ego during the process of signification.

The concept of verisimilitude enables us to discuss the longstanding convention that comedy is – or should be – concerned with 'low' or 'inferior' characters, classes, and life. It also enables us to address the role of stereotypes in comedy, and the idea that comedy is inherently subversive. The concept of verisimilitude specifies adherence to socio-cultural norms as the condition under which the characters portrayed and the actions depicted in any instance of representation can be considered both probable and proper. It also specifies adherence to aesthetic norms and conventions as the condition under which any representation can be both generically recognizable and aesthetically appropriate. However, comedy necessarily trades upon the surprising, the improper, the unlikely, and the transgressive in order to make us laugh; it plays on deviations both from socio-cultural norms, and from the rules that govern other genres and aesthetic regimes. In the case of comedy, therefore, generic conventions demand both social and aesthetic indecorum. It is thus hardly surprising that comedy has so regularly involved the representation of what the ruling and 'respectable' elements in a society might regard as 'deviant' classes and their lives, since the attitudes, speech, and behaviour associated with such classes can be used to motivate the representation of all kinds of impropriety. It is hardly surprising, either, that the position of the stereotype in comedy is so often highly ambiguous, depending upon the extent to which it is used either as a norm to be transgressed or as the ready-made embodiment of the unusual, the eccentric, and the deviant. Thus, while it can be seen why comedy has so often occupied an exceptional position within specific aesthetic regimes and institutions, and why it has so often been regarded as potentially – or actually – subversive, it can also be seen that that potential is severely curtailed by the fact that 'subversion' and 'transgression' are institutionalized generic requirements. Comedy may sometimes go 'too far', but the latitude allowed it is generally – and necessarily – quite considerable.

The issues discussed in section 1 are basic and general. They are of relevance both to comedy on television and to comedy in the cinema. Examples have therefore been drawn both from films and from television programmes. In consequence, however, relatively little attention is paid to their aesthetic and institutional specificities, or to the particular nature of the historical circumstances in which they were first produced. Specificities and particularities of this kind are the major focus of the two remaining sections.

Section 2 is devoted to comedy in the cinema, and in particular to comedy in Hollywood. An initial sketch of the aesthetic and industrial regime prevalent in Hollywood's classical era is followed by a location of comedy within the regime as a whole, and within the range of its genres and forms. Comedy's various, generically appropriate, deviations from the norms of the classical Hollywood film are discussed, as is the extent to which a number of the formal spaces it occupied, like the short and the cartoon, were often considered secondary or marginal. In addition, there is some discussion of the theatrical sources of early silent comedy, and of the difficulties encountered by gag-based and slapstick forms in the move towards feature-length narrative films. Particular reference is made here to the work of Chaplin, Keaton, and Lloyd. The films they made in the 1920s, especially the features, are seen in this context as transitory hybrids produced in response to changing conditions of industrial practice and economic profitability: features were privileged over shorts at the points both of production and exhibition, and features earned more money. In view of these considerations it is suggested that these films are a specific and unstable combination of slapstick and narrative elements rather than the final flowering of an authentic slapstick tradition, which is how they have generally tended to be seen.

The other chapter in this part offers an extensive discussion of the tradition of romantic comedy in Hollywood, focusing especially on the so-called 'screwball' films of the 1930s and early 1940s, but including also some reference to the 1920s, 1950s, and 1980s. The coherence of this tradition is seen to lie in a combination of formal conventions and a consistent concern with heterosexual romance, on the one hand, and with prevailing social attitudes and institutional conditions of censorship on the other. The specificities of any one cycle within the tradition are seen to lie in the way relationships between the sexes are constructed, and in the way love, sexuality, marriage, and the family tend to be figured. Reference is made throughout to contemporary cycles and traditions of Hollywood melodrama. As a genre, melodrama tends to share a number of the concerns and conventions of romantic comedy. Its own particular treatment of the issues of romance is therefore used as a consistent point of comparison and contrast.

Section 3 is concerned with comedy on television. Television is itself identified as a form of variety entertainment, one which shifts the context of viewing from public spaces like theatres (and to some extent the cinema), to the private space of the home. Given television's propensity for self-contained, segmental structures, and for forms of direct address, it is hardly surprising that variety programmes, which exploit these propensities, and variety forms, like the sketch, the double-act and the stand-up solo performance, constitute one of the two major sites of comedy on TV. We examine some of these forms – and the variations worked upon them by particular performers – in some detail. We also discuss at length one of the programmes in the *Monty Python* series. Many of its formal characteristics and innovations, and many of the most striking elements of its humour, are seen to depend upon a particular intersection of these contexts at a particular point in time. The *Python* team were part of a generation of comic writers and performers, most of whom were educated at Oxford or Cambridge, and all of whom grew up at a time when theatrical variety was well past its heyday, and when the conventions and formats of broadcast television, along with the institution of television itself, were becoming firmly established. It is no accident, therefore, that many of the elements characteristic of the *Python* programmes function so as to highlight, mock, and rework either the moribund formats of variety or the newly-established conventions of broadcast TV.

The rest of section 3 is devoted to situation comedy, the other major kind of comedy to be found on television. We trace the origins of sit-com in newspaper cartoons, in cinema series, and, in particular, in radio. We identify and discuss the formal and ideological conventions of sit-com. These include a dependence on repetition and an avoidance of narrative closure; the way each episode in a sit-com tends to involve an encounter between a stable 'inside' (comprising regular characters in an established situation), and an enticing or intrusive 'outside' (which tends to threaten the former's stability); and the way sit-coms tend to structure the relationships between their regular characters along familial, or quasi-familial, lines. And we conclude with a discussion of *Steptoe and Son*. *Steptoe* is a sit-com which centrally depends upon a dislocation between ideological and structural convention. The 'inside' to which it returns each week is the inverse of respectable, familial normality. Normality lies, instead, on the outside.

As such it must remain an unattainable impossibility in order for this particular sit-com to continue. For *Steptoe* the world of conventional domestic sit-com is always, therefore, elsewhere.

Section 1

1
Definitions, genres, and forms

Perhaps the most striking thing about comedy is the immense variety and range of its forms. Historically, these forms have included narrative poems and plays, novels and short stories, *comedia erudita* and *commedia dell'arte*, slapstick and the comedy of manners, the jig, the droll, and the afterpiece, and pantomime, flyting, and farce.[1] Even within the more restricted fields of cinema and television, comedy is, and always has been, marked by its formal diversity. From the variety show to the short, from the sketch to the narrative feature, from cartoons to sit-coms and from double-acts to stand-up routines, the range of forms it can encompass is probably greater than that of any other genre.

Given that this is the case, any single definition of comedy, or any definition of comedy based on a single criterion, is bound to be limited in application, and therefore insufficient. This is true even of definitions based on the criterion of laughter. For while the generation of laughter seems to be the only element common to forms as different as sit-coms and stand-up routines, and to films and television programmes as diverse in structure and content as *The Good Life*, *Rowan and Martin's Laugh-in*, *The Philadelphia Story* (1940), *A Night at the Opera* (1935), *Cops* (1922), *Screwball Squirrel* (1944), and *The*

Rory Bremner Show, there are occasions when things are not quite so straightforward. For example, a number of comedies – like *Going my Way* (1944), or *It's a Wonderful Life* (1946), or *The Apartment* (1960) – are only intermittently funny, and seem designed as much to make us cry as to make us laugh. Equally, many films – *The Big Sleep* (1944), *El Dorado* (1967), and *Stakeout* (1987) among them – contain plenty of funny lines and funny moments, but are not conventionally categorized as comedy. These instances point to the fact that the generation of laughter is not always enough, in and of itself, to define a film – or a television programme – as a comedy. Other criteria can come into play.

This is borne out if we turn to the dictionary for a definition. The *Concise Oxford Dictionary*, for instance, begins its entry on comedy as follows:

> *comedy*, n. Stage-play of light, amusing and often satirical character, chiefly representing everyday life, & with happy ending (cf. TRAGEDY);

This entry usefully highlights a number of points, not only about the multiplicity of criteria comedy can involve, but also about the contexts in which those criteria have often been formulated and comedy traditionally defined.

The first thing to note is that laughter as such is not even explicitly mentioned – though 'amusing' is perhaps an obvious synonym for it. More important is the fact that criteria of content and structure are specified, in addition to criteria of affect and tone, and that equal emphasis is laid upon them. A comedy is not just 'light' and 'amusing', it is marked also by a 'happy ending' and by its concern with the representation of 'everyday life'. This has always, in the west at least, been considered an important aspect of comedy. From Aristotle on, and in contrast to tragedy (a contrast marked by the entry itself), comedy was for centuries the most appropriate genre for representing the lives, not of the ruling classes, of those with extensive power, but of the 'middle' and 'lower' orders of society, those whose power was limited and local, and whose manners, behaviour, and values were considered by their 'betters' to be either trivial, or vulgar, or both. Silent gag-films, the tradition of slapstick, the *Carry On* series, television performers like Arthur Haynes and Benny Hill, and sit-coms like *Steptoe and Son* and *Til Death Us Do Part* are all evidence of the continuing relevance of this particular convention. However, it is worth stressing that the dictionary marks this convention as neither universal nor definitive: comedy is only 'chiefly' concerned with the representation of everyday life. The comedy of manners, many of Shakespeare's comedies, (*As You Like It*, for instance, and *Twelfth Night*), films like *Forbidden Paradise* (1924) and *Holiday* (1938), and television programmes like *To the Manor Born* and *Yes, Prime Minister*, all of them centred on ruling or upper-class characters, or ruling or upper-class life in general, are evidence of that. (So too, of course, as a corollary, are films like *Looks and Smiles* (1981) or *Death of a Salesman* (1985), and programmes like *Edna, the Inebriate Woman*, which represent lower-class characters or everyday life within a generic context quite different from that provided by comedy.) It is worth pointing out, though, that in these instances it is very often the case that upper-class life is represented in its more 'private' (and therefore more everyday and 'trivial') aspects.

A happy ending, meanwhile, is also a crucial, but partial, convention. Usually, as in films like *Moonstruck* (1987), or in television programmes like *The Cosby Show*, it exists alongside, and in combination with, other key conventions, such as the consistent generation of laughter through the multiple use of gags, funny lines, and funny situations, and, in these instances at least, the representation of lower-class characters and everyday life respectively. (The characters in *Moonstruck* are mostly of Italian immigrant stock. The family in *The Cosby Show* is resolutely professional and middle-class, but the programme centres on what it marks as the ordinary misunderstandings, conflicts, and routines of everyday domestic existence.) However, in certain instances, like those cited above as examples of films marked only intermittently by funny moments, a happy ending can be the primary – occasionally, even, the only – convention involved. In these instances, comedy can come surprisingly close, in its concerns as well as in many of its structural features, to the genre we tend now to think of as melodrama. Thus, but for the intervention of God, a comic angel, and a happy ending, *It's a Wonderful Life*, centred as it is on a man who comes to feel so trapped by the pressures and circumstances of his life that he contemplates suicide, would be a melodrama about the frustrations of domesticity and small-town existence. But for a happy ending, *The Apartment*, concerned as it is with a man who falls in love with his boss's mistress, would be a melodrama about unrequited love.

The kinship between comedy and melodrama is evident not just in isolated, individual examples, but in a whole tradition of 'genteel' or 'sentimental' comedy exemplified by films like *State Fair* (1933), *Steamboat Round the Bend* (1935), and the various versions of *Little Miss Marker*. It is evident, too, in various strands of romantic comedy, particularly those in which a melodramatic crisis is resolved by means of a happy ending. Examples here include *Why Change Your Wife?* (1920), *The Shop Around the Corner* (1940), and *The Goodbye Girl* (1977). This generic kinship has its origins in the theory and practice of high bourgeois theatre in the late eighteenth and early nineteenth centuries. A new hybrid genre emerged at this time in a number of European countries. It tended to feature characters of a lower rank and status than those appropriate to tragedy, and the domestic settings, romance plots, and happy endings of comedy. But the characters and the situations they found themselves in were treated seriously, their tragic potential emphasized, in a way inappropriate to comedy hitherto. The genre acted in part as a vehicle and focus for the cult of sensibility and sensitive feeling that was an important component in the formation of a new, ascendant bourgeois culture. One of its major aims was to encourage audiences to empathize with its protagonists, to identify with their plights and dilemmas, to feel sorry for them, and to weep on their behalf – happy ending or not – rather than to laugh at them. Labels for the new genre tended to vary. It bore some resemblance to the older tradition of tragi-comedy. It was sometimes called, simply, *drame* or drama. We would now call it melodrama. In France it was called *comédie larmoyante*, tearful comedy.[2]

This term is indicative not only of the extent to which comedy can be found and classified on the basis of criteria pertaining to narrative characteristics in general, and a happy ending in particular, but also of the extent to which the criteria, and the forms to which they refer, can exist separately from, at times even in contradiction to, those based on the generation of laughter. The theatrical provenance of *comédie larmoyante*, and of the theory that sustained it, is indicative of the extent to which definitions and theories of comedy have their basis in the theatre, a point borne out by what is perhaps the most striking feature of the dictionary definition quoted above: its specification of comedy as a type of 'stage-play'.[3]

Many of these theatrically based theories, definitions, and forms have their roots in Aristotle's *Poetics*, and in the neoclassical theory and practice of the post-Renaissance period (which borrowed from Aristotle, and reworked and refined his ideas and formulations).[4] Neoclassical theory, based as it was in an aristocratic cultural milieu, and concerned as it was to emulate the principles laid down in the *Poetics*, tended to erect a distinction between high and low comedy, and to promote the importance of narrative considerations in general, and the criterion of a happy ending in particular. It tended, as a corollary, to downplay or to denigrate non-narrative forms of comedy, and the importance of the criterion of laughter.

Neoclassical concepts still have their uses, as we shall see in later chapters of this book. But the existence – and importance – of non-narrative forms of comedy, whether historical, like the jig, or contemporary, like the stand-up routine, reveal the limitations both of neoclassical theory, and of the criterion of a happy ending. For, on the one hand, a happy ending necessitates a preceding narrative context, a context lacking, by definition, in non-narrative forms. On the other hand, non-narrative forms clearly qualify as comedy. They do so, however, not on the basis of the way they end, nor on the basis of any other structural features. They do so because, and only because, they are designed to make us laugh. They qualify as comedy on the basis of the very criterion neoclassicism tended, along with non-narrative forms themselves, to undervalue.

This is a key point, not because of what it tells us about the limitations of neoclassical theory, but because of what it tells us about the heterogeneity of forms and conventions comedy can involve. It is indicative, in particular, of two sets of divisions which traverse the field of comedy as a whole – and which require very careful separation. One is the division between the criterion of a happy ending and the criterion of laughter. The other is the division between narrative and non-narrative forms. Although there tends, within neoclassical theory to be a coincidence between them, the two kinds of division are logically distinct. Moreover, they do not always, in practice, correspond with or accompany one another. For while the criterion of laughter can apply only to narrative forms, and while non-narrative forms only qualify as comedy because of the criterion of laughter, the symmetry between the different forms and the different criteria is incomplete: the criterion of laughter is not, like the criterion of a happy ending, restricted to one type of form; it can apply to narratives, as well as to non-narrative forms like double-acts and stand-up routines.

Comedy and the comic

These differences and divisions are to some extent marked in the common terminological distinction between 'comedy', on the one hand, and 'comic' on the other. If we consult the *Concise Oxford Dictionary* again, we find that the principle meaning of 'comic' is 'causing, or meant to cause laughter'. The term therefore embodies one, and only one, of comedy's major generic criteria. It can refer, though, to any of its forms. Indeed, its field of potential reference is extensive – so extensive that it stretches beyond the province of comedy, and beyond the province of aesthetics as a whole. A real event can be comic, as can a real person or an instance of everyday discourse. So, too, insofar as the term refers to effects as well as intentions, to 'causing' laughter as well as meaning to cause it, can a horror film, a war film, or a drama (for reasons we consider later).

'Comedy', on the other hand, is an aesthetic term. (Its use in reference to non-aesthetic events and situations tends always to be explicitly metaphorical, in a way that the use of the term 'comic' is not.) It has two distinct kinds of meaning. It can refer to the genre as a whole, in which case it either explicitly or implicitly includes each of its various criteria, each of its various forms, and each of its various works (as in 'there are many kinds of comedy on television', or, 'comedy is hard to define'). However, it can also refer to particular works (as in, '*Some Like it Hot* is a comedy', or, 'I saw a comedy on television the other day'). In these cases a much more restricted notion of comedy comes into play, as is evident from the fact that certain forms and programmes cannot be referred to by using the indefinite article – 'a'. Thus, *The Two Ronnies* may be comedy, but it is not 'a comedy'. Nor is a Harry Enfield monologue, or a Smith and Jones cross-talk routine. These examples are all, of course, instances of non-narrative comedy. As such, they are an indication of the fact that the use of the indefinite article tends to imply a definite – narrative – form, and definite – narrative – criteria.[5] (This fact incidentally helps to explain why comic avant-garde films like Buñuel and Dali's *Un Chien Andalou* (1928) and Michael Snow's *So Is This* (1982) are not usually referred to as comedies: they lack a conventional narrative structure, as well as a conventional institutional base.)

In considering comedy, then, we are confronted by a set

of terminological distinctions, a variety of forms, and a number of different generic criteria, all of which only correspond with one another to a limited degree. A happy ending and the generation of laughter, the two main criteria, are simply not of the same order. A happy ending implies an aesthetic context; the generation of laughter does not. A happy ending implies a narrative context; the generation of laughter does not. And so on. These differences mean that the conventions involved can either co-exist without impinging on one another, as they do in most instances of narrative comedy, or can remain entirely separate, as they do in non-narrative comedy on the one hand, and in the descendants of *comédie larmoyante* on the other.

In addition, the generation of laughter, as a convention in its own right, accounts to a considerable extent for comedy's formal diversity. For although the generation of laughter depends upon certain principles and certain devices, it does not require any particular type of structural context. The forms designed to give rise to laughter are local, specific, and, often, momentary: the funny line, the joke, the wisecrack, the gag, and so on. These local forms can, of course, exist on their own. Many of the earliest comic films, and many sketch-like interludes in TV variety shows, are simply gags. They can also function as the culminating point in restricted and simple narrative forms like the sketch. They can exist, within the context of a stand-up act or a cross-talk routine, as self-contained units, or as units linked loosely into sequential (rather than consequential) strings. And they can also be introduced into full-length narrative forms like the sit-com and the feature film. Inasmuch, then, as the generation of laughter is a defining generic convention, it can mark all kinds of forms as comedy.

It can also mark all kinds of genres as comedy. Thus there exist comedy westerns, like *Support Your Local Sheriff* (1968), comedy thrillers, like *North by Northwest* (1959) and *Charade* (1963), comedy detective films, like *The Thin Man* (1934), comedy horror films, like *The Cat and the Canary* (1939), and, of course, musical comedies like *Top Hat* (1935), *Carefree* (1939), and *Singin' in the Rain* (1952). Hybrids like these illustrate the extent to which the features of comedy can be combined with the features of nearly all the other major genres. Hybridization is not, of course, unique to comedy. There exist combinations of the western and the horror film (*Billy the Kid vs. Dracula* (1965)), the western and the musical (*Oklahoma* (1955) and *Seven Brides for Seven Brothers* (1954)), the musical and the horror film (*The Rocky Horror Picture Show* (1975)), and so on. Comedy, however, seems especially suited to hybridization, in large part because the local forms responsible for the deliberate generation of laughter can be inserted at some point into most other generic contexts without disturbing their conventions. There are limits, of course, but they are determined largely by considerations of tone, and most genres do not require any single tone to predominate throughout the duration of a narrative. (Some individual generic films do, but that is another matter.)

Parody and satire

Generic hybridization should be distinguished from parody. None of the examples given above involve more than momentary instances of generic parody. They are true generic combinations. There are, of course, many examples of generic parody, from *Blazing Saddles* (1974), a parody western, to *Carry on Cleo* (1964), a parody epic, to *East Lynne with Variations* (1919), a Ben Turpin comedy which parodies both one particular melodrama (*East Lynne*) and the conventions of melodrama in general. But parody is a special case. In contrast to generic hybrids, which combine generic conventions, parodies work by drawing upon such conventions in order to make us laugh. As Linda Hutcheon has argued, parody need not always be comic.[6] However, when it is, and when it occurs within the context of a comedy, laughter is consistently produced, not just by gags and funny lines (as may, of course, be the case with a hybrid), but by gags and funny lines which specifically use as their raw material the conventions of the genre involved. The result is not the combination of generic elements, but the subordination of the conventions of one genre to those of another. *Blazing Saddles* is not a comedy western, but a comedy, albeit one which relies upon a knowledge of the western to work.

We return to the topic of parody later in this book. In the meantime, though, it is worth stressing here that parody is a *mode* of comedy, not a form. Parody has its own techniques and methods, but no particular form or structure. The instances cited above happen all to be narrative feature films. But there exist countless examples of parody in sketch form (like Victoria Wood's 'This Week's Film' sketch, which parodies British stiff-upper-lip war movies), and parodies of documentary in quasi-documentary form (like Woody Allen's *Zelig* (1983) and *The Rutles*). Parody is, in fact, only one of a variety of modes available to comedy. Here, again there is a variety, a range, and probably the best-known, along with parody itself, are satire and slapstick.

Satire is often confused with parody, but the two are quite different. Where parody, as we have seen, draws on – and highlights – aesthetic conventions, satire draws on – and highlights – social ones. Like parody, but perhaps more insistently, satire works to mock and attack. It uses the norms within its province as a basis against which to measure deviations. Sometimes the deviations themselves are attacked, particularly if those who deviate are those who profess to adhere to these norms most strongly. Sometimes the norms are attacked – in the name of other, less prevalent, social values. Thus $M*A*S*H$ (both the film and the television series) uses the democratic and humanitarian values in whose name the war in Korea (and of course, by analogy, Vietnam) is being fought, as a set of self-professed norms against which to measure the undemocratic and inhumane practices both of the American military and governmental establishments, in particular, and of war itself, in general. And thus Chaplin's

Modern Times (1936) attacks what it marks as the predominant and inhuman values of modern industrial society in the name of disappearing values it associates especially with pre-industrial, rural life.

As Linda Hutcheon has pointed out, one of the reasons why parody and satire are sometimes confused is that parody can be used for satirical purposes. One of her examples is *Play It Again, Sam* (1972). *Play It Again, Sam* begins with the central protagonist, Alan Felix, watching the end of *Casablanca* in a cinema. He idolizes Rick, the character played in the film by Humphrey Bogart, and Bogart's image in general. Inspired by Bogart, who (played by a lookalike actor) in fact appears alongside him at various points to give him advice, he seduces his best friend's wife. The affair is short-lived, however, for in an almost exact reliving of *Casablanca*'s final scene, he tells her to return to her husband. According to Hutcheon, these references to *Casablanca* and to Bogart both demonstrate the distinction between parody and satire and also show how the two modes can interact:

> The actual physical incorporation of the earlier film in the opening sequence and the presence of the Rick/Bogart figure point to the parodic inversions. Yet the protagonist is not an antihero; he is a real hero, and his final sacrifice in the name of marriage and friendship is the modern analogue to Rick's more political and public act. What is parodied is Hollywood's aesthetic tradition of allowing only a certain kind of mythologizing in film; what is satirized is our need for such heroization.[7]

Like parody and satire, slapstick is a *mode* of comedy, a mode that can be found in forms as diverse as the sketch, the double-act, the short, and the feature film. As Don Wilmeth explains in his entry on slapstick in *The Language of American Popular Entertainment*, the word 'slapstick' referred originally to a type of prop used to mark violent comic action of the kind to be found especially in pantomime, circus, and 'low' forms of farce. Only later did it come to acquire the more general meaning it has today:

Slapstick: Literally, a comic weapon, originally called a batte, comprised of a pair of lath paddles or long, flat pieces of wood fastened at one end and used by comics (especially in the *commedia dell'arte* and English pantomime) to create a great deal of noise with minimum danger when another person is struck. According to one story, told by Buster Keaton, Harry Houdini used this word during the time of the Keaton-Houdini circus in which Keaton's father worked with the escape artist. Keaton points to the Evans and Hoey's rough-and-tumble act that played the Columbia wheel towards the end of the nineteenth century as the first knockabout act. It is obvious that the literal slapstick was translated into a term to describe physical or broad comedy.[8]

As we shall see the physical – and therefore visual – qualities of slapstick were of crucial importance in the early comedy of the silent era in the cinema. Keaton, of course, was one of its primary exponents a little later, in the 1920s. Rather than discuss slapstick any further at this point, however, a discussion of a film which uses slapstick – and refers to the production of slapstick films – will serve to draw together a number of the points made so far. More than just slapstick, though, the film involves other modes, like parody and satire, and a variety of the forms of comedy discussed earlier in this chapter. Indeed, in many ways the film is *about* these modes and forms, the interrelationships between them, the points at which they are either compatible or incompatible with one another, and, in particular, the values they each embody. It is a film which in other words constructs and works out its ideological and thematic concerns in terms of comedy's various modes and forms. The film in question is *Show People* directed by King Vidor for MGM in 1928.

The story, briefly, centres on a character called Peggy Pepper (Marion Davies), who arrives in Hollywood hoping to become a film star. She meets a young actor called Billy who gets her a job at Comet Studios, in the unit specializing in cheap, slapstick comedies, and for which he himself already works. Initially upset at the blow to her pride and ambition, she nevertheless soon becomes a success, and she and Billy are drawn together. Her success, however, leads her away from Billy when she lands a contract at the prestigious High Art studios. Renamed Patricia Pepoire, she stars there in a series of high-class period melodramas, and attracts the attentions of her smarmy co-star, who claims to be a French count. She now sees little of Billy. She looks down on the work he does, the work she herself has done, and resolves to marry her new co-star. Billy gatecrashes the wedding to persuade her not to go through with the marriage, reminding her of how much fun they used to have together making humble, slapstick films. He leaves, apparently unsuccessful. But Peggy realizes on reflection that Billy is right — 'We're fakes, clowns', she says to her would-be husband, and proceeds to cancel the wedding. Now dressed less showily, and behaving more humbly, Peggy is next seen on the set of another melodrama. But this one has a more contemporary, First World War setting, unlike the period films she had appeared in before, and centres on characters of a lower social class. (The film being shot is in fact highly reminiscent of Vidor's own drama, *The Big Parade*, initially released in 1925, three years before *Show People*, and it is clearly significant that the director on set is played by Vidor himself.) Billy, too, is acting in the film, not knowing that Peggy is also involved, and unaware that she has secured him his part. Shooting begins. Billy is playing the part of a soldier, and is required in the scene being filmed to kiss a French peasant girl goodbye as he leaves for the front. The girl, of course, turns out to be played by Peggy. Billy is at first surprised, confused, and hurt — but the kiss continues long after the cameras have stopped rolling.

Show People is a comedy. It is played mostly for laughs, and it has a happy ending. Its story and setting allow for parody (directed mostly at the costume dramas in which Peggy stars with 'the Count'), slapstick (much of it motivated by the filming in and around Comet Studios), and a degree of satire as well (much of it aimed at overwheening ambition and at social and artistic pretension, each of them mocked in the name of more 'democratic' norms and values). Its romance plot, meanwhile, allows the film to explore the relationship between comedy and melodrama.

The romance between Billy and Peggy is treated seriously and, especially when it deteriorates and Billy becomes unhappy, is the occasion for a number of tearful moments. Such moments, of course, are characteristic not only of romantic, narrative comedy (of *comédie larmoyante*), but of melodrama too. The final reconciliation, the happy ending, is also characteristic of both genres, and the film itself highlights this kinship by setting its own happy ending within the context of the filming of, precisely, a melodrama. An additional point of kinship is suggested here too. It is that the values implicit in the way contemporary melodrama bestows dignity on the lives of ordinary people, giving them both significance and status, are values it shares with the type of comedy *Show People* itself exemplifies. Narrative comedy and contemporary melodrama are both here contrasted with the costume dramas made at High Art studios. These films, with their period settings and their aristocratic protagonists, endorse, not ordinary dignity, but upper-class pride. In fostering Peggy's vanity, they constitute a major barrier to the fulfilment of the couple's romance. Indeed, they encourage an alternative 'romance', a romance based on shared pretence and snobbery, not on mutual love. Thus the obstacle that stands in the way of romance, the obstacle that has to be overcome in order for a generically appropriate ending to be produced, is specified in precise generic terms.

It is this obstacle which leads to what begins as one of the most melodramatic scenes in the film: the confrontation on the day of the wedding. Utterly disconsolate, utterly desperate, Billy pleads with Peggy not to go through with her marriage to the Count. He talks of the love he and Peggy once shared. He tells her she is making a mistake. He speaks of all the fun they once had when they first worked together at Comet. Suddenly, he picks up a soda siphon and proceeds to drench Peggy with its contents. This action is especially significant. It not only recalls (and re-enacts) Peggy's humble beginnings in slapstick, but it specifically recalls (and re-enacts) the very first piece of slapstick in which she was ever involved – a gag at her audition, at a time when, as here, she had high ambitions and artistic pretensions, and when, as here, she least suspected she would function merely as the butt of a crude piece of physical humour.

The gag with the soda siphon is, however, more than a piece of thematically significant repetition. It is an important instance of slapstick in its own right. It is funny. And it serves to shift the tone of the confrontation scene from one of high seriousness to one of low farce. In so doing, and in recalling at the same time the recurrent opposition between Comet's comedies and High Art's costume dramas, it is marked twice over as an alternative to the forms and the values of melodrama – both those associated with High Art films, and those embodied, up to this point, in the tone of the confrontation scene itself. However, the opposition between slapstick and melodrama is not a simple one, and is not in fact ultimately resolved in slapstick's favour. Slapstick is valued for the populist foundation of its aesthetic in a relentless aggression against narcissism, vanity, snobbery, and pride (the things which lead Peggy astray, and which the gags with the soda siphon help both to undermine and to keep in check). It is thus incompatible in all respects with the kind of melodrama made at High Art studios. However, slapstick shares these populist values not only with *Show People* itself but also with the type of melodrama we see being filmed at the end. And here it is not only the case that a distinction re-emerges between different kinds of melodrama. It is also the case that a distinction is established between different kinds of comedy, that narrative comedy and contemporary melodrama are finally aligned, and that they are aligned in such a way as to expose the limitations of slapstick.

As itself an instance of narrative comedy, *Show People*

requires a happy ending – the reconciliation of the couple, the fulfilment of their romance. What is significant is that the ending takes place on the set of a contemporary, populist melodrama, not at Comet on the set of a slapstick film. Slapstick is, in the last instance, inappropriate, inadequate, as a vehicle for either the romance or its fulfilment. It lacks a plot structure capable of sustaining a romance and of producing an ending of this kind (the only narrative structure of which we see any signs at Comet is that of the simple chase). And it lacks the necessary range of values and tone. If slapstick is incompatible with pride, it is also incompatible with dignity. It is thus incapable of taking seriously either the romance or its protagonists. Thus narrative comedy can accommodate slapstick and give it a value, but the reverse is not the case. In the end, narrative comedy is, if anything, more compatible with contemporary melodrama. Indeed, as the couple kiss on set under Vidor's direction, the two forms become indistinguishable. This is not just because they can share and endorse the same values, but also because they share the same kind of narrative structure, and, often, the same kind of ending. It is to the precise nature of that structure and its ending, along with other issues of narrative in comedy, that we now turn our attention.

2
Comedy and narrative

As we have seen, one of the major definitions of comedy – stories with happy endings – implies a narrative form. In this chapter we shall be concerned not only to explore the issues of happy endings and the ways they can figure in comedy but also to discuss issues of narrative structure in general. In addition we shall discuss conventions of narrative motivation in comedy, in particular the extent to which comedy can involve improbable forms of causality and logic. This will involve considering the mechanisms of comic suspense and surprise which, insofar as they concern the articulation of narrative events, and the distribution of positions of relative knowledge and ignorance, show how consideration of narrative must also involve considerations of modes of articulation and modes of address.

Narrative: story and structure

We begin by discussing one particular structural model of narrative comedy, a model first formulated by the fourth-century grammarian, Evanthius, which was extensively discussed during the Renaissance and the ensuing period of the predominance of neoclassical aesthetic ideas. We discuss this particular model here for three main reasons:

first because, as we shall see, it can still productively be used to analyse particular narrative comedies; secondly because, as an ideal to be aspired to, the model was one which dramatists writing comedies used as a guideline; and thirdly, and perhaps most importantly, because it locates happy endings within a broader structural context.

According to Evanthius, then, a narrative comedy consists, or should consist, of the following components or functions in the following order: a *protasis*, or exposition, an *epitasis*, or complication, and a *catastrophe*, or resolution.[1] (A *catastasis*, a new and further element of complication, was proposed during the Renaissance by Scaliger as a possible additional component in the structure, following the *epitasis*).[2] In order to illustrate the workings of this model, and to demonstrate its productive potential, we would like first to use its terms in an analysis of the structure of Blake Edwards' recent comedy, *Blind Date* (1987).

Blind Date can quite easily be divided into the four components proposed by the model, each in their requisite sequential order. First there is a *protasis*, which extends from the opening credit sequence through to the point at which Walter (Bruce Willis) gives Nadia (Kim Basinger) some champagne at a recording studio before going on to a business dinner being held in honour of Mr Yakomoto, a visiting Japanese businessman whom Walter's firm is trying hard to impress. During this part of the film we are introduced to the principal protagonists (usually through the device of having them introduced to one another). Walter meets Nadia and we learn that they like each other. They bump into David, Nadia's ex-boyfriend, who, we learn, is still obsessed with her and hence obsessively jealous of Walter. We learn of the importance of the dinner to Walter's career. And, crucially, we learn of Nadia's susceptibility to alcohol.

Next comes the *epitasis*, beginning with the dinner and extending to the point at which Walter is arrested and jailed. Thanks to Nadia's drunken behaviour, induced by Walter's champagne, the dinner is disrupted, Mr Yakomoto insulted, and Walter fired. The relationship between Nadia and Walter begins to sour. After a nightmare of an evening, Walter is arrested at a party for shooting at David (who has pestered the couple throughout).

Walter is bailed out by Nadia the following morning. But now comes the *catastasis*. Walter still faces a trial and a prison sentence. Despite a fierce argument with him, Nadia, feeling guilty and responsible, attempts to persuade David, who is an attorney, to defend Walter and secure him an acquittal. David agrees – but only on condition that Nadia marries him. She reluctantly promises to do so. David then defends Walter. Walter's case is dismissed and he is set free. However, Nadia now faces marriage to David.

The *catastrophe* comes at the last minute. According to neoclassical theory, the *catastrophe* consists, or should consist, of a definitive *peripeteia*, or reversal of fortune (from better to worse, in the case of tragedy, and as in the modern meaning of the word, but the other way round in the case of comedy). Here the reversal occurs on the day of the wedding. Walter has impregnated some chocolates with alcohol and had them delivered to Nadia that morning (having failed to get to her room the night before). Nadia has eaten all the chocolates bar one. With the wedding ceremony in progress, she drunkenly interrupts the minister to declare that she is not in love with her husband-to-be. Walter calls to her across the swimming pool nearby. They run towards one another and dive into the pool to embrace. A brief epilogue follows:[3] Walter and Nadia are together on a beach. In the foreground close to camera is an icebucket containing, not champagne, but coca cola.

Before moving on to discuss the general applicability of this model to comedy, and issues concerned with the extent to which, as a model, it is in fact generically specific, we would like to stress the extent to which it is capable of shedding light on individual films. In the case of *Blind Date*, for instance, one can see that there are two potential *catastrophes* corresponding to the two different instances of complication, that they echo and invert one another, and that the final dénouement is a resolution of the romance plot, to which other strands of the narrative are therefore, ultimately, subordinate. One instance of resolution follows Walter's arrest and imprisonment, and consists of his rescue by Nadia via the intervention and agency of David. The other instance consists of the rescue of Nadia from marriage to David by Walter, via the agency of the alcohol in the chocolates. The romance links and crosses both phases of complication and crisis. The first resolution is generically incomplete because it leaves the couple in a state, not of happy union, but of separation, a direct threat, in fact, to the dénouement required. Alcohol, meanwhile, emerges as an element with a number of important functions. It is responsible for the complications comprising the *epitasis*. It marks the inauguration of the romance (when Walter gives Nadia the champagne at the recording studios). And it is the agent enabling the resolution of the *catastasis*, indeed the resolution of the narrative as a whole. Its functions fulfilled (and the narrative over), it is finally displaced by the coca cola in the beach scene at the end.

This said, however, the model is so schematic and so general that it can be applied to genres like the western, the thriller, and the detective film, as well as to the genre of comedy. One important reason for this, as David Bordwell has pointed out, is that as far as the American cinema is concerned the convention of the happy ending was almost universal in Hollywood during its classical period (from 1918 to about 1960), and served as a mark, not just of comedy, but of nearly all other genres as well.[4] Moreover, whereas the usefulness of the model lies partly in the way it specifies the function of the happy ending in structural terms, in terms, that is to say, of an overall formal design (and not or not only in terms of content), echoes of the model and its ending can again be found in genres other than comedy itself. Kristin Thompson, for instance, cites a passage from one 1913 scenario guidebook whose structural ideals are very similar to those of the Renaissance and post-Renaissance theorists of comedy:

> Each scene [i.e., shot] should be associated with its pur-
> pose, which is to say that the outline of a play should
> comprehend: First 'cause' or beginning; secondly, develop-
> ment; third, crisis; fourth, climax or effect; fifth dénoue-
> ment or sequence.[5]

The point here, again, is that this advice is not generically restricted, that these structural ideals are not specific
to comedy. The guidebook is proffering advice on general
compositional principles. These principles extend beyond
issues of structure. They also concern motivation: the
extent to which each 'scene' should have a 'purpose', a
justification, and the forms that purpose can, or should,
ideally take. Here the specificity of comedy is much more
apparent, for comedy is often a generic exception to the
rules and regimes of motivation that tend to govern most
other Hollywood genres. The extent to which this is so is
particularly apparent in the way happy endings are handled in comedy. David Bordwell's discussion of happy
endings in Hollywood is again worth quoting here:

> Within the terms of Hollywood's own discourse, whether
> the happy ending succeeds depends on whether it is
> adequately motivated. The classical Hollywood cinema
> demands a narrative unity derived from cause and effect.
> The ending, as the final effect in the chain, should resolve
> the issues in some definite fashion. Screenplay manuals
> from 1915 to 1950 insist that the end of the narrative
> should arise from prior events. . . . The happy ending . . .
> is defensible if it conforms to canons of construction. When
> these canons are not followed, the happy ending becomes
> a problem. Screenplay manuals are dissatisfied with forced
> or tacked-on happy endings. The characters, writes Frances
> Marion, must be extricated in 'a *logical* and dramatic way
> that brings them happiness'. The unmotivated happy
> ending is a failure, resulting from lack of craft or the
> interference of other hands.[6]

Bordwell here has stressed one particular kind of motivation, causal motivation, and its prevalence within a range

of Hollywood genres. He goes on to point out, however, that in certain circumstances causal motivation can be abandoned for, or intermingled with, coincidence, Luck, Fortune, Fate or the intervention of the supernatural. These forms of motivation (or non-motivation) are in fact quite frequent. But they are restricted to certain kinds of films, of which comedy is one of the most important. Thus, while a happy ending is characteristic of a range of Hollywood genres, there is a difference between genres like the thriller, the detective film and the western, where happy endings are successfully appropriate only if motivated by a logic of cause and effect, and genres like the melodrama, the supernatural horror film, the musical, and comedy, where the arbitrary and the coincidental can appropriately play a much greater role.

Thus, to return to comedy specifically, the ending of a film like *After Hours* (1985), is generically appropriate, yet utterly dependent on coincidence: Paul Hackett (Griffin Dunne) is encased from head to foot in a plaster cast and trapped in the back of a van. There seems no way out, no way he can escape to return to the safety and normality of home and the routine of work. Yet suddenly, just as the van is driving past his office at the very hour that work is beginning, it is forced to swerve, the back doors are flung open, Paul falls into the road, and his plaster cast is smashed. Now, miraculously, he can walk into work on time, and take his place, somewhat stunned, at his usual, familiar desk.

Motivation is an issue that affects not just endings but also the events that precede them. Comedy does not seem to require a particular regime of motivation to bind together the events in its stories or the components in its structure. It does not even demand that every event narrated be in any way connected with either story or structure (a latitude crucial to the existence of many jokes and gags). If anything, it not only permits but encourages the abandonment of causal motivation and narrative integration for the sake of comic effect, providing a generically appropriate space for the exploration and use of non-causal forms of motivation and digressive narrative structures.

For these reasons, comedy is a prime site for all manner of unlikely actions – and all manner of unlikely forms of justification for their occurrence. A chemical substance called 'flubber' is used in *The Absent-Minded Professor* (1960) (and its sequel, *Son of Flubber* (1963)) to motivate impossible sporting and gymnastic feats. *Splash!* (1984) posits the existence of a mermaid to justify its plot and to motivate a number of its gags, *Mr Ed* a talking horse, *Francis* (1950) a talking mule, and *My Favorite Martian* an extra-terrestrial with magical powers.

The animated short is, of course, a particularly rich field for examples of the illogical, the impossible, and the absurd. Explicit motivation is usually lacking. Motivation here tends to be generically implicit: all kinds of improbable things simply happen in this kind of comedy. Thus when some kind of explicit and rational motivation *is* provided, it can clash with the ambience of the genre as a whole. Tex Avery's *Screwball Squirrel* deliberately constructs a clash of this kind to highlight the fundamentally artificial and arbitrary nature of *any* form of motivation whatsoever. The impossibly sudden appearance and reappearance throughout the film of the squirrel and the dog (after each, by turns, seems to have escaped from or eliminated the other) is something we come to accept as simply par for the generic course. Having done so, however, we are then asked to rethink our acceptance and its basis. For suddenly, at the end, a rational explanation is provided: both the dog and the squirrel have identical twins. In context, this explanation is itself improbable and absurd, an evident – and evidently arbitrary – imposition.

Coincidence, meanwhile, can play an important role not only in the ending of a comedy, but throughout the plot as a whole. *A Chump at Oxford* (1940), for instance, is pervaded by coincidence, from the opening scenes in which Laurel and Hardy are unwittingly responsible for catching a bank robber, to the scenes at Oxford University where, by being struck on the head by a window, Stan is transformed (or re-transformed) into an English lord (and, eventually, back again).

Whatever the form of motivation, probable or improbable, named or unnamed, motivation is always, in the final analysis, functional to the design of a narrative: George Bailey (James Stewart) is saved from suicide in *It's a Wonderful Life* not because God wills it, as the film itself proposes, but for the sake of a (generically appropriate) happy ending.[7] Narrative design is also at issue in suspense and surprise, two types of narrative strategy fundamental to all kinds of comedy. Here, though, design is a matter of articulation, of narrative considered as a process. Within that process the distribution of narrative knowledge and the spectator's place within that distribution are crucial.

Comic suspense and surprise

Renaissance and neoclassical theory sometimes specified that there should be two components to the *catastrophe* in a comedy's narrative structure. One, as we have seen already, was a *peripeteia*, or reversal of fortune. The other was *anagnorisis*, a transition from ignorance to knowledge, in accordance with Evanthius' original formula: 'The catastrophe is the reversal (conversio) of affairs preparatory to the cheerful outcome, and revealed to all by means of a discovery (cognitio).'[8] A *catastrophe* could therefore appropriately occasion either suspense or surprise, since suspense and surprise are the products of different ways of distributing relative narrative knowledge among and between the characters and the audience, on the one hand, and of the way events unfold, whether predictably or unpredictably, on the other.

Basically, suspense involves the giving of knowledge and surprise its withholding. In the case of suspense, the knowledge given is always partial, and, as George Duckworth has pointed out, different degrees and kinds of knowledge can lead to different forms of suspense:

Dramatic interest or suspense may be of two different types: (1) suspense of anticipation; the spectator knows what is to happen, but not when or how; he follows the progress of the action and awaits with ever-increasing hope or fear the coming of the expected event; (2) suspense of uncertainty; the spectator does not know the outcome and remains in a state of ignorance and curiosity about the later action. The two forms of suspense are not incompatible, for ignorance of details may go hand in hand with a heightened anticipation of the main events, or the immediate action may be foreshadowed and the ultimate result left in uncertainty.[9]

Duckworth is writing primarily here about the spectator's knowledge, and the spectator's involvement in suspense. Yet in the cases of both suspense and surprise the characters' knowledge is at stake as well. (As Evanthius' formulation indicates, *anagnorisis* is a matter of revealing knowledge 'to all'.) Thus, it is a complete surprise both to us, to Paul Hackett (and, presumably, when they find out, to the drivers of the van) when Paul is suddenly and coincidentally deposited outside his office at the end of *After Hours*. In *Trading Places* (1983), on the other hand, it is no surprise to us when Winthorp (Dan Aykroyd) and Billy Ray (Eddie Murphy) turn up at the end at the stock exchange. But it is to the Duke brothers. Suspense builds as we anticipate, along with Winthorp and Billy Ray, that they will make a fortune and ruin the Dukes, since we know they are in possession of secret information about anticipated crop yields, though we do not know precisely when and how the information will be used. The Dukes, on the other hand, once aware of their presence, themselves anticipate the worst, though they do not initially know that the information is in the hands of their antagonists. In *Gregory's Girl* (1980), there is a further variation. Both Gregory and the audience are surprised when Dorothy does not turn up for their date, and when Gregory is met by a series of the girls at his school, each of whom pass him on, as it were, to someone else. The girls though, of course, know exactly what is going on all the time. It is no surprise to them. Suspense both for Gregory and for us is generated around uncertainty as to who, if anyone, he will end up with (and why he is being passed on in this way). Finally, in *Some Like It Hot* (1959) it is no surprise to us or to Joe (Tony Curtis) when Gerry (Jack Lemmon) declares that he is a man. It *is* a surprise to Sugar (Marilyn Monroe), who has just recovered from an earlier double surprise – learning that 'Josephine', the 'woman' in the band for whom she sings, is really Joe, and that Joe is really the man she thought was a millionaire oil tycoon. And it *should* be a surprise to Osgood (Joe E. Brown), who wants to marry 'Geraldine' (really Gerry in disguise). But Osgood's reaction is itself surprising. He is neither shocked, nor hurt, nor even ruffled. To Gerry's final admission that they cannot be wed because he is a man, Osgood replies, simply, 'Nobody's perfect'.

In order to produce suspense or surprise, narrative knowledge has to be distributed among and between the characters and the spectator in certain patterns. These patterns form the basis of a number of longstanding and stereotypical plot structures in narrative comedy, and give rise to the recurrent appearance of certain types of character. Thus many comic suspense plots involve a character engaged in some kind of scheme or plan. This scheme or plan will necessitate either directly duping another character or group of characters (who may in turn be conventionally accorded the traits of gullibility), or at least keeping certain kinds of information secret (not least the existence of the plan itself), thus in turn necessitating that other characters remain in a state of ignorance. The spectator is generally made aware of the plan early on (if not, surprise may result from its revelation). But he or she may remain, like the schemer, unaware of the extent to which or the ways in which it may work out, and hence also of the extent to which or the ways in which other characters will discover its existence. If its existence *is* discovered, a counter-plan may be hatched. The initial schemer or schemers may then become dupes themselves.

Every Girl Should Be Married (1948), in which a single-minded salesgirl sets out to ensnare a prominent bachelor doctor into marriage, is marked by a plot of this kind. So, too, are *The Great McGinty* (1940), *The Lady Eve* (1940), and *Hail the Conquering Hero* (1943), all written and directed by Preston Sturges. (As Brian Henderson has pointed out, Sturges' narratives often build 'an excruciating tension' from the construction of discrepant intentions and discrepant layers of knowledge.)[10] In *The Lady Eve*, scheming, as so often in Sturges, takes the form of disguised identity. Jean Harrington (Barbara Stanwyck) is a con artist. She and her accomplices set out to swindle Hopsy Pike (Henry Fonda) of some of the vast sums of money he possesses as heir to a brewery. She attracts his attention and flirts with him. He falls for her and is later deprived of money in a game of cards. Jean, however, falls in love with her erstwhile dupe. She decides to tell Hopsy who she really is. Before she can do so, however, Hopsy finds out for himself. When she begins to tell him, he pretends he has known all along. The tables are turned. Jean is hurt and angry, accusing Hopsy of playing her for a sucker. She leaves him, vowing later to get her revenge. So a second strand of scheming is set in motion (of which the audience is as fully informed as it is of the first). Pretending to be 'Eve', a rich, charming, and sophisticated young woman, she arrives at a party in Hopsy's family home. The variation here on the conventional formula is that Jean pretends she is someone else without in any way changing her appearance. It is precisely on the basis of this lack of disguise that Hopsy is convinced she is not really Jean: if she were, she would indeed have attempted to disguise herself. Thus Hopsy is duped into falling in love and into marriage. On the wedding night, Jean gets her revenge. Hours are spent as she reels off a list of all the men with whom she has been romantically involved. Hopsy is shocked and disappointed. He now wants a divorce, to which Jean agrees – for a price. But Hopsy must meet her in New York to complete the divorce on her terms. He refuses, deciding to leave the country altogether. Having been informed by the narrative all along as to who is planning what, thus anticipating the outcome of events set up in advance, we are now in a state of ignorance as to what will happen next and as to how the plot will be resolved. We next see Hopsy on a liner. He bumps once more into Jean (as before, to him this is accidental, to us and to Jean it is the result of prior planning). Still thinking Jean and Eve are two different people, Hopsy is delighted. He cannot believe his luck. They head for Jean's cabin. Hopsy says they cannot go in together because he is married – Jean replies that it doesn't matter – she is too. They enter the cabin and close the door.

There is an interesting feature of this ending, one which has retrospective repercussions across the narrative as a whole. There is no scene at the end in which Hopsy finally learns the truth we and Jean have known all along. In accordance with the conventions of romance, we assume that the couple's feelings for one another are now genuine, that Jean will tell Hopsy what has been going on, and that he will forgive her and she him. But these remain the assumptions of romantic convention. And the conventions of romance have been firmly challenged and undermined elsewhere in the film, notably when Hopsy repeats verbatim to Eve an earlier declaration of love he had made to Jean. This repetition is comic, according both Jean and the spectator a privileged position of knowledge. However, it is interestingly not used by the film to judge Hopsy as cynical and insincere. It is clear he means what he says both times. If anything he is judged as naive, since in both instances he does not really know, as we do, to whom he is declaring his love. Thus the convention of the unique, spontaneous expression of true love, prevalent elsewhere in the Hollywood feature film as the mark of romantic authenticity, is doubly undermined.

The film's final shot, meanwhile, emphasizes the lack of a final revelation of the truth to all the characters – thus modifying the conventions of *anagnorisis*, and producing an equivocation about the status of knowledge in the film, a split between the knowledge inherent in convention, and the knowledge actually provided by the process of narration itself. In this final shot, Muggsy, Hopsy's body-guard-cum-valet, lets himself out of the cabin as the couple go in. He has been suspicious of Jean all along. It was Muggsy who discovered that she was a con artist, and it was Muggsy more than anyone who suspected that Eve might be Jean. He was never, however, quite sure. He is still not quite sure, even at the end. 'Positively the same dame', he mutters as he stands outside the cabin door. But positive is precisely what he is not. Can we, then, be so sure that our conventional expectations will be borne out? Can we be sure that Hopsy will learn the truth – especially given the way the film has firmly undermined the assumptions of romantic convention? Like Muggsy we are perhaps almost sure, but never certain. The certainties we normally derive from our knowledge of convention are thrown into question because they are never fully aligned with (hence confirmed by) those we derive from the knowledge actually given by the narrative.

Many other examples could be discussed here of films and television programmes which adopt the formulae of scheming and plotting, pretence and disguise, to produce comic suspense. Such examples would include *Fawlty Towers* (Basil always scheming to get things done on the cheap, or to improve the nature of the clientele at Fawlty Towers and to keep his plans hidden from Sybil), *Trouble in Paradise* (1932), *The Major and the Minor* (1942), *Kind Hearts and Coronets* (1949), *The Ladykillers* (1955), and *Teacher's Pet* (1958). In *Tootsie* (1982), *Victor/Victoria* (1982), and *Some Like It Hot*, pretence and disguise take the form of men masquerading as women (or vice versa), while *The Phil Silvers Show* each week centres plots of this kind around the schemes of Serjeant Bilko.

Bilko is, of course, only one in a longline of comic characters whose primary trait is scheming, from Walter Burns, to Wile Coyote, just as Phil Silvers is one in a long line of actors whose personae are similarly marked by this trait, from Groucho Marx, to Walter Matthau. In his television show, George Burns, also shares this trait to some extent, though, as a variant, his scheming abilities tend to be used more to extricate him and Gracie (and their neighbours) from the complicated consequences of *Gracie's* plans and actions. He can only intervene when he finds out what is going on, when he has access to the information necessary to understand what has been happening. Here, the show's famous device of the on-screen TV set, on which George can watch what is happening elsewhere in the narrative, is crucial, as Burns himself has explained in one of his books:

> All the situation comedy shows had one thing in common; somebody was always eavesdropping, either listening at a door, peeking through a keyhole, looking through a window or whatever, so they could find out what was going on and plan their counterattack. Week after week I was spying on Gracie and it was getting pretty monotonous. Well, one day my writers and I came up with a new idea we were all excited about. We decided we should put a television set in my den. That way, instead of eavesdropping I could just turn on the television set and tune in Gracie and see what nutty things she was up to.[11]

Another type of suspense plot is one in which misunderstanding and ignorance are the consequence not of deliberate planning, but of the disposition of events, a disposition of which the spectator, but none of the characters, is fully aware. Here, accident and coincidence replace scheming as the primary form of motivation for the evolution of the plot. Events are the result of chance rather than human manipulation, and mistakes are the consequence of innocence rather than of deliberate deception. *The Gold Rush* (1925) is a good example.

A final plot pattern used as the basis of comic suspense is one in which a number of characters are engaged in schemes whose interaction across the pattern of events tends to ensure that each of their goals either fails or needs to be modified. The characters each have a partial awareness of, and influence on, the course of events, but their awareness and influence are limited. The spectator knows their plans and the extent of their knowledge, and can perhaps anticipate, though never with full certainty, the evolution of events in full. Such is the case with films like *Open All Night* (1924), *The Great Race* (1965), and *It's a Mad, Mad, Mad, Mad World* (1963), in which a series of different characters all engage in a search for a stash of money, and in which one of the central narrative questions thus becomes: who will get to it first?

To an extent, of course, many of the films cited earlier as examples of plots involving schemes and plans could be cited here too. For however successful the outcome of a schemer's plans may eventually be in these films, they often have to be modified or reworked in the light of the course the events planned actually take (while in addition suspense is constructed from the possibility that these plans may be found out). Even Bilko occasionally finds himself in difficulties. We may foresee these difficulties, either because we are privy to information the schemer is not, or because our sense of the order of probability underlying events leads us to foresee that they will evolve in a certain way.

There are two important points here. The first is that suspense can arise on the basis of the system of motivation governing the chain of events – rather than from information explicitly given us by the narrative. The second is that, however much a comedy may involve or depend upon suspense, it will usually at some point also involve surprise. Of course, some of the characters in a suspense plot will always, at some point, be surprised – if they discover they have been duped, if their plans go awry, or whatever. But in these instances, their surprise will usually contrast with the spectator's knowledge and expectations, marking the discrepancies in awareness between the position of the spectator and the character or characters concerned. However, there may be moments in any comedy in which the spectator, too, is surprised. It is to this form of surprise that we now briefly turn.

However much we may expect the unexpected, we can never be sure of the form it will take or the point at which it will occur in the course of the narrative. As with suspense, surprise can be based on the course of events that constitute the plot and the system of motivation that appears to govern their occurrence, and the connections between them, in the process of narration (in particular the points at which and the ways in which knowledge and information are given to the viewer), or else on a combination of the two. Thus, given only the information accorded to us by the narrative (rather than that available to us through familiarity with the performer's persona), it comes as a surprise when, in *College* (1927), Ronald (Buster Keaton) is suddenly able to perform a whole series of almost superhuman athletic feats in coming to the rescue of the heroine. For, earlier on, we have witnessed only the extent to which he has been pathetically incapable of performing any single one of them. Similarly, it comes as a surprise when in *Blind Date* we learn that the judge at Walter's trial is David's father. It also comes as a surprise when, at the end of the episode of *Hancock's Half-Hour* entitled 'Lord Byron Lived Here', we discover that a handwritten draft of a famous poem really does exist beneath the wallpaper at Railway Cuttings. Sid (Sid James) had earlier forged some poetry on the walls hoping to attract tourists to make some money. We know it is forged because we see him do it (and because the poetry is so awful). The ruse fails because the Ministry says there is no evidence that Byron (who, Sid and Hancock claim, has written the poems) ever stayed in East Cheam, and because the souvenirs and antiques that Sid and Hancock try to sell to tourists are so unconvincing. The discovery of the real poem is thus a surprise because we have been given no prior knowledge that it is there, because all the internal narrative evidence (and the system of probability it involves) lead us to conclude that no major poet ever stayed at Railway Cuttings, and because, as a consequence of watching other episodes of *Hancock*, we have come to expect Hancock's schemes and delusions of grandeur to be ill-founded. The final irony, of course, is that Hancock does not recognize the poem ('The Charge of the Light Brigade'), and regards it as incompetent doggerel.

Comic surprise, then, stems from the occurrence of

unforeseen and unforeseeable events. The events in question have not been pre-signalled. Nor do they follow any pre-established system of logic. Surprise, indeed, can stem on occasion from the fact that an event bears no relationship whatsoever either to the plot or to causal motivation, as when, in *The Cocoanuts* (1929), Harpo Marx picks up a telephone and eats it, or when, in *Son of Paleface* (1952), Painless Potter (Bob Hope) finds himself in a car being chased across the Prairie. The car loses a wheel, but Potter keeps it upright by holding it up with a rope from the inside ('Hey, this is impossible!').

These examples are instances of gags, jokes, and local comic moments within larger, feature-length, narrative contexts. They are extreme instances of the extent to which such moments involve surprise, a confounding of expectations based on certain forms of logic, certain regimes of plausibility, certain systems of motivation and certain types of aesthetic convention. They are also, of course, moments at which laughter occurs.

3
Gags, jokes, wisecracks, and comic events

Although it is important to distinguish between gags, jokes, wisecracks, and comic events, it is also important to recognize that they share a number of basic characteristics.

They share, as we have already seen to some extent, a fundamental reliance on surprise. Hence they share certain ways and means of constructing and undermining expectation, certain means and modes of playing with logic, convention, and meaning, and certain principles of temporal articulation (notably the building of a structure around one or more culminating moment). Many gags, jokes, and wisecracks also share the property of being potentially, or actually, self-contained. Although in practice many gags, jokes, and wisecracks exist in the cinema or on television within some kind of narrative setting, relying on and using that setting to provide the fields of knowledge, convention, and meaning necessary for them to work, they can and do exist either autonomously (as single, one-off jokes, shorts, or skits) or in other, non-narrative contexts (like variety shows and revues). They all share, finally and fundamentally, the fact that they are instances and examples of the comic – forms whose principal function is to be funny and thus to occasion laughter.

Comic events

The first form we want to discuss here is a form we shall call loosely, 'the comic moment' or 'comic event'. It is a form characterized, unlike the others, by the extent to which it can exist only within a narrative context – as a consequence of the existence of characters and a plot. To give an example, towards the climax of Howard Hawks' *Monkey Business* (1952), Edwina Fulton (Ginger Rogers) is seen lying asleep on a bed. A male toddler wanders in from the house next door and climbs up beside her. She wakes and stretches, touching the baby lying unseen beside her as she does so. Puzzled, she turns to look at him. An expression of shocked realization slowly fills her face. 'Barnaby!', she exclaims.

There is nothing inherently funny either about the action and its articulation, or about the word Edwina utters. The scene neither takes the form of a self-contained visual gag nor builds to a one-line wisecrack or joke. The scene is only funny because of its narrative context. Barnaby is the name of Edwina's husband (played by Cary Grant). He has been trying to invent an elixir of youth. A substance with age-reversing properties has, in fact, been produced accidentally by a laboratory chimpanzee. Unknown to the characters in the film, it is contained in a dispenser of drinking water. Just prior to the scene with the baby, Edwina and Barnaby, having drunk the water, have been behaving like 10-year-olds. They have childishly quarrelled and parted, which is why Edwina is alone when the baby enters the room. In context then, having all this necessary information, we are in a position to recognize the name Edwina utters, the misunderstanding it marks, and the reason she makes the mistake. We know that she is wrong, that the baby is not her husband, because we are given this information in a previous sequence. Yet we also know the mistake is both possible and logical given the prior events in the film and the system of cause and effect that underlies them.

This particular comic event, and the comic moment

within it, is so integral to its context that it gives rise to further events of relevance to the plot. Edwina's mistaken concern leads her to take the baby to the laboratory in search of a cure instead of searching for her real husband – who is meanwhile busily engaged in persuading a gang of youngsters to help him scalp the man he childishly believes is his rival for Edwina's affections.

There are instances of comic events or comic moments less integral to the structure of a plot, either because their comic value depends upon a form of preparation itself inessential to the narrative (though the event itself may be crucial), or because, vice versa, the event is prepared for by the plot, but has no narrative consequences.

An example of the former would be the scene in the first episode of Alan Plater's *The Beiderbecke Affair* in which Trevor Chaplin (James Bolam), in response to a ring at the door, opens it to discover, in comic astonishment, 'a beautiful platinum blonde'. Trevor's meeting with this woman is a key moment in the story, leading both him and Mrs Swinburne (Barbara Flynn) into the mysterious sequence of events that constitute the bulk of the serial. The scene thus has many narrative consequences. It is primarily funny, however, because it follows directly an inessential narrative sequence in which Chaplin and Swinburne discuss (somewhat sardonically), Trevor's fantasy that one day 'a beautiful platinum blonde' will come to the door.

An example of the latter type would be the point in Jack Rosenthal's *The Bar Mitzvah Boy*, at which the boy's father, Victor, is driving the family in his taxi to the synagogue for the bar mitzvah ceremony itself. A man in the street hails the cab – and Victor automatically breaks to stop and pick up a fare ('force of habit'). The event is funny only because of its narrative context. Where usually it would be appropriate for Victor to pick up a fare in his cab, it is highly inappropriate on this occasion. The drive to the synagogue is a narrative event. But its comic moment is totally inconsequential: the next scene takes place in the synagogue itself – and the family have all arrived safely.

One particular mode of comic event is verbal. There are, of course, various types of verbal humour, and various kinds of funny lines and funny remarks. The form we are thinking of here is one which is rarely discussed. It is distinguishable from jokes and wisecracks insofar as it is integral to, and dependent entirely upon, the existence of a narrative context to make it funny. Where jokes and wisecracks are self-contained, and inherently humorous, the type we are thinking of is not. The difference can perhaps best be illustrated by considering two different lines of dialogue uttered by the same character at different points in the same film, Billy Wilder's *The Fortune Cookie*.

In *The Fortune Cookie* (1966), Harry Hinckle (Jack Lemmon) has an accident covering a football match as a television cameraman. The accident is not particularly serious. But under the influence of his scheming attorney and brother-in-law, Willie Ginritch (Walter Matthau), Harry pretends that his back may be permanently injured in order to claim insurance. The insurance company, suspicious of the claim, decides to hire a detective agency to bug Harry's apartment. Willie discovers that the apartment is under surveillance. Any reference to Harry's real condition, or to the existence of the scheme, is therefore forbidden. At this point, Harry's ex-wife, Sandy, returns, unaware of the scheme, and unaware that the apartment is bugged. She asks Harry about his injury. Keeping up the pretence, he tells her that he is suffering from a 'compressed vertebra'. 'Too bad it's a phony', she says. At this point, both Harry and we, the audience, think she is referring to his injury, and thus that she has given the game away. We laugh precisely, and only, for this reason – because within minutes of her arrival Sandy has uttered the very type of remark Willie and Harry have been at scrupulous pains to avoid (though it turns out she is referring to something else entirely). We do not laugh because the remark is in any sense inherently funny. (In this sense Sandy's 'Too bad it's a phony' is rather like Edwina's

'Barnaby!'). By contrast, later on in the film, Sandy returns to Harry's apartment after seeing Willie about 'annulling' her divorce. Harry asks if such a thing is possible. Willie will find a way, she replies, 'He can find a loophole in the Ten Commandments.' This line, like the previous one, arises in a specific narrative context. It refers to a character who exists within that context, and with whose traits it has made us familiar. However, it is neither contained nor determined by this context, nor dependent upon it to raise a laugh. It could be said by any of the characters at any point in the film. Indeed, it could be inserted into virtually any film and still be funny, provided a referent with Willie's traits has been introduced in one way or another.

Jokes and wisecracks

Sandy's remark about Willie is probably best characterized as a wisecrack, a term defined in Harold Wentworth and Stuart Flexner's *Dictionary of American Slang*, as 'A bright, smart, witty or sarcastic remark'.[1] It could also just be called a joke, an intentionally funny comment, line, anecdote, or story. The terminology is less important at this point than a set of important distinctions. One concerns the contrast between self-contained forms and forms, like Sandy's first line, which are bound by their context. The other concerns a contrast between lines and remarks which the character or performer who speaks them intend to be funny, which exist therefore, in part at least, as a display of the speaker's wit, and lines and remarks which are unintentionally funny, which result from stupidity, ignorance, or misunderstanding.

One of the reasons why many jokes, wisecracks, and funny lines are rarely integral to a plot is that they all require formal closure, often in the form of a punchline. Because of this degree of closure, they are structurally unsuited to narration. They can, and often do, involve narrative preconditions. But it is difficult to use them as a springboard for narrative development. They are instead much more suited to constructing or marking a pause or digression in the ongoing flow of a story. Such is certainly the case with Sandy's remark about Willie.

Precisely for this reason, special motivation is often provided for wisecracks and jokes by having them spoken by characters particularly given to verbal wit and repartee: Trapper and Hawkeye in *M*A*S*H*, Buddy and Sally in *The Dick Van Dyke Show*, Carla in *Cheers*, and so on. In many films and television programmes, of course, the context is one in which a performer simply stands up and delivers a string of jokes (*Richard Pryor Live in Concert* (1979), for instance, or stand-up spots in variety shows). Here, a narrative context is often absent altogether. What counts is not the persona of a fictional character, but the persona of a professional performer.

It is worth noting in this context that an important site for joking and wit is provided by the songs in musicals, revues, and variety shows. Variety-style comics like Arthur Askey, Eddie Cantor, and Victoria Wood are well-known for their comic songs, while lyricists and song-writers like Ira Gershwin, Dorothy Fields, Cole Porter, and Howard Dietz are famous for the wit of their lyrics.[2] Here, the formally self-sufficient and enclosed nature of the wisecrack or joke is underlined and reinforced by the formally self-sufficient and enclosed nature of a song (both a distinct entity in itself, and an entity marked internally by the potential closure of a line, rhyme, verse, or refrain). Hence Dietz' lines about *Hamlet* in the song 'That's Entertainment' from *The Band Wagon* (1953):

> 'Some great Shakespearian scene
> Where a ghost and a prince meet
> And everyone ends in mincemeat'

Witty songs in particular, perhaps – but jokes and wisecracks in general – imply a *control* of language: language manipulated deliberately for the purposes of humour. And insofar as language is the site of understanding, communication, logical thought, and the demonstration of an awareness of decorum and the rules of social intercourse, its intentionally witty use implies all kinds of other abilities. But linguistic humour can result from an unwitting *misuse* of language, or rather a comic misuse of language marked as unintentional in some way (as the product of linguistic or cultural ignorance, some kind of physical impediment – deafness, for instance, or a stammer – or an uncontrollable psychological propensity for mixing metaphors, perhaps, or for mispronunciation).

Examples can be contained within the space of a single utterance (Jimmy Durante in *What! No Beer?* (1933) talks of millions of parched lips, 'straining at the leach'), or they can take dialogue form, as in the following exchange from *The Bob Newhart Show*:

> 'I think I'm overcoming my agoraphobia.'
> 'I didn't know you had a fear of open spaces.'
> 'I thought it was a fear of agricultural products. Anyway, wheat doesn't scare me anymore.'

Here, the requisite lack of understanding is specific and linguistic. It centres on the meaning of one particular word. A more general cultural ignorance is implied, often, in *Hancock's Half-Hour*:

> 'Does Magna Carta mean nothing to you?
> Did she die in vain?'

Generalized as a character trait, linguistic and cultural ignorance can form the basis of a consistent persona, as in the case of Inspector Clouseau (Peter Sellers) in the *Pink Panther* films. A persona like Clouseau's can be used to motivate all kinds of unintentionally funny lines.

On a more general level, misunderstanding and ignorance mark a disturbance in the communication process. Such a disturbance is very often the basis of verbal humour in films, programmes, and sketches. The following extract is from a sketch by Alan Bennett. He is trying to dictate a telegram over the phone. Comic disturbance is here amplified by the fact that the telephone limits the means by which meaning can be verified and checked:

> '. . . the telegram is going to a Miss Tessa Prosser, that's Tessa Prosser, 130 Chalcott Square, S.W.19.

Right. Right. Er – no, "Right, right" is *not* the telegram – what I will do, I will say "Here is the telegram", and then anything I say subsequent to that will be the telegram.

Here is the telegram. Are you there? No, no, no . . . that's not it, no – the telegram is "Bless – your – little" . . . "Bless your little" . . . "Bottibooes".'

Comedy, of course, stems not just from the use or misuse of language. It stems also from physical action. And it stems on occasion from an interaction between the two, as when in *Horsefeathers* (1932), Groucho declares a document illegal – 'There's no seal on it. Where's the seal?' and Harpo pulls a seal, complete with flippers, from out of the drawer. Groucho's line here sets up a semantic field, a frame of meaning and reference, to which Harpo's action is a logical, but unexpected (and incongruous) response. The comedy takes the specific form of what Leonard Maltin has called the 'visual pun'.[3]

The visual pun is only one of the forms taken by the comic interplay between language and action. In *The Navigator* (1924), rich, spoilt, and hapless Rollo Treadway (Buster Keaton) journeys from one side of the street to the other in a chauffeur-driven limousine to propose marriage to the woman living opposite. She turns him down. He leaves her house, and on reaching the pavement declares to his chauffeur that 'I think a long walk would do me good'. He strides off – but only back across the road to his mansion. The dialogue here sets up an expectation of an action which the action that actually follows undermines. The same kind of device can be found in a stand-up performance. In one of his television shows, Tommy Cooper blows up a paper bag and declares 'Now I shall produce a white dove'. He bangs the bag. A couple of feathers drift to the ground. Sometimes, instead of preceding the action, a line of dialogue will follow. In these cases, verbal comments often constitute a character's incongruous, ingenious, or insufficient attempts to restore a control and dignity lost during the course of the action itself. Thus when in *The Return of the Pink Panther* (1975), Inspector Clouseau falls over on a heavily-waxed floor, and when

he is asked if he is alright, he replies, 'Of
alright, I'm examining the wax'.

Gags

From discussing instances in which action and dialogue
are combined, we can now turn to the field of visual,
physical action, the field of the gag. There is a good deal
of imprecision and variation in the use and history of this
term. Different writers on comedy use it in a number of
different ways to talk about a number of different things.
It can in fact be used quite legitimately to refer to verbal
jokes and humour. Comics like Bob Hope often refer to
their jokes as gags, and Don Wilmeth claims that in vaudeville a gag was 'a joke or a pun'.[4] We shall here restrict
the meaning of the term to 'non-linguistic comic action',
in order to give it some precision and consistency. It should
be clear, though, that our decision to do so is rather an
arbitrary one.

In its original meaning a gag was 'an improvised interpolation'. Only later did it come to mean 'a pre-prepared
piece of action', the meaning it still tends to have today.
This distinction corresponds to some extent with one distinction made by Jean-Pierre Coursodon in his discussion
of the features of a gag.[5] For Coursodon, there is a fundamental difference between gags, on the one hand, and
what he calls 'comic effects', on the other.[6] An example
of the former would be the sequence in *Cops* (1922) in
which an anarchist at a parade tosses a bomb from the
roof of a building. The bomb lands next to the character
played by Buster Keaton, who is driving past at the time
in his cart. Keaton picks up the bomb, then lights his
cigarette with the burning fuse and tosses it into a group
of marching policemen. The sequence contains three
linked but separate stages:

> 1. a laying out of its basic components (an anarchist pre-
> pares to throw a bomb just as Keaton and his cart appear in
> the parade); 2. development of the situation in a particular
> direction (the bomb lands next to Keaton); 3. reversal and

'punchline' (Keaton lights the cigarette and tosses the bomb away like a match).[7]

An example of a comic effect would be a 'pratfall' (like Clouseau slipping over on the waxed floor), or a double-take, slow-burn, or some other kind of comic expression. For Coursodon, these effects lack the structured complexity of the true gag. They are single one-off comic occurrences.

We would agree that there is a difference between Keaton's comic sequence and a pratfall or double-take. However, because the term 'gag' can apply equally to any kind of visual comic effect, it can legitimately be used to refer to all of these forms. Coursodon's distinction can perhaps best be marked by calling comic effects simply 'gags', and sequences involving complex elaboration 'developed' or 'articulated' gags.

More importantly, perhaps, the term 'gag' is appropriate to all these forms, because they all share a property marked in its meaning as interpolation: they each constitute digressions or interruptions in the progress of a plot or a piece of purposive narrative action. They hence each tend also to involve a degree of surprise.

In the case of single or simple gags, the interruption is momentary. J. B. Ball (Edward Arnold) is on his way to breakfast in *Easy Living* (1937). He sees a black cat, trips, and falls down the stairs, then picks himself up and resumes his progress to the breakfast table. In the case of articulated gags, the interruption is sustained, and the internal structure of the gag is marked by variation, digression, and a number of instances of comic surprise. In *Busy Bodies* (1933), Stan Laurel and Oliver Hardy are supposed to be working as carpenters in a factory. Stan has pushed Ollie over (first interruption). Stan decides to engage in a purposive action – he begins to help Ollie to his feet. But a workman asks Stan to put his jacket in the closet (second interruption). Charles Barr describes what happens next:

Stan opens the closet and the door hits Ollie in the face.

Ollie . . . bangs the door shut: the impact loosens a piece
of metal that's hanging on the wall: it crashes down on
Ollie's head.

Stan, returning, has to open the door again – it hits Ollie
in the face.[8]

This gag is an instance of what Barr calls a 'triple gag',
a suite of actions linked by a logic of variation: 'gag,
reversal, new reversal'.[9] Although by no means all articulated gags are triply structured (in *One A.M.* (1915)
Chaplin makes eleven consecutive attempts to pull his
Murphy bed down from the wall and get into it safely),
they all work by producing surprising variations on a
single action or a series of linked actions. The elements of
an event or situation are established. Then the action takes
an unexpected turn. Expectation may derive from our
general cultural norm as to the course an action should
typically take or as to the type of action appropriate in a
particular kind of situation. It may derive from prior narrative development. Or it may derive from a logic of repetition (a similar action has been performed in a particular
way earlier in a sketch or story). This action may then
itself become the object of unexpected variation. In this
way, what would otherwise be a single, one-off gag can
become part of a series, an integral component in an
articulated gag. (As when Ollie's being struck on the head
in *Busy Bodies* comes through repetition and variation to
form the first phase of an extended triple gag). Such a
development need not be restricted to a single narrative
occasion. It can be interspersed as a running gag across
the wider span of a story. An example would be the
three separate occasions Groucho and Harpo try to set off
together on a motorbike and sidecar in *Duck Soup* (1933).
The first time Groucho is in the sidecar and Harpo on the
bike. Harpo starts the engine and rides off leaving Groucho behind. The second occasion is almost an exact repetition of the first. The third time, Harpo gets into the
sidecar and Groucho onto the bike. But when Groucho
revs up the engine, it is Harpo who roars off into the
distance.

A number of further points need to be made about narrative, digression, and surprise. First, few gags are as gratuitous as the gag in *Who Killed Who?* (1943) in which an animated detective in pursuit of some villains stops and opens a door marked 'Do not open until Christmas' – and finds himself face-to-face with Santa Claus (a Santa Claus so irate he promptly slams the door shut in the detective's face). Even here, though, pure surprise is still a function of narratively-based expectation. Secondly, certain gags can help to dispel digressive actions rather than build or prolong them, to switch us back in the direction of a plot rather than constitute a detour in its path (to interrupt an interruption). In the films of Keaton and Lloyd, gags located at a point near the dénouement frequently serve through a mixture of luck, ingenuity, and determination to complete a task central to the plot. The surprise factor here lies in the sudden and unforeseen manner in which an obstacle to narrative progress is overcome (as when at the end of *Safety Last* (1923) Lloyd's foot is caught in a cable on top of the high building he is climbing. He is knocked off his feet, but swings through mid-air to land safely at the feet of the heroine up on the roof). There has of course to be an obstacle established in the first place in order for any gag to function in this way. Thirdly, whether gags are digressive or not, they share with true narratives all the properties of narration, all the devices necessary for the sequential presentation of events and their components in space and in time. Consider, for instance, Brad Ashton's description of a developed gag in one of Dave Allen's television shows, and the selective sequential articulation the description implies:

> Four boys (or men dressed as boys) are standing round the pond. Each has a string in his hand, the other end of which is attached to their toy yachts in the water.
>
> One by one we see the yachts keel over and sink. Each time we cut to a close-up of its astonished owner to show his angry reaction.
>
> After the fourth yacht has sunk, the camera pulls back so

that we see for the first time a man in German naval uniform. He is holding a string too. He pulls his string in and we clearly see that attached to it is a toy submarine. He picks up the submarine and, with a smug expression on his face, goose-steps off.[10]

The articulation of the event here is also an articulation of relative knowledge. The same kinds of structures of knowledge are involved in gags as in plots. This means that gags can involve suspense as well as surprise: 'You can do wonders in a scene by letting the audience in on a secret the character doesn't know, like you show them an open manhole, and then you're Charlie Chaplin walking towards it, innocently swinging his stick'.[11] There can thus be a set of correlations between characters occupying positions of knowledge in a plot and in a gag, and characters who in both cases occupy a position of ignorance. Such correlations imply traits typical of characters in comedies: they can be intelligent, smart, and ingenious (like Chaplin and Keaton) or naive, stupid, or ignorant (like Laurel and Hardy). In sound films there can then be a further correlation between such traits and verbal wit and facility on the one hand (Groucho Marx and Bugs Bunny) and verbal ignorance and failure on the other (Inspector Clouseau).

Suspense implies a degree of predictability. It may hence seem to contradict the proposition that gags depend on surprise – particularly because, if anything, there is a tendency in suspense gags for the predictable to become the inevitable. If there is a banana skin around, *someone* will fall on it. Two points need to be made here. One is that knowledge in suspense is never total, even in this context. There is always room for surprise in the way the anticipated event takes place: in who will fall on the banana skin, and in where, when, and how it actually happens. (Thus in *Blind Date* we see Walter drunk at a party. He staggers outside near a swimming pool. It isn't he who falls in, though, but one of the waiters, when Walter pulls away the rug on which he is standing.)

The second point is that surprise can reside not at the

level of the event itself, but at the level of the way the event is narrated. In *From Soup to Nuts* (1928), Laurel and Hardy are waiters at a dinner party. Ollie has slipped on a banana skin and fallen headlong into a cream gateau. He returns to the kitchen to fetch another. The banana skin, meanwhile, now lies just outside the kitchen door. We fully expect him to slip and fall into the second gateau. And sure enough, he does. But variation – and surprise – are provided. As Ollie is about to fall we cut to a shot of Stan's face first anticipating, then confirming, then reacting to what happens off-screen. There is an unexpected digression at the level of narration, in the form of an interpolated close-up. We expect Ollie's pratfall. Our expectations are confirmed. But we also expect to *see* Ollie's pratfall, and instead we are shown Stan's face.

If the process of narration can be crucial to the production of comic surprise, it can be crucial also to the timing of a gag. Gags, like jokes, are organized around a nodal point (a point in jokes Walter Nash has called a 'locus', and in gags Sylvain du Pasquier has called a 'caesura').[12] It is at this point that laughter occurs. Whether anticipated or not, a comic point is always momentary. It is always possible, though, to string a series of such points together in rapid succession. Thus in *The Three Ages* (1923), Keaton jumps from the top of one high building to another. He slips, then falls through an awning, grabs a waste pipe, falls further as the wastepipe gives way, then shoots through a hospital window, slides across the floor, falls through a hole, slides down on a fireman's pole, goes and sits on the back of a fire-engine to recover – and is driven off into the distance. As here, the comic point is always simultaneous with a comic occurrence (a fall, a look – the driving off of a fire-engine). In a gag involving suspense, therefore, its introduction is delayed while the narration provides the information necessary to generate anticipation, or slowly unfolds the events with which it will culminate. In a gag of pure surprise, on the other hand, where the comic point cannot be foreseen, the event in which it occurs will be presented as rapidly as possible.

It is thus no accident that the gags of Laurel and Hardy and Harry Langdon, in particular, are known for their suspense *and* the slowness of their pace, while Tex Avery's cartoon gags, by contrast, are renowned both for their speed and surprise.

Gags and comic structures

Because gags so often constitute digressions within a story or story-based action, and because there is a degree to which they are inherently incompatible with coherently organized and tightly motivated plots, they have at times formed the basis of comic structures marked neither by developmental narratives nor even by happy endings. We would like to conclude this chapter by looking at some examples.

Non-narrative, or non-developmental, structures can be found most frequently in the field of the sketch and the short (in all its guises, from the single-reeler to the cartoon). The restrictions on length that apply to these forms means that any narrative content need only be minimal. Sometimes the gag itself is the only action, especially in the earliest comic films or in the type of short sketch represented by Dave Allen's boat-sinking episode. Over and above this, though, the basic principles of the gag can be used to structure sequences and films lasting longer than single gags, however developed. In these cases, the principle of serial variation can be used either to explore the multiple ramifications of a single situation, task, or event (many of the films produced by Hal Roach are structured in this way), or to generate a series of distinct but repetitive actions. The supreme example here would perhaps be Chuck Jones' *Road Runner* cartoons. Individually and in series, these constitute what are in effect running gags without the interruptions of a plot, or articulated gags which extend the number of variations on an action from three to eleven or twelve.

Chuck Jones has himself described how the *Road Runner* films are marked by the themes of 'ineptitude' and 'frustration'.[13] Michael S. Cohen has characterized their implicit temporal structure as 'perpetual'.[14] Both sets of remarks are important. The *Road Runner* films are cartoon shorts. But given the structuring principles of serial repetition, they could in theory be extended to feature film length and beyond. In practice, where longer films do incorporate such principles, they tend to do so by inserting running gags into the ongoing flow of a story, either by systematically alternating or interrupting narrative scenes with gags, or by using the gags to mark the fundamental similarities between otherwise distinct narrative actions. In both cases, as in the *Road Runner* films, gags and repetitions (and repetitious gags) can be used to mark and articulate 'ineptitude' or 'frustration', or both. If so, they can also be used to produce endings which are by no means unambiguously 'happy'.

Gags are suited to the articulation of ineptitude and frustration because they are suited to the articulation of failure. They are suited to the articulation of failure because of the potential ingredient of interruption (just as they are suited to the articulation of sudden success because of the ingredient of surprise). Even the simplest one-off gags can hence be built on failure – as when in *Modern Times* (1936) Chaplin's Tramp tries to take an early morning dip and fails, because, as he discovers when he dives in head first, the water near his cabin is too shallow. If repetition is added and the gag developed, the increment of frustration and failure is thereby increased – as when Ollie tries again to serve the gateau in *From Soup to Nuts*. A sketch or short consisting solely of a gag or series of gags of this kind must of necessity end in failure (like the gags themselves). Many short films end this way, from the earliest and shortest (like *The Treacherous Folding Bed* (1897) or *Scenes From My Balcony* (1901)) to the later and more developed (like Laurel and Hardy's *The Finishing Touch* (1928)). In films of feature length, any tendency to build or interpolate narratives with gags and comic repetitions of this kind increases the potential increment of frustration and failure still further. Inasmuch as this is the case, though, such a tendency is in potential contradiction with the demands of a happy ending, and the success (not failure) it implies.

In episodic forms like the television sit-com, this is not necessarily a problem, for there need never be an ending of any kind. Sit-coms like *Fawlty Towers* and *The Rise and Fall of Reginald Perrin* can thus build on endless frustration and failure. However, repeated failure – to the point of a down-beat or catastrophic ending – can occur in one-off features. This is especially true of comedies built around incurably incompetent characters, like *Take the Money and Run* (1968), *Love and Death* (1975), and *Annie Hall* (1977), all featuring Woody Allen, and, hence, Allen's familiar, incompetent persona. More often, though, the need for success and a happy ending necessitates some kind of transformation, hence a change in the nature and the fortunes of the protagonist, and a change in the nature of the gags. In most of Keaton's feature films, for instance, the gags begin at some point not to articulate ineptitude, but to articulate the protagonist's growing capability, as Daniel Moews, among others, has pointed out:

> Such gags . . . both in combination and individually, reiter-
> ate in their structure the larger forms, the larger gags, of
> the hero and his fate, his initial and often unbelievably
> prolonged state of farcically active but unchanging failure
> and then his sudden transformation into surprising
> success.[15]

In films like *The General* (1926) and *College*, gags and situations are systematically repeated, but second time round they are symmetrically inverted or reversed so as to result in triumphant success.

In Keaton's features, the central protagonist is transformed – he loses his incompetence. In the films of Harry Langdon, Jerry Lewis, and Norman Wisdom, the incompetence ramains, but there is a change of consequence and fortune: innocence and good intentions are rewarded by a beneficent fate, and everything works out alright in the end. As Frank Capra has put it, 'Langdon trusted his way through adversities, surviving only with the help of God or goodness'.[16]

Capra himself wrote gags for Langdon, and directed some of his films. The later films he made often embody a similar pattern, in which failure leads to frustration and despair, and in which a happy ending appears almost out of the blue (*It's a Wonderful Life* is the supreme example, but *Mr Deeds Goes to Town* (1936), *Mr Smith Goes to Washington* (1939), and *You Can't Take It With You* (1938) all more or less adopt this pattern). In this kind of context, a happy ending can come across as pure fantasy. It can also come across as ironic. Capra's protagonists tend to be aware of their failures, bitterly conscious of their frustrations and their lack of power. In this context, a happy ending, a sudden reversal of fortune, can emerge, not as the final and triumphant fulfilment of their wishes, but as yet further evidence of their lack of control. Such endings are the mark of a power much greater than themselves, a power whose primary characteristic is its arbitrariness.

Insofar as this is the case, arbitrary happy endings, like the gags and repetitions that precede them, can mark an insistence of symbolic castration: the fundamental condition of lack and insufficiency that underlies (and can always undermine) any narcissistic self-image or fantasy. Happy endings usually fulfil such self-images and fantasies. Here their foundations can, to some extent at least, be exposed.

Alternatively, and in conclusion, happy endings can become merely the last stage in a paranoid fantasy, the final mark that the central protagonist is the object of universal, and malevolent persecution. A good example here would be *After Hours*. We have already noted the extent to which this film's protagonist lacks knowledge, and the extent to which the ending is markedly arbitrary (see pp. 31, 34). The narrative as a whole is constructed around his repeated failure to extricate himself from ever more complex and ever more dangerous situations. The more he tries, the worse things become. These repetitions, dangers, and failures are all marked or engendered by encounters with a succession of female characters. All of them seem at first concerned to seduce him or to help him. But the seduction is ambiguous. They all end up leading him still further into danger. Lack, insufficiency, failure, and frustration – and the castration to which they all testify – become thus identified with the women that he meets. The key moment in the film, in this context, thus becomes the moment in which he fantasizes the terrifying possibility that one of these women might be horribly scarred. The image of the lack he suffers is thus projected onto the female body – figured precisely as a male dread of women and the difference that women represent.

Throughout *After Hours*, while we as spectators tend to share the protagonist's perspective on events, we are also distanced from him – distanced enough, at any rate, to laugh at things that he himself finds increasingly horrific. We are thus positioned as immune from the lack that he suffers, from the failures he uncannily repeats. Where the protagonist's narcissism is undermined, ours is secured. Insofar as this is the case, *After Hours* is a film which exemplifies not only a particular use of gags, repetitions, and a happy ending but also a number of the psychic mechanisms Freud has identified as belonging to certain kinds of humour, and to certain forms of the comic. It is to humour and the comic – and to formal and psychological factors involved in the generation of laughter – that we now turn.

4

Laughter, humour, and the comic

As we have already indicated, laughter, humour, and the comic are by no means synonymous with comedy, and have by no means always functioned as primary generic criteria. Ben Jonson, for instance, wrote:

> Nor, is the moving of laughter always the end of *Comedy*.
> ... For, as Aristotle saies rightly, the moving of laughter
> is a fault in Comedie, a kind of turpitude, that depraves
> some part of man's nature ...[1]

Jonson's view is part of a tradition that stretches back to Plato and forward into the twentieth century. Christopher Herbert has spoken of the 'persistence with which modern commentators deny the significance of laughter in comedy':

> laughter forms no significant element in comedy, we are
> repeatedly admonished – or if it does it shouldn't, for
> laughter is 'erratic and unreliable,' incompatible, that is,
> with maximum seriousness. The disavowal of laughter in
> comedy originates in modern times in George Meredith's
> 'Essay on Comedy' ... and is echoed in increasingly
> uncompromising terms by later writers. ... Genuine
> humour, says Landor in a passage approvingly quoted by
> Meredith, can only come from 'grave' minds; 'Comedy is
> essentially a serious activity,' declares Knights; many of

the greatest comedies, says Potts, 'have a rather sobering effect.'[2]

We need to distinguish here between a range of different attitudes and theories: those that view laughter as *characteristic* of comedy and those that do not, those that view laughter as *definitive* of comedy and those that do not, and those that *approve* of laughter (whether characteristic, definitive, or otherwise) and those that do not. For Potts, Knights, and Meredith, laughter is a characteristic product of comedy. But it is unstable, unpredictable, and frivolous. It is neither definitive nor important enough to be worth sustained attention. For Gerald Mast, on the other hand, comedies are characteristically funny and funniness is a good thing. However, he does not discuss it directly at all.[3] For Ben Jonson, laughter is neither characteristic, nor central, nor something of which he can approve. The neoclassical cultural context that produced an attitude like Jonson's viewed laughter as always potentially unseemly because 'it was a sign of disturbed bodily control'.[4] It was thus particularly improper for courtiers, aristocrats, and gentlemen. This is partly why the period gave rise to so many plot-based discussions of comedy. A little later, once modified in particular by a middle-class view that laughter, especially scornful laughter, required a suppression of the sensibilities, and was thus in potential conflict with the increasingly influential ideologies of sympathy and sensitivity, *comédie larmoyante* was born; this was a form of comedy shorn of any attempt to produce any kind of laughter.

However, if laughter and humour are not by themselves definitive of comedy, they *are* definitive of the comic and its forms – gags, jokes, wisecracks, and plot-based comic moments. Most comedies contain examples of these forms. It is for *this* reason that the consideration of humour and laughter is important.

The ridiculous, the ludicrous, and the absurd

Laughter is not, of course, caused solely by humour and the comic. It can also be caused by tickling, pseudobulbar palsy, laughing gas (nitrous oxide), Kleine-Levine syndrome, and so on. Equally, as we all know, specific instances of the comic do not always engender laughter. Degrees of laughter change from audience to audience and from occasion to occasion. Indeed, this is one of the reasons sometimes given for avoiding the topic of laughter in discussions of comedy.

Anthony Ciccone has usefully addressed this problem, pointing out that a separation needs to be made between the representation, the laughter it may engender, and the circumstances both may involve. Laughter intrinsic to the comic (as opposed to laughter generated for extraneous reasons) is generated on the basis of an *interpretation* of the representation, an interpretation shaped both by textual cues and by institutional cues or conditions:

> Each spectator observes the same activity, yet if the conditions necessary for the comic interpretation are not generated or acknowledged, either he does not laugh, or laughs for reasons which are not intrinsically related to the activity observed.[5]

A similar argument has been made by Jerry Palmer. What can count as comic is dependent in part upon sociocultural rules, conventions, and conditions:

> In 'The Social Control of Cognition' Mary Douglas argues that a joke must be both perceived as a joke and permitted as a joke, in other words that two processes must occur. A given utterance or event must be seen as having something funny about it (intentional or otherwise), and this something funny must be allowed to be funny.[6]

Laughter can occur only in conjunction with certain kinds of utterance on certain kinds of occasion. Cues are provided by institutional contexts. Within our society, formal comedy is marked as potentially comic because it is produced and circulated within the institutions of 'entertain-

ment' and because these institutions designate some of
the utterances they circulate in this way. The utterances
themselves are invested with cues in the form of generic
conventions: comedies tend to involve certain familiar performers and they tend to be titled in certain ways rather
than others (*Written on the Wind*, *Winchester 73*, and
Night of the Living Dead are unlikely titles for comedies).
These conventions can be marked outside the confines of
the utterance itself, forming a part of the 'narrative image'
of a film or programme.[7] Within the space of the utterance
itself, cues can exist in the form of conventionalized music.
In stand-up performances, comedians often use routine
phrases like 'Have you heard the one about . . .' and 'I
was in the pub the other day when . . .' to introduce and
signal their jokes.

However, cues themselves can never guarantee that an
utterance will be recognized as humorous or that laughter
will always occur. It could therefore be argued that funniness is not a property of utterances themselves, but a
property of circumstance (social or individual), a property
thus subject to negotiation and dispute. But, as Palmer
goes on to point out, 'negotiation does not occur at
random points'.[8] We may or may not laugh; we may or
we may not 'interpret' (to use Ciccone's term) any point
in an utterance as humorous; we may even laugh at something which has not been cued as humorous; but wherever
and whenever the processes of negotiation, interpretation,
and laughter take place, they do so at points in an utterance which all always share certain features.

The points themselves are instances of the comic, and
the features that mark them are features of humour. A
situation in life can be interpreted as comic, an utterance
cued as serious – like a horror film or a tragedy – can be
interpreted as comic, if the features of humour can be
located within them. Within the realms of comedy, as we
have seen, the comic can be cued and inscribed in the form
of the joke or the gag. The joke and the gag explicitly
embody the formal features of humour. But humour is
also a matter of psychic features and properties. The term

implies a faculty of the mind and a set of mental operations as well as a set of formal properties. Broadly speaking, the latter is the field of the 'what', the former the field of the 'why'. In order to deal with the why, we need first to deal with the what. We need first to turn, then, to the formal characteristics of the comic.

Both for classical and neoclassical theory, the comic is characterized in terms of 'the ludicrous' and 'the ridiculous':

> Comedy is an imitation of baser men. These are character-ized not by every kind of vice but specifically by the ridicu-lous, which is a subdivision of the category of deformity. What we mean by 'the ridiculous' is some error or ugliness that is painless and has no harmful effects. (Aristotle)[9]

The site of the ludicrous and the ridiculous may either be the mind (in the form of ignorance, imprudence, credulity, the making of an error or mistake) or the body (in the form of ugliness, deformity, ill-fitting or inappropriate gar-ments, and so on). Elder Olsen has sought to theorize a distinction between the ludicrous and the ridiculous in terms of the relations between an action or situation and its agent. For Olsen, the comic requires a set of basic components:

> the *agent* must be contrary to the kind required to make the act serious, *or the person or thing affected, the manner, instrument used, purpose, result, the time, the place.*[10]

A distinction can then be made as to the degree of responsibility of the agent involved. Where the agent is at fault, the action is ridiculous, where the agent is not to blame (because of '*ignorance of circumstances, or because of chance*'[11]), the action is ludicrous. Beyond the actions and their agents, these categories can then be applied to other characters, and to people in general:

> People are ludicrous or ridiculous in appearance as well as in speech or action: because of bodily or facial expression, or gesture, or motion, or physical activity, or dress.[12]

The categories can clearly be of use in describing or

distinguishing between various kinds of comic characters and performers, and various kinds of comic action. Thus where Inspector Clouseau is basically ridiculous in appearance, speech, and action, most of the characters played by Jerry Lewis are basically ludicrous. Where Ollie's pratfall in *From Soup to Nuts* would be an instance of the ludicrous (because of the degree of chance and unwitting ignorance involved), the scene in *Fawlty Towers* in which Basil's car breaks down while he is hurrying back to the hotel, and in which he proceeds to beat it with the branch of a tree, would be an instance of the ridiculous. There can then be instances of cross-over between the particular nature of an action and the general nature of its actant. If Ollie's pratfall is ludicrous, Ollie himself tends generally to be ridiculous – because of his impatience, and because of his sense of his own importance.

For Olsen, 'the basis of the ridiculous and the ludicrous ... is the unlike'.[13] All instances of the comic involve a departure from a norm, whether the norm be one of action, appropriate behaviour, conventional dress, or stereotypical features. However, the unlike must be tempered by the like, for as 'we approach the wholly unlike, we approach the monstrous, and the monstrous is never ridiculous'.[14] There must in other words be a degree of normality in the abnormal, a degree of the appropriate in the inappropriate, a degree of the logical in the illogical, and a degree of sense in the otherwise nonsensical. Comedy that relies on the grotesque (like the Jerry Lewis films or *Monty Python* or a great deal of early film comedy) risks verging either on the monstrous, as Olsen points out, or on the silly (something so ridiculous or ludicrous it isn't even funny). Whether it does or not depends in part on personal taste and in part on different cultural and aesthetic standards and values: norms change from group to group, class to class, historical period to historical period, society to society. They also differ from work to work, cycle to cycle and type to type within the field of comedy itself. Works and comic performances establish their own norms, and their own particular balance between the ludicrous, the ridiculous, the grotesque, the monstrous, and the silly. Thus *The Meaning of Life* (1983) is as different from *Bringing Up Baby* (1938) as *Bringing Up Baby* is different from either *Local Hero* (1983), on the one hand, or *Something Wild* (1987), on the other. Similarly, Ben Elton is as different from Dave Allen as Dave Allen is from Bob Monkhouse or Lenny Bruce. And while both the so-called screwball cycle in America and the Ealing comedies in Britain share the marking of departures from the norm as an eccentricity of character and behaviour, the latter is far less abrasive, far more whimsical, than the former.

The notion of the unlike, of departures from a norm, underlies a great deal of comic theory that stresses incongruity (where departures from the norm are discussed in terms of semantics and logic) and surprise (where departures from the norm are identified, conceived, measured, and addressed in terms of their temporal articulation). Jerry Palmer's theory of the absurd – his global term for the ludicrous and the ridiculous – combines these concerns.

Palmer takes the gag as his primary model. His example is a gag from *Liberty* (1929), in which Laurel and Hardy, stuck on top of some scaffolding, find their way to a lift. At the bottom of the lift is a cop. The lift plummets to the ground. Stan and Ollie get out. The lift is raised to reveal not, as we expect, the body of a dead cop, but a midget in policeman's uniform. This gag, like all gags, consists of two elements or moments, a logical moment and an aesthetic or narrative moment, a syllogism and a *peripeteia*. The *peripeteia* is a sudden reversal, 'a shock or surprise in the story the film is telling'.[15] The surprise in this case is that the cop isn't dead, merely squashed. Any *peripeteia*, and therefore any gag (and by extension any instance of the comic, including the joke) requires two stages, 'the preparation stage and the culmination stage'.[16] There is therefore always a degree both of narrative and of temporal articulation. The moment of surprise is the moment of the 'punch-line'. But surprise and shock need not be comic. Comic surprise is characterized specifically by its logical structure. This structure consists of two syllogisms, or systems of reasoning and deduction. One is plausible, the other implausible. They are thus in contradiction with one another, though the implausible syllogism carries greater weight. In the *Liberty* gag the process works as follows:

one line of reasoning tells us that what we see on the screen is intensely implausible:
a) the result of squashing in a lift shaft is death – a well-known state of affairs, the major premiss;
b) i) the cop is squashed – empirical observation, the minor premiss;
     ii) the second minor premiss: he survives;
c) conclusion: the event is implausible.
But a second, contradictory, line of reasoning tells us that the event does in fact have a measure of plausibility:
a) the result of squashing is a reduction in size;
b) the cop comes out smaller;
c) therefore the event has a measure of plausibility.[17]

Palmer stresses finally that 'the two moments of the gag are in practice absolutely inseparable',[18] and that 'the logic of the absurd' is what guarantees the status of gags and jokes as comic (rather than anything else that involves surprise, like horror, or anything else that involves a combination of syllogisms, like metaphor and poetry, or anything else that involves implausibility, like nonsense – which lacks sense and logic altogether).

'The logic of the absurd' thus, in addition, helps to produce what Palmer calls 'comic insulation'.[19] It helps, in other words, to guarantee that 'ugliness' and 'error' are 'painless' (to return to the terms used by Aristotle). It does so by marking events, actions, and characters with a degree of implausibility sufficient to ensure that they are not taken seriously. This is partly a matter of psychology, to which we shall turn in a moment. But it is also worth noting that it is partly a matter of history and culture, since plausibility is always relative to a culture's social and aesthetic norms. These norms are subject to variation and change, which is one reason why what one age or culture finds plausible, another may find unconvincing. It is therefore also why 'old' horror movies and 'old' melodramas may be found funny by contemporary audiences. These genres are both particularly reliant upon convention to render the implausible plausible (in depicting the monstrous, for example, or in motivating passion and coincidence). When conventions change, helping thereby to establish new regimes and standards of plausibility, films using outmoded conventions can appear, precisely, absurd.

All instances and forms of the comic are fundamentally semiotic. Inasmuch as they involve expectation and logic they necessarily also involve meanings and signs. This is as true of accidental or discovered instances of the comic in everyday life as it is of formal instances of the comic like the joke and the gag (which only exist in utterance, and therefore only in purely semiotic form). A man in a pinstripe suit and bowler hat striding head-in-air down the road and slipping on a banana skin can only be funny because it *means* something, in particular because the meanings involved produce a contradiction that leads to a surprise. (The meanings of dignity, purpose, power, and control are suddenly contradicted by the meanings of incompetence, failure, and indignity.)

Palmer's model can therefore be reformulated. Any term, word, or item, as Palmer puts it, is capable of evoking a set of connotations: it belongs to a paradigm. Within the context of a particular chain of terms in an utterance (a syntagm), a connotation may be evoked which is apparently incompatible with the sense of the rest of the chain. There occurs a 'semantic anomaly' – an attribute incompatible with its context – which results in a 'predicative impertinence'. Thus, in the case of the gag in *Liberty*:

> the midget connotes survival, that is life, whereas squashing in a lift shaft connotes death. To phrase it in slightly different terms, squashing the policeman predicates his death, the emergence of the midget predicates his survival.[20]

However, a second reading is possible, one which locates another connotation from the paradigm to which the term belongs. This connotation is much more compatible with a predicate pertinent to the rest of the utterance: in addition to connoting survival, the midget can also connote smallness, a reduction in size; reduction in size is a predicate pertinent to being suddenly squashed.

Nevertheless, though this second reading is possible, the first remains preponderant. Thus the relationship between the two readings is analogous to the relationship between the two syllogisms in the logical structure already outlined: just as in logic the comic is characterized by a predominance of the implausible, so in semiotic terms it is marked by a preponderance of anomaly and impertinence.[21]

Jokes and the comic

We have discussed some of the formal features of humour and the humorous. We need now to consider how and why they make us laugh, how and why they produce the pleasures that laughter marks. We need to consider in particular why the generation of laughter requires 'comic insulation', what connections there may be between the aggressive connotations of 'ridicule' and the concept of the ridiculous, and the connotations of 'play' inherent in a term like 'ludicrous'. And we need to consider the nature of the psychic functions and processes involved in forms marked by such peculiar and specific semiotic operations as those outlined by Palmer. To do so, we turn to Freud, who begins his discussion of *Jokes and their Relation to the Unconscious* at the point where Palmer leaves off, the point precisely of form and technique.[22]

In *Jokes and their Relation to the Unconscious*, Freud distinguishes between joking and wit, on the one hand, and what he calls 'the comic' on the other. The distinction rests in part on their semiotic status, in part on the ensuing differences in their structures of address, and in part on the different psychic instances or levels they tend predominantly to involve.

For Freud a joke is *made* (constructed, produced); it exists only in utterance; and its immediate material is language and signs. The comic, by contrast, is *witnessed* (discovered, observed). It can exist, beyond the realms of formal utterances, in situations encountered in everyday life. Jokes characteristically involve a tripartite structure of address: the joker, his or her addressee, and the target or butt of the joke. The comic involves only the observer and the observed (a perceiver and a butt). Jokes can be divided into two main kinds: 'tendentious' jokes and 'innocent' jokes. 'Innocent' jokes derive their pleasures from technique, from the play with words and meanings that the exercise of wit always involves. 'Tendentious' jokes involve an additional source of pleasure. Technique and word-play function as 'fore-pleasure', allowing the pleasurable articulation of aggressive and erotic wishes, and, thus, the pleasurable circumvention of repression. The pleasures of the comic derive from a process of comparison, in which the difference between the superior position and capacities of the observer and the inferior position and capacities of the observed results in an economy of psychic energy in the observer which is discharged in laughter. In its articulation of repressed wishes across the mechanisms of language, the joke is marked by its central involvement of the unconscious and primary processes. The comic, by contrast, tends mainly to involve the conscious and preconscious systems of the mind.

It will be evident that Freud's category of the comic is not synonymous with ours. As we have already pointed out, a semiotic component is involved in the comic situations of everyday life. These situations, however, are not *constituted* in discourse, nor are they uttered by an agent of address: they lack an enunciator. In comedy, however, if a situation occurs sharing the characteristics of the comic in Freud's sense (a pratfall, perhaps, or an instance of ignorance or naïvety), that situation is present only in semiotic form. It is uttered, enunciated, and as such involves the triadic structure of address characteristic of the joke: a narrator, a spectator, and a butt. This further means that the enunciation of the comic in a film or television programme can share the technical and formal characteristics of joke-making (precisely the semiotic and logical mechanisms outlined above), and may thus, in an exact sense, be witty. It means also, on the one hand, that the position of spectatorial superiority characteristic of the comic has to be constructed (something to which the structures of relative knowledge so crucial to the articulation both of comic narratives and of gags are clearly important). On the other hand, it means that the pleasures of joking can be as crucial to the representation of the comic in comedy as the pleasures of the comic themselves.

Hence there are many gags and comic moments, in addition to the many diegetic jokes and wisecracks, that articulate aggressive or erotic wishes in the guise of semiotic or formal play. The gag from *Liberty* (its aggression directed against the cop) would be an obvious example of the former. It could also be seen as an example of the latter. Throughout the film, Laurel and Hardy have been trying to take off their trousers in conditions of privacy (in order, ostensibly, to swap them: Ollie has Stan's trousers on and Stan Ollie's). A whole series of gags and comic moments have been built around their failure to do so: they keep being observed and interrupted by policemen. An unconscious homosexual wish is clearly in play here. The squashing of the cop can thus be read as an aggression in the service of this wish: an aggression directed against the agency responsible for its repeated frustration. However, the erotic wish involved in this case is evident only in symptomatic form. It is thus distinct from the way in which many of Groucho Marx's wisecracks, for instance, use wit and word-play to permit the articulation of very evident aggressive, erotic (and aggressively erotic) desires. In the case of *Liberty*, the wit involved in the construction of the gag permits the articulation of an aggressive wish which is overdetermined by an erotic wish that remains, by and large, unconscious, censored and repressed. This incidentally is likely to be the case with most gags and wisecracks (including Groucho's: the wishes they evidently articulate are likely themselves to be embodied in wishes that remain unstated). As with *Liberty*, the generation of the wish takes place across the span of the narrative as a whole. The gag itself is the point at which it merely receives comic – or rather witty – (but still *symptomatic*) expression.

Two issues arise as a consequence of these points. The first concerns the site of the wish involved both in *Liberty*'s case (and in others), and thence the site of the pleasures and psychic processes each instance of the comic – in our sense – also involves. The second concerns the fact that neither in the case of *Liberty*'s unconscious wish, nor in the case of Groucho's wisecracks (nor in any instance of joking in everyday life or in formal performance) is the wish, strictly speaking, *fulfilled*. Rather, it is *articulated*, a fact which points, once again, to the importance of the semiotic, and which will lead us finally to address (and to question) Freud's category of 'innocent' joking.

The focus of Freud's discussion of the pleasures and processes of the comic is the figure of the observer. With jokes he seems more interested in the processes involved in the formation of the joke, and therefore in the joker. However, one of his major points is that it is the addressee, not the joker, who laughs. For the addressee, the pleasure lies in the work done by the joker, work the addressee is thus spared (though work is done by the addressee in comprehending the joke).

In a film or television programme, the spectator is in the position of the addressee (and of the observer, if addressed by the comic). The spectator, too, is spared the work of formation. As with the joke, therefore, and in addition, the spectator's unconscious and its wishes are not in the first instance involved in, or responsible for, the *production* of the gag or wisecrack or comic moment with which he or she is addressed. However, the spectator becomes identified with the wishes at stake through accepting, understanding, and laughing at a wisecrack or gag. (The mechanisms and pleasures of wisecracks and gags thus simultaneously secure the expression of a wish and identification with it). Yet, and partly in consequence, there can often occur a point at which the spectator's identification is disavowed. This is true of the gag in *Liberty*. First, if the aggression is directed against the cop, he nevertheless survives. (This indeed is the very point of the gag.) Secondly, once the gag is over, he angrily pursues Stan and Ollie as they scurry away off screen left. Thus, in a second comic moment, an aggression is turned against those acting as (in this case unwitting, but nevertheless responsible) vehicles for the aggression (and the erotic wish) that the first gag involves. The spectator's complicity is absolved – but at the cost of another instance of aggression.

Aggression is therefore neither avoided nor repressed. It is merely displaced. This is because aggression is always fundamentally involved in any instance or form of the comic (both in Freud' sense and in ours). This in turn is because what is always at stake in the comic is a position of superiority – hence narcissism and its object, the ego.

Humour

Freud himself discussed narcissism most extensively in this context in a paper on humour written some time after his book on jokes, at a point when narcissism had become for him a much more central issue.[23] For Freud humour is distinct both from joking and the comic. The example he cites is one of gallows humour: a criminal being led to the scaffold on a Monday morning remarks, 'Well, the week's beginning nicely'.[24] For Freud gallows humour is typical of all humour in that it involves a disavowal of what he calls 'the provocations of reality', thus marking and constructing 'the triumph of narcissism, the victorious assertion of the ego's invulnerability'.[25] Inasmuch as this is the case, there is a butt, a target of aggression, involved in all humour, despite the variations in its structure of address. That target is, to use Freud's term, 'reality' itself, and specifically the reality of castration – the marking of the limits and insufficiencies of the ego, of which death, as in Freud's example, is the ultimate instance. However, *this* target, *this* reality has then to be distinguished from the *ostensible* target of humour in any particular instance (whether a person or character, or the arrangement of events in a story). For the true butt of humour is always *repressed* (as again Freud's example serves to illustrate: death is precisely what constitutes the target of the criminal's remark, yet death is precisely what is absent from the utterance).

This is one reason why the ostensible target of humorous comment or narration (if there is one) tends if anything to be treated as much with indulgence as contempt. For it itself is not the true target. Thus, particularly in 'sentimental' comedy, a tolerant stance is taken towards characters and a wryly ironic (rather than bitter) one towards the events. The faults and weaknesses of the characters are things we, in our position of superiority, may laugh at, but they are excusable foibles rather than major flaws. Interestingly, in films like *Little Miss Marker* (1934) and *On Moonlight Bay* (1951), the characters who come in for most criticism, and who function as major obstacles to a satisfactory conclusion, are fathers or father figures – avatars, precisely, of an oedipalized threat of castration. But interestingly, also, they are eventually won round – they forgive the younger characters their weaknesses (as we forgive theirs). They too adopt a tolerant stance.

In *On Moonlight Bay*, this transition occurs when the father is reminded that he, too, was young once. He has blocked his daughter's proposed marriage because he does not approve of her fiance. Then his young son breaks a window with a catapult. It turns out the catapult once belonged to the father when *he* was a high-spirited boy. His wife, meanwhile, reminds him that they were married at an early age – and the age his daughter wishes to marry. Thus he is doubly reminded of his youth. And once this has happened, the son is forgiven, and the daughter allowed to marry the man of her choice.

This shift exactly parallels the structure of humour itself. For in humour, as Freud notes with respect, in particular, to self-directed humour, the position of superiority corresponds to a position of indulgent adulthood, and the position of inferiority to one of childhood. The latter is an instance of 'what one once was', one of the major forms of identification.[26] It is also the source of the very narcissism with which the position of 'adult' superiority itself is invested, and thus the object of a fond nostalgia for a time when one imagined one was the all-powerful centre of adult attention, and when the world was unmarked by sorrow, danger, and death. Hence Freud's description of the fundamental 'intention' of humour:

> The main thing is the intention which humour carries out, whether it is acting in relation to the self or other people. It means: 'Look! here is the world, which seems so dangerous! It is nothing but a game for children – just worth making a jest about!'[27]

Inasmuch as humour makes of the world 'a jest', inasmuch as it renders the world, therefore, absurd, humour, and the narcissism it articulates, is a major source of 'comic insulation', of the lack of pain which Aristotle specifies as a condition of comedy and of which the lack of suffering and death in slapstick, despite all the pratfalls, would constitute a major example.

Narcissism, childhood, and identification are also at stake in the comic, where, again, the butt, 'the comic person', 'behaves exactly like a clumsy, ignorant child'.[28] Here, though, the aggression inherent in the position of the superior observer is directed precisely and solely at the person observed. Thus where in humour the butt is often merely and affectionately ludicrous, in the comic the butt is always rendered, exactly, ridiculous – worthy of ridicule. Laughter marks a disavowal of what one once was, a refusal of identification, a differentiation of ego and other. The aggression involved, though, stems not from any impossibility of identification, from any absolute distinction between other and ego. It stems from an identification that the laughter disavows, thus from an ambivalence inherent in identification itself. This ambivalence is especially evident in the role of identification in the very constitution of the ego that here seeks to mark its autonomy. For the ego is constituted simultaneously in a recognition of the *likeness* of an other, and in a recognition that the other is distinct. Lacan's model for this is the mirror phase, in which:

> Though still in a state of powerlessness and motor incoordination, the infant anticipates on an imaginary plane the apprehension and mastery of its bodily unity. This imaginary unification comes about by means of identification with the image of the counterpart as total *Gestalt*; it is exemplified concretely by the experience in which the child perceives its own reflection in a mirror.[29]

The ego is thus founded in alienation. The self is in a sense inherently other. And the other here is both an image of the control to which the subject aspires, and, inasmuch as it *is* other, nevertheless itself beyond the subject's own control.

The infantile image that is central to the comic evokes and involves the complexity – and aggression – that marks the ambivalence of this process. The image of childhood engenders an identification inasmuch as the child is what one once was. But the image itself specifies childhood in terms of the *lack* of co-ordination and control characteristic of the subject prior to the mirror phase itself, and in opposition to the nature of image with which the subject identifies there. The comic thus involves an image that is exactly the reverse of the image in the mirror, that is exactly the obverse of the model of the unified, co-ordinated ego. Meanwhile, and in addition, the lack of control that marks the comic's image of childhood evokes the lack of control inherent in the mirror phase itself, inasmuch as the image is other. Thus in an almost perfect illustration of the processes and elements involved here, when W. C. Fields in *The Old Fashioned Way* (1934) vents his aggression on Baby LeRoy by kicking him firmly in the rear, he thereby violently differentiates himself from the child. But his kick is in response to the child's unruliness. It is a mark, therefore, not only of the child's lack of control, but of his own. When we ourselves laugh, we identify with his aggression against the child (thus incidentally sharing the articulation of a socially prohibited wish), but we also disavow that identification. We laugh aggressively at Fields' own aggression insofar as it is a sign, not of his mastery, but of his own infantile lack of control. By contrast, when we laugh at the magical self-control of someone like Chaplin, at his ability to manipulate his environment as he wishes (of which his pantomimic skill is both evidence and instrument), our laughter echoes the 'jubilance' (to use Lacan's term) with which we first appropriate an image of co-ordinated unity during the mirror phase itself.[30] It is hardly surprising, then, that Chaplin's performance is so pervaded by a narcissistic exhibitionism, nor that through the use (particularly in the earlier films) of frontality and frequent glances to camera it is addressed so markedly to the superior position of the spectator.

Chaplin's performance is in part a demonstration of his power, hence a source of identification for the narcissistic ego of the spectator. If, however, the power of the other is too great, the other can become neither admirable, nor ridiculous, but monstrous.

The monstrous marks the extent to which, in Jeffrey Mehlman's words, the subject can 'lose control of the process of oscillation between self and other', a process central to identification itself.[31] While a monster can be as absurd as any comic butt, a horror film as improbable as any comedy, there is a difference, and the difference lies in the relationship between the degree of power with which the other is invested. It can be precisely exemplified in terms of an image of the childlike and infantile: it is the difference, in *Psycho* (1960), between Norman Bates as Mother's timid and dutiful son (the comic Norman Bates), and Norman Bates as the (phallic) Mother herself, or between the uncontrollable powerlessness of a 'natural' human child (like the babies in *Raising Arizona* (1987)), and the uncontrollable power of Frankenstein's new-born creation.

In dealing so centrally with an image of the other for the purposes of precise emotional effect, it is hardly surprising that horror and comedy are so different, yet so close. It is no accident, for instance, that they share shock and surprise as fundamental devices of narration, nor that horror can so easily be both intentionally and unintentionally funny. In both genres, surprise is the point at which the spectator's position is most at stake – the point at which the physical articulation of affect (in the form of laughing or screaming) is more likely to occur. The spectator's laughter, specifically, marks in each instance the restoration of superiority and power: the point in a horror film at which the monster strikes us as unconvincing and ridiculous, or when the build-up of tension is a deliberate false alarm (the monster isn't there behind the door after all).

It is in this context that laughter and the comic emerge quite plainly as forms of defence. It is thus no accident that most of the research on the development of smiling, laughing, and a sense of humour in children has stressed the extent to which they are linked to the development of motor co-ordination and control, an ability to manipulate symbols – and to the sudden defusing of anxiety and fear.[32] Jean Guillaumin has, indeed, sought precisely to specify the psychic function and significance of laughter in terms of the physiology of expulsion that laughter involves: the 'spasmodic and convulsive discharge of laughter' corresponds, for Guillaumin, to a psychic ejection of the threatening object.[33] In particular, the repetition inherent in the fact that this discharge is 'automatically reiterated' leads to 'the satisfaction of control'.[34]

However, he notes that for Freud repetition is a feature of the death drive, of a principle beyond both pleasure and control. And the unexpected and uncontrollable nature of laughter is itself an indication that 'satisfaction' and 'control' are profoundly contradictory and fragile.

Thus, if a position of superiority can be found, it can equally be lost; if the other can be ridiculous, it can equally be monstrous; if repetitions can be pleasurably made, they can equally and at times uncomfortably, insist; if laughter is a mark of control, it itself is uncontrollable. These points serve to indicate that what is at stake is a position of power, and also that that position, far from being stable, permanent and real is the object of a wish, and hence can find articulation only in fantasy. This is nowhere more evident than in the interplay between expectation and surprise and sense and nonsense fundamental to the comic in its broadest sense, in which if the spectator's position is finally one of power, it is a power entirely dependent upon the narration that constructs it.

Here, the two moments of the comic as Jerry Palmer has described them – the moment of disruptive surprise, and the moment of semantic and logical resolution – articulate respectively the loss and restoration of the position of power and control. The moment of surprise undermines the power inherent both in the predictability of a course of events and in the predictability of conventional sense and logic. The moment of resolution reinstalls a position of control by making (witty) sense, and by enabling the spectator to construct retrospectively a logic behind the course which events have taken. Quite apart from any quota of comic aggression and superiority that may additionally be involved, quite apart from any narcissistic disavowal, or from any articulation of forbidden wishes (source of pleasure dependent upon the specificities of particular examples), pleasure derives in general from four principal features of the comic: first, from the fact that any loss of control occurs in a heavily cued context, one which marks the loss as 'playful', therefore 'safe', because it includes a promise that control will be rapidly restored; secondly, from the compensatory pleasures of an aggression against convention that the moment of loss necessarily involves; thirdly, from the suddenness both of the loss and of the restoration (Palmer's insistence that the two moments are in fact simultaneous both highlights the minimal nature of the loss and pinpoints the extent to which the comic, on the one hand, and the psyche, on the other, are inherently contradictory, conflictual, and multidimensional); and, finally, from the absurd and 'magical' nature of the moment of resolution, from the evident properties of fantasy with which it is endowed.

To an extent, these characteristics are shared by many other aesthetic forms. Gags and jokes, though, are distinguished by the predominance of the absurd in a context of comic insulation. This predominance is crucial to R. Howard Bloch's view of the fundamental function of jokes, a view he outlines in his book on medieval fabliaux.[35] For Bloch, jokes are profoundly ambiguous. They exploit, indeed highlight, the arbitrary nature of language and signification. But they avoid pure nonsense. Their illogicalities are always to some degree logical, their absurdity to some degree meaningful. There is always an element of motivation, of justification, in any joke or gag, an element which places limits upon the degree of arbitrariness involved. Thus, in a play of displacement, condensation and substitution which always engenders – and always rewards – a search for motivation, 'the joke disrupts the assumptions of a "natural" relation between language and meaning and, at the same time, serves as a screen for the fact that such a relation never existed in the first place'.[36]

This particular ambiguity underlies a number of other ambiguities about jokes, gags, and the comic, and about the aesthetic and ideological roles of comedy in general. For if comedy has been seen as inherently 'subversive' because it involves breaking aesthetic and ideological conventions, it has also been seen as reactionary, because it involves the use of cultural stereotypes, and because the breaking of convention is itself a conventional generic requirement. In order to examine the issues involved here in a little more detail, we now consider the comic and comedy in terms of the concept of verisimilitude. This concept, as we shall see, helps both to identify and explain the logic underlying most of the techniques, devices, and conventions discussed so far, and to locate with precision the reasons why comedy can be viewed in such very different, and contrasting, ways.

5
Verisimilitude

In his discussion of gags and jokes, Jerry Palmer points out that there are two principal sources of comic surprise: first, the sudden contradiction of expectations founded in the narrative itself; and secondly, 'the contradiction of knowledge, or values, or expectations about the outside world that the audience may be assumed to derive from their ordinary everyday experience'.[1]

The examples he gives of the latter include the 'indignities of farce' (the pratfall, the pie in the face, and so on), which contradict our cultural beliefs and expectations concerning the body as the locus of human dignity and, more generally, the nature of events and the causal connections between them:

> gags can be either totally unpredictable or totally predictable, but never either: the universe of the gag is always one or the other. This contradicts our commonsense everyday knowledge of chains of events in the ordinary outside world, for common sense tells us that causality is such that events are neither totally predictable nor totally unpredictable. Totally predictable events, moreover, commonly contradict such commonsense items as 'nobody's that stupid', or 'once bitten, twice shy'. Totally unpredictable events are likely to be so because the natural laws of the known

universe have been apparently dislocated, as they were in the lift/cop gag.[2]

The issues of predictability and human dignity both refer us to the allied concepts of decorum and verisimilitude. Decorum means what is proper or fitting, verisimilitude what is probable or likely. Both concepts therefore centrally concern the relationship between representations, cultural knowledge, opinion, and beliefs, and, hence, audience expectations. The field of knowledge, opinion, and belief as a whole can, however, be divided into the broadly socio-cultural, the specifically aesthetic and the even more specifically generic, thus giving rise to at least two kinds of verisimilitude, as Tzvetan Todorov has pointed out:

> If we study the discussions bequeathed us by the past, we realize that a work is said to have verisimilitude in relation to two chief kinds of norms. The first is what we call the *rules of the genre*: for a work to be said to have verisimilitude, it must conform to these rules. In certain periods, a comedy is judged 'probable' only if, in the last act, the characters are discovered to be near relations. A sentimental novel will be probable if its outcome consists in the marriage of hero and heroine, if virtue is rewarded and vice punished. Verisimilitude, taken in this sense, designates the work's relation to literary discourse: more exactly, to certain of the latter's subdivisions, which form a genre.
>
> But there exists another verisimilitude, which has been taken even more frequently for a relation with reality. Aristotle, however, had already perceived that the verisimilar is not a relation between discourse and its referent (the relation of truth), but between discourse and what readers believe is true. The relation is here established between the work and a scattered discourse that in part belongs to each of the individuals of a society but of which none may claim ownership; in other words, to *public opinion*. The latter is of course not 'reality' but merely a further discourse, independent of the work.[3]

These two kinds of verisimilitude thus give rise to two kinds of decorum: one which consists in respecting the norms embodied in 'public opinion', and another which consists in respecting the rules of a genre or form. Thus it was both decorous and verisimilitudinous, proper and believable, to endow aristocrats, courtiers, and kings with dignified actions and weighty thoughts in a Renaissance play, just as in postwar European Art Cinema these attributes were more appropriate to *Angst*-ridden bourgeois intellectuals. It was at one time proper, and likely, that epics would be written in a high style, and that operas would consist of 'extraordinary and supernatural adventures',[4] just as now it is proper for pornography and slapstick to be filmed in a 'low' style, and likely that characters in musicals will suddenly burst into song.

Inasmuch as this is the case, verisimilitude and decorum give rise to, and draw upon, generic and cultural stereotypes which, as Gerard Genette has pointed out, often function as implicit sources of aesthetic motivation.[5] Thus, just as in the eighteenth century it would have been improper and therefore unbelievable for a king to be portrayed – against type – as ill-mannered and cowardly, so in a prewar British drama, it would have been improper, improbable, and unbelievable for a working-class character, male or female, to be portrayed as intellectual or heroic. As soon as these types appear in their proper context, no further explanation of their traits and motivations is needed: kings are by definition well-mannered, courageous, and heroic; working-class characters are by definition deferential, of limited intelligence, and ignorant of the finer things in life. And so on.

However, as the centrality of 'the extraordinary' to opera serves to indicate, while there can be a correlation between common opinion, cultural stereotypes, and generic conventions, there can also be discrepancies: 'the extraordinary' is, by definition, contrary to what a culture conceives or defines as probable or likely. Comedy, even more than opera, was, and is, an extreme case in point.

Essentially this is because, as a genre, comedy is often concerned with the lives of 'ordinary' classes and people, and thus with what is, from a ruling-class point of view, the *indecorum* of the speech, behaviour, actions, and manners of those of a lower social rank. It is also because all instances of the comic, of that which is specifically designed to be funny, are founded on the transgression of decorum and verisimilitude: on deviations from any social or aesthetic rule, norm, model, convention, or law. Such deviations are the basis of comic surprise. But the forms the comic can take are as multiple and varied as the norms that govern any society, any social practice, any cultural regime, or any aesthetic form, as we shall see.

Comic transgressions

To begin with, the norm or norms in question may be specifically aesthetic. If so, the comic often takes the form of parody. As discussed briefly in chapter 1, parody can itself take a number of forms, depending upon whether its target is a general representational regime, like the documentary, or specific fictional genres, like the detective thriller or the disaster movie, or even comic forms themselves, like the sketch. (We discuss this particular type of parody later on, in chapter 7.) Outside the realms of parody, the comic may involve deviations from the more general norms that govern aesthetic representations in a culture. For instance, it may take the form of unmotivated interpolations or digressions within the context of norms and ideals of aesthetic coherence and unity, or it may insist on the artifice of coincidence and the arbitrariness of disorder against the rules of 'realistic' aesthetic narration.

Moving beyond the province of aesthetics, comic parody may take as its target other kinds and modes of cultural discourse. Brother Maynard's blessing of the Holy Hand-grenade of Antioch in *Monty Python and the Holy Grail* (1974), for instance, parodies the discourse of the Bible. Reg's dialogue in *The Life of Brian* (1979) parodies the discourse of the British ultra-left ('Judean People's Front!??? We're the People's Front of Judea'). Alternatively, the comic may involve, or derive from, deviations from the norms of discourse itself. This can take the form of absurdity, nonsense, logical incoherence, non sequiturs, mispronunciations, and so on. Most examples of dialogue-based humour, specifically, involve deviations from the norms that govern conventional conversation. They consistute what Walter Nash has called 'defective exchange':

> such exchanges violate the maxims of 'ordinary' conversation ... the obligation to give adequate and accurate information, not to be prolix, not to get into conversational deadlocks, not to be snagged on *non-sequiturs*, to pay attention to what is said, to try to make relevant assertions and responses.[6]

The following exchange from *Duck Soup* breaks practically all of these maxims in order precisely to generate laughs:

> Groucho: 'Now, listen here. I've got a swell job for you, but first I'll have to ask you a couple of questions. Now what is it that has four pairs of pants, lives in Philadelphia, and it never rains but it pours?'
>
> Chico: 'At'sa a good one. I'll give you three guesses.'
>
> Groucho: 'Now, lemme see. Has four pairs of pants, lives in Philadelphia. Is it male or female?'
>
> Chico: 'I think so.'
>
> Groucho: 'Is he dead?'
>
> Chico: 'Who?'
>
> Groucho: 'I don't know. I give up.'
>
> Chico: 'I give up too.'

Groucho's discourse, in particular, tends not only to be marked by deviations from logical norms, or from the maxims of conventional communication, but also by insults and hostility, by deviations from the norms of decorum and good manners implicit in the rules of polite conversation and behaviour:

> Mrs Claypool: 'Mr Driftwood ... would you please get off the bed? What would people say?'
>
> Groucho: 'They'd probably say you're a very lucky woman. Now will you please shut up, so I can continue my reading?'
>
> (*A Night at the Opera* (1935))

The comic insult is a forte not only of Groucho's but also of Blackadder, and Basil and Sybil Fawlty (hence lines like 'You ageing, brilliantined stick-insect'). It constitutes a particular form of wit. At a more general level the rules of politeness and decorum are crucial to all kinds of comedy. The so-called 'comedy of manners', which bases plot complications as well as comic lines and comic moments on deviations from these rules, is an obvious source of examples (from *The Marriage Circle* (1924) to *The Philadelphia Story* (1940)). The comedy of manners most usually sites its stories in milieux of the upper classes, the milieux of those who define what constitutes manners, politeness, and taste in any society. But deviations from decorum, whether inside or outside this particular kind of comedy, can result not only in what a particular sector of society might regard as 'bad taste', but in the transgression of more general social taboos. Hence the example of the *Monty Python* sketch about a man who takes his mother's body to the undertakers. They offer to cook it for him in case he's feeling hungry: 'Look, tell you what . . . we'll eat her. *Then* . . . if you feel guilty about it afterwards, we'll dig a grave and you can throw up in it.' Norms, laws, and taboos of this kind are, of course, usually codified in systems of censorship. It is no surprise then that this sketch was omitted from a repeat of the programme when broadcast in the early 1970s, or that a sequence from W. C. Fields' short *The Dentist* (1932), which showed Fields trying to extract a woman's tooth in a pose modelled on sexual intercourse, was cut from most of the prints.

The Dentist as a whole works by constructing a series of deviations from our sense of what a dentist should be like (just as in *The Barber Shop* (1933) Fields is hardly a model barber: 'Is that a mole?' 'Yeah, I've had it all my life.' 'You don't have it anymore.') Given the prevalence in any culture of models and stereotypes of people, professions, races, nations, and roles, it is hardly surprising that deviations from type (usually in the form of paradigmatic substitution, of the transfer of traits appropriate to one type to a type of a different and inappropriate kind) are so frequently a source of comic improbability and, hence, comic surprise. Thus one of Russ Abbott's TV sketches involves a judge who behaves like a chat-show host. *Star-Spangled Rhythm* (1942) includes a sketch in which a group of men playing cards are invested with conversational traits stereotypically associated with women (they discuss, among other things, furniture, fashion, and food). *The Odd Couple* (1968) features a character who is both hypochondriac and suicidal. *Police Academy* (1984) founds its comedy on having characters, who between them incorporate all the traits that make them unsuited to police work, train precisely as policemen. *Static* (1986) includes a sequence in which a group of elderly citizens are caught in the hijack of a bus. But instead of behaving with outrage or timid infirmity (instead of behaving according to type), they enjoy the adventure and excitement. Woody Allen in *Sleeper* (1973) says 'I'm not the heroic type. I was beaten up by Quakers', thus making explicit the principle behind both the joke and his general image. And finally when in *Roxie Hart* (1942) Roxie's parents are told that their daughter has been found guilty of murder, their subsequent dialogue is funny because it is not what we would normally expect of a mother and father in a situation of this kind:

Father: 'They're gonna hang Roxie.'
Mother: 'What did I tell you.'

We have norms, models and stereotypes, not only of people and roles, but also of actions. These are very frequently the foundation of gags, from J. B. Ball's pratfall (hardly the conventional means for a full-grown, respectable man to get down stairs), to the point in the chariot race in *The Three Ages* (1923) at which one of the dogs pulling Buster Keaton's chariot collapses – and Keaton simply gets a 'spare' from the 'boot'. Here, actions and elements appropriate to one mode of transport are (ingeniously, unexpectedly, and anachronistically) transposed to another. Keaton's gags often taken this transpositional form. So, too, do Chaplin's (though, like the sequence in

The Pawnshop (1916) in which a watch is examined the way a doctor would examine a patient, they tend to rely much more on mime).[7]

As has already been discussed, many gags, like the gag in *Liberty*, contradict our models and norms of actions and the behaviour of the universe to the point of complete impossibility. In *Go West* (1940), Harpo is stretched to twice his normal length while suspended between two rail cars. Television 'snow', in *The Disorderly Orderly* (1964), starts to blow into the room. In *Fast and Furry-ous* (1948), the coyote draws a roadscape on a cliff-face – and the roadrunner runs right through it. And in *Slap-Happy Lion* (1947) a kangaroo hops into its own pouch and disappears.

The cartoon in particular is, of course, precisely unhampered by what Creighton Peet has called 'such customary necessities as the laws of gravity, common-sense, and possibility'.[8] If comedy in general, and the Hollywood cartoon in particular, can stretch the rules of narrative motivation to the point of impossibility, and if, through parody, it can transgress and thus highlight the conventions of a particular film, genre, mode, or type of discourse, it can, in doing so, highlight its own fictional, conventional, and artificial status. In doing *this*, it can provide both isolated and systematic examples of 'self-awareness' and 'self-reflection', of what the Russian Formalists called *ostranenie* – estrangement, foregrounding, the exposure of the poetic or aesthetic device.[9]

Direct address to camera (in the form of a look and/or comment) and references to the fiction as a fiction are just two of the most obvious – and obviously transgressive – devices used very frequently in comedies to draw attention to their artifice, to highlight the rules by which it is governed and, thus, to raise a laugh. Jerry Lewis, Charlie Chaplin, and Laurel and Hardy all frequently address the camera, while in *Horsefeathers* Groucho at one point comes forward to tell us that 'I've got to stay here. But there's no reason why you folks shouldn't go into the lobby until this thing blows over.' In *Road to Utopia*

(1945), on the other hand, fiction and artifice are marked both by Robert Benchley's narration and by incidents like the one in which a man enters a scene to ask Bing Crosby for a light:

Hope: 'Hey, what do you do around here?'
Man: 'Nothing.'
Crosby: 'You in this picture?'
Man: 'No, I'm taking a short cut to stage ten.'[10]

Tex Avery's cartoons contain a constant stream of self-referential devices. One of the characters in *A Feud There Was* (1938) turns to camera and tells us that 'In these here cartoon pictures, a fellow can do about anything'. In *Lucky Ducky* (1948), the characters change from colour to black and white as they chase past a sign that reads 'Technicolor Ends Here'. And so on.

Comic verisimilitude

We have so far principally discussed the ways in which comedy and the comic involve transgressions of decorum and verisimilitude. But of course, comedy and the comic have their own – generic – regimes of verisimilitude, their own – generic – decorum, their own – generic – norms, conventions, and rules. In comedy, we expect the unexpected. If gags and jokes often function as neuralgic points, as points at which the conventionally censored or repressed find expression, they are performing a permissible, indeed institutionalized, function. Thus comedy in general, and the comic in particular, become, somewhat paradoxically perhaps, the appropriate site for the inappropriate, the proper place for indecorum, the field in which the unlikely is likely to occur. A prologue sequence from *Cheers* provides a perfect illustration of this last point in particular. Sam has come in late for work at the bar. He proceeds to explain to Rebecca, his boss, why he has been delayed:

'Boy, you will not believe what happened to me. I made a right hand turn on the Boyle centre and ran right into this

stupid parade. When my car backfired it scared the tar out
of these two cute little poodles in tutus who were dancing
by . . .'

Rebecca interjects in cynical disbelief: 'Dancing poodles?'
Sam continues:

'Yeah. Anyway the dogs spooked and ran away and this
little girl in blue sequins ran right in front of this little car
full of clowns that swerved to miss her. And the car ran
right in front of this elephant. The elephant reared up and
threw this swarmi guy who was riding on his trunk . . .'

Rebecca interjects a second time. Sam's story is ridiculous,
unlikely, improbable, and therefore totally unconvincing:
it lacks all verisimilitude:

'Sam, this is the lamest excuse you have ever given me.
Why didn't you just say "I'm sorry Rebecca. I overslept.
It won't happen again." '

But this is a comedy. As she finishes her sentence we cut
to a shot of the bar room door. In walks a girl in a blue
sequined dress followed by two little poodles in tutus.

This paradoxical combination of layers and levels of
verisimilitude and non-verisimilitude accounts for a
number of ambiguities. It accounts first for the fact that
while comic indecorum can on occasion disturb and
offend, it usually does not – precisely because we *expect*
indecorum of a comedy. It accounts secondly for the ambiguity of the role of the stereotype in comedy. For if the
comic involves the deformation of socially conventional
stereotypes in certain fields, certain respects, and certain
circumstances, it draws on them in others, particularly
and precisely for its own generic types. We have already
mentioned stupidity and dim-wittedness as stereotypical
forms of motivation for unconventional speech and behaviour in comedy. We might add insanity and intoxication.
Where these traits are stabilized as permanent characteristics, they form the basis of many basic comic stereotypes:
the imbecile or fool (Clouseau, Laurel and Hardy, Harry
Langdon), the drunk (Chaplin quite often, Dickie Hender-

son, Lord Charles, Leon Errol), and the lunatic or the eccentric (Woody Woodpecker, Screwball Squirrel, Mortimer's relatives in *Arsenic and Old Lace* (1944) ('Insanity runs in the family. It practically gallops.'), the family and hangers-on in *You Can't Take It With You*, the heroine in *Bringing Up Baby*, the Aunt in *On the Avenue* (1937), and so on). These are all stereotypes of social and cultural deviance. To them might be added the 'grotesque' and the 'ugly' (stereotypes of physical deviance), the old, the very young, the scatty female, the foreigner, and so on: it is hardly surprising that comedy often perpetuates prejudice, or draws uncritically on racist or sexist stereotypes, since they provide a ready-made set of images of deviation from social and cultural norms. The level of generic verisimilitude accounts, thirdly, for the *non* avant-garde character of even the most formally adventurous of comedies. As is often the case in all types of art, 'self-reflexive' devices can function as much to *intensify* a generically appropriate effect (in this case laughter), as to estrange conventions and their audiences, to hence *renew* a genre as much as to fundamentally disturb or alter its boundaries. Tex Avery and *Monty Python* may well foreground their own devices, and those of other forms, but, leaving aside for the moment the issue of the differential effect of such devices as looks and remarks to camera within the distinct structures of address marking cinema and television, they remain, first and foremost, innovative practitioners of institutionalized generic entertainment.

To sum up, we have argued that *all* instances of the comic involve a degree of non- or anti-verisimilitude, that *all* instances of the comic involve a deviation from some kind of norm, rule, convention, or type, whether culturally general or aesthetically specific. However, since this is the basis of comedy as a genre, since it is what we expect of the comic, neither comedy nor the comic can be regarded as inherently subversive or progressive, or as inherently avant-garde. If, in the words of Mick Eaton, the comic always involves a 'transgression of the familiar', it also always involves a 'familiarisation of the transgression'.[11]

More often than not, therefore, as we have argued elsewhere, 'comic pleasure is . . . inextricably linked to a replacement of transgression in relation to ideology, a resetting of the boundaries'.[12]

Section 2

6
Hollywood, comedy, and The Case of Silent Slapstick

In this chapter we locate comedy within the general aesthetic and industrial regime of classical – and preclassical – Hollywood cinema. We look at one of the ways in which it has been divided theoretically into two broad kinds or traditions. And we discuss in particular the role of gagbased comedy and slapstick in Hollywood, the theatrical contexts and traditions from which it stems, and some of the issues involved in the attempts made to produce feature-length slapstick films during the course of the 1920s.

Classical Hollywood cinema

The term 'classical Hollywood cinema' refers to the industrial structure, mode of production, and aesthetic regime marking the commercial cinema in America from (roughly) 1917 to 1960.[1] In the period from about 1917 to the mid–1920s, control of the film industry in America passed into the hands of a small group of companies. These companies were vertically integrated: they produced and distributed films, and they showed them in chains of cinemas which they themselves owned, or which belonged to other companies within what has been called 'the oligopoly'. The coming of sound and the early years of the Depression involved and produced some modifications to the number of these companies and their ranking in the hierarchy, but by the mid–1930s a stable structure had emerged. There were five large, vertically integrated companies, Loew's MGM, Paramount, RKO, Twentieth Century-Fox, and Warner Brothers. And there were three smaller companies, Columbia, United Artists, and Universal, who either produced or distributed films, but who did not own either large, first-run cinemas, or large-scale cinema chains. This structure characterized the American film industry until the late 1940s and early 1950s, when an anti-monopoly government decree forced the major companies to divorce their exhibition interests from their interests in distribution and production. By the end of the 1950s, all these companies had complied with the terms of the decree, and, thus, the nature of the industry, its practices, and its films had irrevocably changed.[2]

During the classical period, the companies were known as studios. The term referred both to the companies as corporate structures and to the sites of production they owned. In both instances, it implied a particular mode of production, and a particular type of corporate organization. The studios were factories employing large numbers of people in specialized jobs and roles, often on long-term, exclusive contracts. They produced and distributed a large and regular volume of films to fill all the cinemas to which they were guaranteed access.

The primary staple product of the classical cinema in America was the narrative feature film. Its general stylistic and structural features have been described by David Bordwell in Bordwell, Staiger, and Thompson's book, *The Classical Hollywood Cinema*.[3] The classical feature film was usually somewhere between 80 and 120 minutes in length. Its cinematic means and devices – editing, lighting, special effects, and so on – were geared principally to the intelligible unfolding of a story, to the delineation of strongly-profiled characters, settings, and actions within a coherent fictional space and time, and, secondarily, to the provision of spectacle. The narrative itself was organized according to the principles of the nineteenth-century 'well-made' play and the contemporary short story. It had a beginning, a middle, and an end. Stress was laid on causality ('the careful and logical working out of the laws of cause and effect'),[4] the preparation of events and actions, and consistent psychological motivation. Events, actions, and characters were legibly presented and plausibly motivated. Typically, there were two causally interrelated lines of action, one of which generally took the form of a heterosexual romance, and both of which tended to be geared to the goals of the principal protagonists. The narrative consisted primarily of a series of modulated scenes, scenes which would each take up, develop, or conclude a previous chain of events and actions, and open up a new one. Such scenes could be interspersed with transitional sequences usually depicting a transition in time and space. By and large, each narrative was self-contained. Narration was designed to display events, actions, characters, and their settings rather than its own devices and forms. The narrative flow was usually punctuated by moments of spectacle, but such moments were tied to, and hence motivated by, narrative action, narrative setting, and their respective components. The mode of address of the classical feature film was usually impersonal. The process of narration rarely acknowledged the spectator directly, or drew attention to itself.

The narrative feature film was the standard (and standardized) product of a highly organized industry which produced films on a factory-like, assembly-line basis. Because its product was an *aesthetic* product, however, the industry was faced with an in-built requirement for a degree of novelty, difference, variation, and originality, however standardized and similar it may have liked that product to be from a purely cost-effective point of view. In an industry like the motor car industry, there is, if anything, a requirement for each car within a range to be identical. Ranges and models only exist to renew and to stimulate demand. Aesthetic production, on the other hand, including the production of films, involves the requirement that, even within a range or model (or their equivalent), each work (though not, of course, each copy of that work) be in some way distinct. Thus, even within the American film industry, each product had to some extent to be different, individual, unique. No two films could be identical. There was an in-built need for variation and novelty, as well as a pressure for similarity and standardization.

One of the principal means of product differentiation during the classical period was by genre. Genres were particularly important, and particularly useful, because within each genre difference is minimal and systematic, variation on a format rather than absolute novelty. Genres thus combine the advantages of differentiation with the advantages of an in-built (and preponderant) requirement for repetition and standardization. Each film was unique, but each film was also just a variation on a formula or type. Thus, to take an example, *The Maltese Falcon* (1941) and *Shadow of a Doubt* (1943) are different from one another in a number of ways. The former is set in the city, the latter in a small town in the mid-west. The former centres on a male protagonist, the latter primarily on a female. *The Maltese Falcon* has a group of villains, *Shadow of a Doubt* only one. But both films are thrillers. Criminal villainy, whether spread over a variety of characters, or focused only on one, is a threat to the central protagonist in both films. This threat is coupled with an investigative process which in turn is a source of suspense. *The Maltese Falcon* features an experienced, professional detective who accumulates knowledge, and anticipates and wards (or fights) off danger throughout the course of the narrative. *Shadow of a Doubt* centres on a young woman who is unaware of the danger until late on in the film, and who then has to decide how to deal with it. Each film therefore handles the investigative process and the construction of suspense in a different way. But, along with criminal villainy and the dangers it poses (dangers concretized in both cases in moments of physical attack), they are necessarily included in both films as standard generic ingredients.

The different genres themselves – the horror film, the

gangster movie, the western, the war film, the epic, and so on – each provided a regularized set of variations on the format, components, and pleasures of the Hollywood feature film itself: different stresses in the story and its telling, different kinds of goals for its protagonists, different sources and kinds of spectacle, different sources of drama and conflict, different types of balance between spectacle and narrative. Thus where the source of primary conflict and narrative disturbance in the horror film was a monster of one kind or another, in the war film it was either the onset of war itself, or the threat posed by the enemy. Where the source of spectacle in a western was a specific type of landscape, costume, and setting (as well as generically necessary moments of physical conflict), in many horror films it was the physical appearance of the monster itself. And where the thriller tends to privilege the pleasures of plot complexity and narrative drive over the pleasures of spectacle, with the musical the reverse is often the case.

Thus genre and genres provided the advantages of contained variety and standardized differentiation both within and across the range of Hollywood's output as a whole. They minimized the financial risks inherent in the need for novelty. And they encouraged the systematic exploration and exploitation of the characteristics of the classical feature film and of Hollywood's technical and stylistic resources. During the classical period, each studio provided its own range of genres, but they could afford to some degree to specialize, to fully exploit their own particular resources, since the output of each of the studios complemented and extended the output of all the others. The full range was thus provided by the oligopoly as a whole.[5]

Comedy in the Hollywood regime

Comedy was part and parcel of this industrial and aesthetic regime. Comedy was always regularly produced. And comedy was always popular. As is well known, Bob

Hope, Bing Crosby, Jerry Lewis, and Dean Martin regularly topped polls in the 1940s and 1950s for the most popular performers in Hollywood. Their films, together with those of Abbott and Costello, were nearly always box-office hits.[6] However, it is important to point out the extent to which, and the ways in which, comedy, however regular and popular, was either exceptional or marginal, or both.

The first thing to point to here is the difficulty of defining either the characteristics and conventions of comedy as a genre in Hollywood, or its limits and boundaries. It is, of course, an important truism that other genres are difficult to define in anything other than banal tautologies, in part because they constantly evolve. Thus a western is a film set on the western frontier, a gangster film is a film about gangsters, and so on. However, comedy is especially hard to pin down. Here, as elsewhere, the multiplicity of comedy's conventions and forms is both striking and important. Important, too, is comedy's close relationship with melodrama and the musical. We have discussed already the kinship between melodrama and narrative comedy. The kinship between comedy and the musical is evident in the fact that one of the major forms of the Hollywood musical is, precisely, the 'musical comedy'. Musical comedy includes films like *Top Hat* (1935), *On the Avenue* (1937), *Cover Girl* (1944), and *Singin' in the Rain* (1952), all of them marked by comic plots, gags, and jokes, and all of them involving specialist comic performers. In these films singing and dancing tend to constitute the primary point of attraction, they thus tend to be thought of as 'musicals' first and foremost. However, where singing and dancing do not predominate, musical comedy can become, simply, comedy, as in the Marx brothers' films, the Hope and Crosby 'Road' films, and the films of Abbott and Costello.

Another reason why comedy is hard to define as a genre is that, quite apart from its kinship with melodrama and the musical, it has a specific and privileged capacity to combine with, or take over, all the other Hollywood genres. These genres can all be rendered comic, and can all be parodied. We have discussed generic parody (and generic hybridization) already, in chapter 2. We would like here to stress the extent to which this can blur (and extend) generic boundaries, particularly those of comedy itself. And we would like to emphasize the extent to which its capacity for parody places comedy in a generically unique position. It can either refer to or incorporate the rules and devices of all the other genres. Thus comedy can in itself, to a considerable extent, explore and exploit many of the possibilities of the Hollywood feature film that the other genres exist to embody. It can also both parody – and break – most of the conventions of the feature film itself.

The extent to which comedy can be an exception, both within Hollywood's generic regime, and with respect to the conventions that govern its films, has been noted by Bordwell. Comedies can rely on coincidence. They can employ *deus ex machina* endings. They need not, especially in the case of slapstick or comedian-oriented comedy, adopt the romance plot convention. They can abandon the convention of the modulated scene. Many scenes in Hollywood comedies exist almost solely for the display of gags, comic incident, and comic performance. Although they usually include characters relevant to the story, and settings pertinent to the narrative and its fictional world, they need neither pick up and advance, or introduce and develop, a line of action related to the plot. For example, although in each case there is a degree of important thematic motivation, neither the scene in *It's a Gift* (1934) in which Harold Bisonette (W. C. Fields) tries, and consistently fails, to get to sleep, first in bed, then on a bench on the porch, nor the scene in *The Great Dictator* (1940) in which Adenoid Hynkel (Charlie Chaplin) plays with a globe, in any way advance or develop the plot.

For Bordwell, comedy's exceptional status with respect to the norms and conventions of the classical feature film is its capacity for 'artistic motivation', the exposure of artistic devices and, thus, the systems to which they

belong. While other genres can draw attention to their
own devices and rules of construction (Bordwell significantly stresses the melodrama and the musical), comedy's
capacity for artistic motivation can at times override all
cannons of plausibility, coherence, narrative dominance,
and impersonal address:

> We must ask what limits classical cinema imposes on artis-
> tic motivation. Generally moments of pure artistic motiv-
> ation are rare and brief in classical films. Compositional
> motivation leaves little room for it, while generic motiv-
> ation tends to account for any flagrant devices. Indeed,
> baring the device has become almost conventional in cer-
> tain genres. Comedies are more likely to contain such *outré*
> scenes as that in *The Road to Utopia* (1945), in which
> Bing Crosby and Bob Hope, mushing across the Alaskan
> wilds, see the Paramount logo in the distance.[7]

There are two points to make about Bordwell's comments. First, he is right to stress the 'conventional' nature
of comedy here, in line with its more general capacity for,
indeed reliance upon, deviation from rules, norms and
laws of all kinds, as discussed in chapter 5. But secondly,
both in this particular passage and elsewhere in the book,
he tends to skate over the extent to which moments like
these depart fundamentally, albeit in a generically appropriate way, from the very conventions of the classical
feature film he has been at pains to describe in some detail.
It is this particular aspect of certain kinds of Hollywood
comedy that is stressed and discussed in Steve Seidman's
book, *Comedian Comedy: A Tradition in Hollywood
Film*.[8]

Seidman's basic thesis is that there is a distinct tradition
of comedy in Hollywood, a tradition he labels 'comedian
comedy'. In a number of ways, and for a number of
different reasons, it is a tradition marked by features which
run counter to those predominant elsewhere in Hollywood
films. He begins by noting the extent to which a great deal
of Hollywood comedy has involved performers who began
their careers, and established their acts, their styles of

performance, and their personae, in media other than the cinema itself. Stan Laurel and Charlie Chaplin began their careers in music hall and vaudeville, the Marx brothers, the Ritz brothers, Eddie Cantor, and Mae West in vaudeville and musical theatre, Jack Benny and Bob Hope in vaudeville and radio, Danny Kaye and Jerry Lewis in resort hotels and nightclubs in the Catskills, and Woody Allen in nightclubs and on television. Characteristic of these institutions and contexts is a structure of address in which an audience is witness to a live (or would-be live) performance, and in which the performance itself is directly and explicitly aimed at those listening and watching. When they appear in films, therefore, these performers bring with them not just an extra-cinematic persona, but a persona, and a style of performance, established in extra-cinematic terms.[9] These terms can conflict with or contradict the structure of address characteristic of the narrative film. Devices like direct address to camera, references to the fictional nature of the films in which these performers appear, quotes from, or references to, other films, and references to the world of showbiz outside the fictional universe of any one film, are all endemic to comedian comedy.[10] Seidman gives a number of examples. One would be the moment in *The Road to Bali* (1952) when, as Bing Crosby goes off to serenade the heroine (Dorothy Lamour), Bob Hope turns to camera and says, 'He's going to sing now, folks; now's the time to go outside and get some popcorn'. Another would be the moment in *Whistling in Brooklyn* (1943) in which Red Skelton, playing a fictional radio personality, mistakes an angry mob for a crowd of adoring fans. 'Boy', he says, 'if Jack Benny and Bob Hope could only see me now.' All these devices conflict with the dominant Hollywood convention that events have, so to speak, already happened, that they are plausibly motivated, that they take place in a self-contained fictional world, that narrative performance is unmarked, and, thus, that direct address to camera is forbidden.

Through the use of devices like these, the comedian becomes, in comedian comedy, an anomalous and privileged figure within the world of the films in which he or she appears, able to step outside its boundaries, and to play with its rules and conventions. A common device, one which re-emphasizes the point made earlier about the relationship between comedy and other genres, is to mark the rule-bound nature of this universe by making it specifically generic. Thus the comedian and his 'deviant' behaviour are set in playful conflict with the conventions of the western (Bob Hope in *The Paleface* (1948)) or the detective thriller (Buster Keaton in *Sherlock Junior* (1924)) or the horror film (Dean Martin and Jerry Lewis in *Scared Stiff* (1953)). In each of these films, it is as if the comedian – the disruptive element in the smooth functioning of the genre – is dropped into the fictional world by accident and, like a child, proceeds to toy with the rules. The comedian is therefore in conflict with the conventional laws of the genre concerned. On the one hand the comedian 'interferes' with the ostensible fiction, on the other the fiction 'constrains' the comedian. It is the play between the two that is responsible for much of the comedy.

Take the example of *The Paleface*. Jane Russell plays a bandit who is sprung from prison by the federal authorities who want to enlist her aid to defeat a band of gun-runners. Already there is some sign of deviance – the location of Russell, a 'woman who can take care of herself', as hero – but it is a familiar deviance that can be coped with in terms of the fictional mode of the western (see, for instance, non-comic westerns like *Johnny Guitar* (1954) and *Forty Guns* (1957)). However, instead of the federal agent, who can set her on the trail of the villains, she meets Bob Hope's incompetent dentist, 'Painless' Potter. Hope is the very inverse of the typical western hero, and the comedy elaborates his 'aberrant' characteristics – he is a show-off, a coward, and a useless shot, and he continually fails to consummate his marriage to Russell. But of course, this 'deviance' is precisely the mark of the comedian's talent as a comedian, his special status in the film. He is *playing* the misfit, playing with generic expectations, even, at the extreme, playing for the sake of play itself.

The comedian, then, is aberrant, disruptive. But his disruptiveness tends to be contained, and therefore motivated, by a (culturally conventional) opposition between eccentricity and social conformity. For Seidman the specificity of this opposition within the tradition of comedian comedy is that it is internalized as an opposition *within* the individual, and thus 'tied to the formation of a coherent personality'.[11] The comedian is therefore not simply a misfit-hero, but deviant with respect to the more general 'rules' of identity and 'adult' maturity, with regard to general social and familial norms. Deviance, confusion, and eccentricity are here suggested in a number of different, but recurrent, ways: dressing-up (Woody Allen as the robotic servant in *Sleeper* (1973), Danny Kaye in *The Inspector General* (1949)), crossdressing (Eddie Cantor in *Ali Baba Goes to Town* (1937), Bob Hope in *The Princess and the Pirate* (1944)), the feigning of madness (Bob Hope in *My Favorite Brunette* (1947) and *Son of Paleface*), and the playing of dual roles (Danny Kaye in *Wonder Man* (1945) and Jerry Lewis in *The Nutty Professor* (1963)). In addition, many of these comedians play characters who are childlike and infantile, a feature especially marked in their naïvety (Harry Langdon), their physical non-coordination (Jerry Lewis), and their preference for a world of daydreams and fantasy (Danny Kaye in *The Secret Life of Walter Mitty* (1947) and Woody Allen in *Play It Again, Sam*). Thus the very attributes that set these comedians apart – their performance skills, their verbal and physical dexterity, their ability to assume another identity through mime and through disguise, their ability to transform situations and objects at will – become, in comedian comedy, the hallmarks of abnormality, maladjustment, and, at times, potential insanity.[12]

Seidman not only contrasts the features and devices of comedian comedy with those of other kinds of Hollywood film. He also produces a distinction between comedian comedy, and comedy of a more stylistically conventional kind. He argues that similar cultural oppositions and issues are at stake – non-conformity, eccentricity, sexual difference, the lack of fit between individual characteristics and desires and institutional norms and requirements. And he acknowledges that some non-comedian comedies, like *His Girl Friday* (1940) and *The Palm Beach Story* (1942), contain instances of self-reference. But his main point is that because comedies like these do not revolve around the performances of comedians, they tend to be governed much more by the dominant conventions of the Hollywood feature film.[13]

We shall in our next chapter discuss the case of romantic comedy in Hollywood, referring specifically to *His Girl Friday* and *The Palm Beach Story* (among others), and concentrating in particular on some of the cultural oppositions and issues Seidman has identified. We want now, though, to extend our discussion of the ways in which the institutional position and aesthetic characteristics of comedy in Hollywood during the classical era were often exceptional, marginal, or in other ways non-standard. In order to do so we turn to the field of shorts and cartoons.

Shorts and cartoons

As well as producing and circulating feature films, the major Hollywood studios regularly produced and/or distributed shorts and cartoons through the classical period. Columbia, for instance, produced and distributed the Three Stooges films, RKO the animated Amos 'n' Andy series, Paramount the Robert Benchley shorts, MGM the Tom and Jerry cartoons, and Warner Brothers the Joe Palooka and Joe McDoakes films, and the cartoons that featured Bugs Bunny, Daffy Duck, Elmer Fudd, and the others. During the 1920s and 1930s in particular, cartoons and shorts were also produced by a number of smaller, specialized companies. The Hal Roach studios produced the Our Gang series and the Laurel and Hardy shorts, Disney produced the cartoons that featured Mickey Mouse, Donald Duck, and Goofy. Fleischer Brothers made the Betty Boop and Popeye cartoons. And Educational Pictures made shorts starring Lloyd Hamilton, Lupino

Lane, Harry Langdon, and the Ritz brothers, among others. These companies all had distribution deals with one or other of the majors.[14]

The examples given here are all, of course, examples of comedy. Comedy was by no means the only genre to figure live and animated shorts. Musical shorts, documentaries, and sports films were all also made.[15] But comedy – along with the musical – was the major fictional form. The point here is that shorts and cartoons, and therefore short and animated comedies, were secondary in status to feature films, both industrially and aesthetically, and were not necessarily governed by the same aesthetic rules and conventions. Thus shorts and cartoons were made usually on strict and limited budgets. They circulated as supports to features, and were thus institutionalized neither as primary attractions, nor even as attractions in their own right. And this was related, part as cause, part as effect, to the fact that the standards and conventions that governed the feature film either did not, need not, or could not apply. Shorts and cartoons were of sub-standard length. Newsreels – and individual newsreel items – did not tell self-contained stories. Documentaries could, and did, adopt some narrative conventions, but the status of the events depicted was different. And documentaries tended to use voiceover commentaries rather than the editing devices of the classical narrative film to provide information and to guide the spectator's attention. Some musical shorts, certainly, had plot lines and narratives. A film like *Ranch House Cowboy* (1939), with Ray Whitley and his Six Bar Cowboys, even has an intertwining double plot. One is about the Whitleys losing their ranch in a swap for a worthless goldmine. The other concerns an actress stranded with the Whitleys on her way to California. The two plots are linked to one another when the actress helps Whitley swap the ranch back again and gains the car she needs to complete her journey as part of the deal. These events are narrated in the classical style. But if classical norms are adhered to in some respects, they are abandoned in others. Most notably, *Ranch House Cowboy* is marked by an unconventional, unclassical balance between spectacle and narrative. Nearly half of the film's running time is occupied by singing and playing songs and instrumentals. Many other musical shorts, of course, like *Symphony of Swing* (1939), with Artie Shaw, have no plot at all. They consist solely of a string of separate numbers.

Given the secondary, marginal, or other non-standard nature of the short, it is hardly surprising that comedy (itself, as we have seen, prone to deviations from classical norms) should feature so heavily. Nor is it surprising that so much short comedy is of the comedian comedy kind. This is even true of the animated short. Characters like Bugs Bunny, Tweetie Pie, and Daffy Duck often address remarks and looks to camera. The films they appear in frequently contain all kinds of self-referential devices and moments. And characters like Daffy Duck, Screwball Squirrel and Wile Coyote embody and exhibit precisely the same oppositions, splits, and disorders as the performers discussed by Steve Seidman. Of course, the 'performers' in these films have no previous careers in other fields of comic entertainment. But cartoons like *The Big Snooze* (1946) and *Duck Amuck* (1953) do suggest that they have careers and contracts in the movies, and that they only play the parts they do in order to fulfil them.

We have here only noted the relationship between comedy and the short. In order to examine the relationship further to look again at the relationship between comedian comedy and the classical feature film, we turn now to silent slapstick. Here we shall pay particular attention both to the characteristics and the functions of slapstick in the cinema prior to the advent of the feature film (when all films were 'shorts'), and to its encounter with the feature film – and *its* characteristics and functions – during the course of the 1920s.

Early cinema, silent slapstick, and the 1920s

By the 1920s, the cinema in its classical form had been firmly established in America. The industry was now organized along vertically integrated lines, and most of the companies that were henceforth to dominate it had now emerged. The feature-length narrative film was now not only the industry's primary product, but also, because of its relative expense, the foundation for the oligopoly's control.[16] Henceforth the short film, the single-reeler and the two-reeler, the industry's staple product in the early 1910s, would be either secondary, or marginal, or both.

One of the reasons for the emergence, and rapid dominance, of the feature film, in America as elsewhere, was its cultural prestige, and hence its ability to generate profit and income. It was felt that feature films could attract middle-class audiences, audiences with a high disposable income, and that more could be charged to see them than the average programme of shorts. *The Birth of a Nation* (1915), for which the hitherto unheard-of price of a $1 was charged for admission, and which earned the hitherto unheard-of sum of $5 million on its initial release alone, was to prove them right.[17] For Hollywood, feature-length films meant extensive and carefully organized narratives. Both on this count, and because of its low cultural standing among the classes Hollywood was seeking to attract and maintain as a regular audience, there was a great deal of adverse criticism of slapstick comedy in the trade press during the late 1910s and early 1920s, and concomitant demands for a type of comedy with greater capacities for narrative organization and feature-length development. The *Moving Picture World*, for example, argued in September 1919 that:

> Slapstick must be taboo. The public has gone beyond the rough-and-tumble performances that used to be classed as humorous. Instead, a more subtle, clean-cut production, with at least some semblance of a story, is the current demand in the comedy line.[18]

Three years later, Frederick Palmer, in his *Photoplay Plot Encyclopaedia*, wrote that:

> Burlesque and farce are becoming less and less popular,

and there is no real demand for stories of this type. The comedy producers are desirous of polite, plausible situation comedies, preferably founded upon an amusing situation that might very naturally occur in the life of almost any spectator.[19]

A tradition of 'plausible situation comedies' of what Tom Dardis, Kalton Lahue, and Donald McCaffrey have all loosely called 'polite' or 'genteel' comedy, already existed within the field of the single-reeler. According to Dardis, it was indeed precisely this tradition that provided the basis for most feature-length comedies in the late 1910s and early 1920s:

while many feature-length comedy films *were* being made in 1919–22, they were nearly all 'story' films, usually based on popular novels and plays and *Saturday Evening Post* serials. They would star performers like Constance Talmadge, Will Rogers, and Mabel Normand. The story was always the main thing.[20]

Thus what is significant about the comments of Frederick Palmer and the *Moving Picture World* (and others) is not that they sought the invention of a new kind of comedy, but that they represented a threat to the old kind, one which hitherto had clearly been important (important enough, at any rate, to be singled out for attack). For the producers of slapstick comedy this threat carried with it, as we shall see, very particular financial implications. More than that, though, it marked a final shift away from a form and conception of cinema in which slapstick was not just important, but central, a shift away from a period in which, prior to 1906, at least, slapstick was fundamental, not just to film comedy, but to the aesthetic nature, cultural function, and institutional location of films as a whole.

As Tom Gunning has pointed out, the cinema prior to 1906–7, was a 'cinema of attractions', its films, both individually and collectively, a series of effects and points of interest and astonishment aimed, often directly, at the viewer.[21] In fact during this period, as Gunning goes on to argue, 'the cinema' as we know it, an industry and institution with its own specific product, its own internal organization, its own ancillary activities, did not exist. There were no sites or buildings dedicated solely, or even primarily, to the showing of films before the advent of the nickelodeon in 1905. And there was no distinct and interlocking system of film production, distribution, and exhibition. Hence there was no concept of 'going to the cinema', nor any concept of 'cinema' itself. Films – moving photographic pictures – were produced for exhibition and consumption within frameworks, sites, and contexts that existed already, and that had been developed for the presentation of magic lantern shows, scientific novelties, magical displays, theatrical entertainments, and so on. In addition to the limitations and characteristics of contemporary film technology, these contexts greatly determined the forms and modes of the films that were made. They account, in particular, for the characteristics that follow from the status of the films as attractions, and for the forms of internal organization used to display the attractions they contained.

Among these contexts were the forms and institutions of variety entertainment. Some, like fairs and circuses, involved travelling from place to place. Others like vaudeville and music hall were located in fixed sites and specialized buildings. Whether permanently sited or itinerant, though, the hallmark of these forms and institutions was the range of very different types of entertainment they each provided, and the way these entertainments were presented and programmed. All of them, in one way or another, adopted a modular format in which a variety of acts, and a variety of *types* of act, each unrelated to the others, would appear before an audience for a fixed and limited period of time.[22] Usually, the mode of presentation was sequential, but occasionally, as in circuses and fairs, it could be simultaneous as well. Each form or institution had its own particularities, either specializing in a certain array of acts, or having its own unique, individual structure. However all of them aimed, in the words of Garff

Wilson, 'to satisfy the tastes of a polyglot audience by providing novel and varied entertainment', entertainment which would be both diverting, and 'easily understood'.[23]

Given this structure, and given these aims, every act within each of these forms and institutions tended to be highly self-contained, to build rapidly towards a powerfully marked climax, and to strive for novelty, immediacy of impact, and instant appeal. Since films and programmes of films were initially nearly always shown as acts within one kind of variety format or another, they, too, were subject to these aims and concerns. They too were marked by these formal characteristics. Not surprisingly, comedy was a key generic component, both in live acts and films.[24] Not surprisingly either, the predominant kinds of comedy were slapstick and gag-based: instantly intelligible, full of powerfully marked effects designed to produce an instant (and audible) audience response, and internally structured so as to build across a series points to a climax without the aid of a plot. In the words of one contemporary commentator:

> The great demand ... is for low comedy with plenty of action. Broad sweeping effects without too much detail are wanted. The artistic 'legitimate' actor wastes too much time in working up to his points, but the skilled vaudevillist strikes them with a single blow and scores. A successful vaudeville sketch usually concentrates in one act as many laughs and as much action as are usually distributed over a three-act comedy.[25]

Many of the earliest – and therefore shortest – film comedies consisted simply of gags, with more or less time devoted to the stage, and the task, of preparation. In order to constitute a ten- or fifteen-minute 'act', a number of films would be shown, each of them individually providing some kind of 'point'. In an English film, *The Miller and the Sweep* (1897), a miller, dressed in white, and carrying a bag of flour, approaches the foreground space of the frame from a mill located at the back. A sweep, dressed in black, and carrying a bag of soot, enters the frame from the left. There is virtually no preparation at all. The two men simply collide with one another and begin to fight. The gag is a visual one: the miller gets covered in soot and turns black, while the sweep gets covered in flour and turns white. (Significantly, given the importance of nineteenth-century variety to early comedy, the origins of this gag seem to lie in the circus.)[26] In *The Treacherous Folding Bed*, a French film of 1897, there is more preparation. A group of soldiers enter a room, make adjustments to a bed, and leave. Another soldier comes in, sits on the bed, and the bed, of course, collapses. There is a minimal narrative here. Two distinct events are presented in sequence, linked by a logic of cause and effect. There is even a degree of characterization. The group of soldiers are pranksters. The individual soldier is an unwitting dupe. But, again, the 'point' is the gag. Any narrative there may be exists solely to set up the pratfall. Any characterization there may be is simply an effect of the structure of the gag.

From this earliest period to the mid–1910s, films, and the institutional context in which they were made, shown, and viewed, underwent a number of significant changes. The cinema itself began to emerge as a distinct cultural entity, a distinct nexus of socially recognized characteristics, features, and practices. Cinemas were built. Audiences increased in size. A large-scale industry devoted almost exclusively to the production, distribution, and exhibition of films now existed. As a result, the films themselves changed, both in nature and in function. First, they increased in length. By 1908, the standard length of a film had increased from one or two minutes to ten or twelve minutes (the length of a single reel). Secondly, films were no longer just 'attractions' in theatrical variety. Cinemas now existed, devoted either solely or primarily to the showing of programmes of films. Thirdly, films were made increasingly and specifically to attract 'respectable' (and relatively wealthy) middle-class audiences, and hence to cater to middle-class tastes, and to embody middle-class aesthetic values.

The consequence of all these developments was an increasing abandonment of the aesthetic of attraction, an increasing attention to the values of narrative, and an increasing narrativization of the films themselves. Just as one reform group in America in the early 1910s attacked the aesthetics of variety on the grounds that it was dependent upon 'an artificial rather than a natural human ... interest',[27] so the trade press and contemporary commentators on the cinema began to demand 'art' and coherent narration:

> To secure art in a motion picture, there must be an end to be attained, a thought to be given, a truth to be set forth, a story to be told, and the story must be told by a skillful and systematic arrangement or adaptation of the means at hand subject to the author's use.[28]

One of the consequences of *this* was the development of a new kind of comedy in the cinema, the genteel tradition mentioned earlier. Another was an increasing uncertainty, on the part of commentators and critics, as to the value (and values) of slapstick, and an increasing attention to what came to be perceived as its exceptional and anachronistic characteristics.

One of the earliest genteel comedies is D. W. Griffith's *The Peach Basket Hat* (1909). According to Tom Gunning, Griffith had been largely responsible for shifting the emphasis at Biograph, the studio for which he worked at this time, away from slapstick comedy and towards what he calls 'domestic' modes and forms.[29] *The Peach Basket Hat* is one of a series of films Griffith made about a fictional couple called Mr and Mrs Jones. Like the others in the series, it exemplifies a commitment to the representation, within the field of comedy, of 'respectable' middle-class characters and 'respectable' middle-class institutions like the family and marriage. Significantly, in using a name like 'Jones' it marks the characters, their values, and their settings as ordinary, unexceptional, and familiar – in direct contrast to the emphasis in slapstick on the extraordinary and the grotesque. More than that, though, *The Peach*

Basket Hat exemplifies a commitment to the values of narration. As Gunning points out, the extent of this commitment can be measured by comparing it with *The Lost Child* (1904), an earlier Biograph prototype.[30] Both films concern the apparent disappearance of a baby. In *The Lost Child*, a man with a large basket is suspected of stealing the child. In *The Peach Basket Hat*, the suspects are gypsies. In *The Lost Child*, the baby has been hidden from view by a dog kennel. In *The Peach Basket Hat*, its disappearance is due to a large cardboard box. Although there are similarities, then, the films are different. But the difference between them lies not so much in their respective narrative detail, nor even in the number of shots they involve (eleven in *The Lost Child*, thirty-four in *The Peach Basket Hat*). It lies rather, as Gunning points out, in the relative attention they accord to spectacular comic action on the one hand, and to narrative exposition and motivation on the other, something the distribution of the shots serves to measure:

> In *The Lost Child*, the first shot set up [sic] the basic narrative situation: the baby's disappearance and the beginnings of the search for him. The following 8 shots are devoted to the chase and capture of the supposed culprit (the last two shots revealing where the child really is). In Griffith's film, 22 shots are spent setting up the situation: Mr. Jones reading the newspaper about a kidnapping; the arrival of Mrs. Jones' new hat; the box falling over the baby. Only the last 11 shots are devoted to the chase.[31]

The chase was a key device in the cinema at the time *The Lost Child* was produced. It marked the increasing length of films at this time, and allowed them to move in the direction of edited narration, articulating one particular kind of narrative action across a variety of shots, locations, and spaces. It also functioned, within comedy in particular, as a new kind of slapstick attraction. Of particular significance, then, is the way that *The Peach Basket Hat* both absorbs its chase into an elaborated narrative context, and uses editing to construct a distinct and consistent narrative voice:

In 1904, the chase was the narrative form *par excellence*. By 1909, filmmakers felt the need to embed it in a story that provided some characterization and motivation (Mr. Jones has read in the newspapers about a kidnapping and is anxious ... however, the superstitious nurse invites some gypsies in to tell her fortune, and therefore ...).

The filmic expression of the chase sequences in the two films also involves some important differences. The earlier film followed the usual format, including pursuers and pursued in the same shot and linking shots together on the movement of characters from one location to the next. Griffith introduces parallel editing into the chase sequence, but in a curious fashion. The gypsies and the group of pursuers led by Mr. Jones both appear in each shot; there is no parallel editing between them. Rather, Griffith interpolates 4 shots of the baby-concealing box back at home into the chase sequence. The effect is clearly ironic. The omniscient *narrator-system* reminds the audience of the babby's [sic] actual situation, still unknown to the characters. ... Even in this simple comedy a sense of *voice* is revealed in the ironic contrast of frenzied pursuit with baby safely at home.[32]

Having made these points, it is important to stress that 'genteel' comedy and the values of well-made narration did not displace silent slapstick during the early 1910s. It rather grew up alongside it. The single-reel format could be used either to produce self-contained, internally developed, consistently motivated, and coherently narrated narratives. Or it could be used to pile gag upon gag, chase upon chase, in an escalating frenzy of movement. Griffith himself made a number of slapstick chase films, including *The Curtain Pole* (1908) and *The French Duel* (1909), both of them more or less contemporary with *The Peach Basket Hat*. And the continuing viability of slapstick, both aesthetically and economically, was still to be marked by the advent of Mack Sennett's Keystone comedies in 1912. Critical comment, however, drew increasing attention to the aberrant and old-fashioned nature of slapstick. Referring to the basis of a great deal of slapstick in French comedy, *The Moving Picture World*, for instance, criticized *The Curtain Pole* in the following terms:

> One is disposed to wonder why the Biograph company with its splendid organization has felt forced to adopt the worn-out scheme of foreign producers and introduce these long chases and destruction of property as part of their amusement films. No fault can be found with the picture technically, but the plan under which it is worked is not quite so satisfactory.[33]

More neutrally, the same paper some two years later merely noted the general difference between slapstick and other forms in matters of characterization and narrative: 'In farce-comedy alone', it declared, 'can characterization be *subordinated* to incident and action'.[34] But other commentators usually sought, in marking differences such as these, to imply disapproval or contempt. Thus *Photoplay* in 1912:

> The moving picture play has altogether outgrown themes of single individuals in a series of incidents that have no relation to one another except for the presence of the main character. For instance, the mischievous small boy in a series of pranks; the victim of sneezing powder in various mishaps, the near-sighted man, etc. They are all passé.[35]

And thus film director, James Kirkwood, writing in 1916:

> I believe that the most desirable sort of play today is modern and American, whether a swift-moving drama with strong, human characterization, or a comedy devoid of extravagance, its incidents growing out of the foibles of human nature rather than produced by one of the characters smiting another with what is commonly called a slapstick.[36]

With Kirkwood's criticisms, and the year in which they were made, we are back again in the era of the feature film, and the kinds of criticisms quoted earlier in the chapter.

As already mentioned, Sennett's Keystone Studios had, in the interim, played a major part in sustaining the slapstick tradition. A new wave of comic performers from vaudeville, the circus, pantomime, and English music hall,

among them Ford Sterling, Chester Conklin, Charlie
Chaplin, and, a little later, Ben Turpin, all featured in
Sennett's films. Their success led other variety comics, like
Stan Laurel and Buster Keaton, to make films too, thus
helping to establish a second phase of comedian comedy
in the cinema (following a first phase dominated much
more by French performers like 'Rigadin', 'Boireau', and
Max Linder.)[37]

By the early 1920s, therefore, despite criticism throughout the 1910s, slapstick seemed still to flourish, and slapstick shorts continued to be made. Now, though, they
were made against prevailing trends, in very different,
and increasingly circumscribed, industrial and economic
conditions. The feature film had arrived, marking the
ascendancy of narrative values. It was now the industry's
principal product. Thus whereas in the early to
mid–1910s, slapstick's format, the single-reel short, was
at one and the same time the format best suited to its
aesthetic characteristics, and the format to which the
industry as a whole was geared as its standard commodity,
there was now a discrepancy. The industry was geared
to one form, slapstick to another. Slapstick's form was
secondary. Its industrial position was weaker, much more
marginal. So too was its financial position. Hitherto,
because its form was standard, slapstick comedy was able
to make as much money at the box office as any other
kind of film. Now, although slapstick tended to be made
as much in double-reel as single-reel formats, and although
the films of Chaplin, Lloyd, and Keaton, in particular,
made a great deal of money, its earning capacity in any
short form was simply not as great as feature-based genres
and modes.

It is therefore significant that the renewed demands in
the late 1910s and early 1920s for 'genteel' comedy and
narrative values – the values of the feature film – were
now not just ignored. They could not afford to be. And
it is even more significant that two of the most popular
slapstick performers, Keaton and Lloyd, were among those
who publicly acknowledged these demands, in articles they

wrote for a book called *The Truth About The Movies*, first published in 1924. Keaton, for instance, expressed the view that 'explosives, cops, stock situations, flivvers, pie throwing and bathing girls' were *passé*: 'A comedian today no longer finds his dressing room filled with slapstick, property bricks, stuffed clubs and exploding cigars. Comic situations have taken the place of these veteran laugh getters.'[38] Lloyd's view is similar: 'We have noticed ... that audiences are drawing closer to an appreciation of comedy wherein gags are mingled with story than in [sic] just straight gag comedies – pictures built entirely for laughs.'[39]

Lloyd and Keaton, of course, along with Chaplin, were among the first of the slapstick comedians to move into features. Chaplin made *The Kid* in 1921, Lloyd the four-reel *A Sailor Made Man* in 1921 and the five-reel *Grandma's Boy* in 1922, and Keaton *The Three Ages* and *Our Hospitality* in 1923. The financial stakes involved can be gauged by comparing some figures. In 1920, Lloyd made a two-reel short called *Bumping Into Broadway* for $17,274. The film was a success. Within three years of its initial release it had grossed over $150,000 at the box office.[40] However, three years later Lloyd made a feature called *Safety Last*. It cost $120,963. But it grossed more than $1,580,000.[41]

A move into features could clearly be profitable. But it could also be problematic, for it entailed a dilution of the characteristics of slapstick and an accommodation to genteel values and the demands of well-made narration. Buster Keaton has pointed to some of the aesthetic issues involved:

> In one or two of my later two-reelers I tried putting in a story-line. But this had not always proved feasible, and the faster the gags came in most short comedies, the better. In the features I soon found out that one had to present believable characters in situations that the audience accepted. ...
>
> One of the first decisions I made was to cut out custard-

pie throwing. It seemed to me that the public by that time
– it was 1923 – had had enough of that. . . .

We also discontinued using what we called impossible
or cartoon gags. These can be very funny in a cartoon
short, and sometimes in a two-reeler. . . .

But that sort of gag I would never use in a full-length
picture – because it could not happen in real life, it was
an impossible gag.[42]

We would like to conclude this chapter by taking a more
detailed look at some of the issues Keaton has identified
here, together with a number of others raised by the
encounter between slapstick, genteel comedy, and well-
made, feature-length narration. We take as examples for
discussion Harold Lloyd's *Grandma's Boy*, Buster
Keaton's *Our Hospitality*, and Chaplin's first sound feature, *City Lights* (1931).

Slapstick and narrative cinema

It is Donald McCaffrey's thesis that Harold Lloyd's work
is, from 1917 onwards, increasingly marked by a combination of genteel and slapstick elements.[43] Abandoning his
earlier slapstick style and 'Lonesome Luke' persona, and
influenced in particular, according to McCaffrey, by contemporary genteel performers like Charles Ray, Douglas
McLean, and Johnny Hines, Lloyd now develops what
he called his 'glass' character, and turned much more to
plausibility, plot, and the humour of situations. Lloyd
himself discussed the changes in his style and persona in
precisely such terms in his autobiography, *An American
Comedy*, first published in 1928.

The glasses would serve as my trademark and at the same
time suggest the character – quiet, normal, boyish, clean,
sympathetic, not impossible to romance. I would need no
eccentric make-up, 'mo' or funny clothes. I would be an
average recognizable American youth and let the situation
take care of the comedy.[44]

McCaffrey suggests that Lloyd rather overstates the extent

to which he abandoned slapstick elements. While his 1920s films *are* marked by a more genteel persona, and while they are marked also by plots and situations which provide motivation for the gags, the pratfalls, and the chases, are still there.

McCaffrey discusses *Grandma's Boy*, along with *Safety Last* and *The Freshman* (1925), in order to pinpoint both the nature of its genteel and slapstick components, and the way these components are used. *Grandma's Boy* tells the story of a young man whose timidity and cowardice lead him firstly to be beaten up and thrown into a well by a rival for his girl (Mildred Davis), then intimidated by a brutal-looking tramp. He goes to visit the girl, but suffers further humiliation on account of his old-fashioned clothes. He is asked to join a posse in search of the tramp, but separated from the others he runs home in terror. Grandma hears of his cowardice, and tells him about his grandpa. Grandpa, too, was a coward. However, inspired by a voodoo talisman, he conquered singlehandedly a group of Union officers during the civil war. Now in possession of this selfsame talisman, the young man finds the tramp and finally captures him in hand-to-hand combat. Finally, congratulated by grandma and the girl, he learns the truth: grandma's story was only a story, and the talisman only an ornately carved umbrella handle. But the young man then realizes that courage is only a state of mind. With his newfound knowledge and self-confidence he convinces the girl that they must get married at once.

Grandma's Boy contains a number of slapstick elements: several comic fights, a lengthy chase, eccentric costume, and numerous gags and pratfalls. However, they are all related either to the nature (and transformation) of the central protagonist, or to the development of the narrative, or both. Thus the chase is embedded in a story, indeed it marks the culmination of a narrative thread concerning the pursuit and the capture of the tramp. It features characters introduced much earlier in the film. And it marks the transformation undergone by one of these characters – the young man – and hence a reversal in the relations between them. One of the gags in the film, meanwhile, occurs during the course of the young man's visit to the girl's house. He gets his finger stuck in a vase and frantically tries to remove it while keeping it hidden from the girl and, therefore, avoiding impropriety and social embarassment. Here there are direct links to the genteel tradition. The visit itself constitutes an episode in the romance plot that provides the film with its basic narrative frame. It is the location of the gag with the vase within this frame, and the consequent production of humour not just from a physical incident but also from its social and situational context, that marks the way the film consistently integrates slapstick material into both genteel and narrative contexts. A similar strategy is at work early in *Grandma's Boy* when the young man is embarrassed by having to walk past a group of children wearing wet and shrunken clothes. There are clear echoes here of the way the slapstick tradition uses ill-fitting clothes and bodily exposure for laughs. But in this case, ill-fitting clothes are the consequence of a previous narrative incident – the ducking in the well – an incident itself related both to a consistent character trait (the young man's cowardice) and to the romance plot (the young man is dumped in the well by his rival). The stress, moreover, in the presentation of this sequence is as much on the way the young man suffers humiliation as a consequence of wearing the clothes as it is on their ludicrous nature.

McCaffrey sums up many of the differences between earlier slapstick films and the way slapstick is used in Lloyd's films of the 1920s as follows: 'The difference between Lloyd's works and the early works can be explained in one word – motivation.'[45] Motivation – of various kinds – is also a feature of Keaton's *Our Hospitality*. It is a feature stressed, in particular, by Bordwell and Thompson, in their discussion of the film in *Film Art*.[46]

Our Hospitality concerns a young man, Willie McKay (Buster Keaton), who journeys to the south from New York to inherit what turns out to be a derelict mansion.

On the journey he meets a young woman, and is invited to her home. She is a member of the Canfield family, and, unknown to either of them, the Canfields are sworn enemies of the McKays. Willie visits the Canfield home, where, ironically, the rules of southern hospitality mean that he is safe from attack. He stays the night, but is forced to leave in the morning. During a chase through the countryside and down to the river Willie eludes his pursuers, then, spectacularly, rescues the daughter from drowning. The Canfield men return home disappointed, but determined to continue the feud. They are surprised to discover, however, not only that Willie is there in the house, but that he and the daughter are now being married by a local minister. Confronted with a *fait accompli*, the elder Canfield eventually relents, and decides that the feud should now end.

As Bordwell and Thompson have noted, nearly all the elements in *Our Hospitality* – including the gags – are multiply motivated: used to advance the narrative, used to delineate character, and, often, presented in such a way as to ensure a high degree of narrative economy. Thus

> virtually every bit of behavior of the figures functions to support and advance the cause-effect chain of the narrative. The way Canfield sips and savors his julep establishes his Southern ways; his Southern hospitality in turn will not allow him to shoot a guest in the house. Similarly, Willie's every move expresses his diffidence or resourcefulness. Even more concise is the way the film uses the arrangement of figures and settings in depth to present two narrative events simultaneously ... the Canfield boys in the foreground make plans to shoot Willie, while in the background Willie overhears them and starts to flee.... Thanks to depth in spatial arrangement, Keaton is able to pack together and connect two story events, resulting in tight narrative construction, and in a relatively unrestricted narration.[47]

Multiple motivation, and this particular kind of narrative economy, helps give the film compositional coherence. Such coherence is also provided by the way in which elements of *mise en scène*, and actions and gags, are inter-linked as recurring motifs. One example would be what Bordwell and Thompson call 'the fish on the line motif':

> Early on in *Our Hospitality* Willie is angling and hauls up a miniscule fish. Shortly afterward, a huge fish yanks him into the water. . . . Later in the film, through a series of mishaps, Willie becomes tied by a rope to one of the Canfield sons. A great many gags arise from this umbilical-cord linkage, especially one that results in Canfield's being pulled into the water as Willie was earlier.
>
> Perhaps the single funniest moment in the film occurs when Willie realizes that since the Canfield boy has fallen off the rocks, so must he. . . . But even after Willie gets free of Canfield, the rope remains tied around him. So in the film's climax, Willie is dangling from a log over the waterfall like a fish on the end of the line.[48]

One particular point worth noting about 'the fish on the line motif' is that its development serves progressively to narrativize a type of action – a figure – which begins as an incidental gag. The catching of a miniscule fish early on in the film serves no plot purpose whatsoever. In the climax, however, the figure is crucial to the outcome of the story. For it is by swinging on the rope – like a fish on the end of a line – that Willie is able to rescue the daughter from the waterfall.

In all these ways, *Our Hospitality* exemplifies all the virtues and characteristics demanded of the well-made narrative feature film. But what of the genteel tradition? As Bordwell and Thompson have noted, one of the film's recurrent elements is a sampler bearing the homily 'Love Thy Neighbor':

> It appears initially in the prologue of the film, when seeing it motivates Canfield's attempt to stop the feud. It then plays a significant role in linking the ending back to the beginning; it reappears at the end when Canfield, enraged that Willie has married his daughter, glances at the wall, reads the inscription, and resolves to end the years of feuding.[49]

The sampler here not only plays a significant role in the provision of compositional and narrative unity. It also plays a role in the way the film uses its genteel components. It helps to cement the romance, and thus provide a happy ending, while it is also used ironically, to mark the differences between two incompatible sets of southern values: the values of genteel propriety (which mean among other things that a guest must be treated hospitably) and the values of 'chivalry' and 'honour' (which mean that Willie is in mortal danger as soon as he steps out of the Canfield house). The film takes a distance from those who hypocritically espouse both at once. But it finds in the outsider, Willie, both someone who acts in a truly chivalrous manner (he rescues the daughter) and someone who, almost-literally, loves his neighbour (so much so, of course, that he marries her). In this way, Keaton, the slapstick comedian, finds himself playing the part of a character who incarnates all the genuine genteel virtues.

Before turning, lastly, to *City Lights*, it is worth recalling the extent to which Chaplin and his films were criticized during the 1910s and the early 1920s for their slapstick values, and for the vulgarity of much of their humour. Writing in *Variety* in 1915, for instance, Sime Silverman described Chaplin's films and persona as 'mussy, messy and dirty': 'never anything dirtier was placed upon the screen than Chaplin's Tramp'.[50] Even those who liked Chaplin felt compelled to acknowledge, and to deprecate, these qualities. This is from *The Little Review*, again in 1915:

> the stuffy, maddening 'bathos' that clings to the mob like a stink is dispelled, wiped off the air. Charlie Chaplin is before them, Charles Chaplin with the wit of a vulgar buffoon and the soul of a world artist. . . . He is absurd; unmanly; tawdry; cheap; artificial. And yet behind his crudities, his obscenities, his inartistic and outrageous contortions, his 'divinity' shines.[51]

Photoplay, meanwhile, considered that Chaplin was facing a choice:

What is to become of Charlie Chaplin? Will the little genius of laughter relegate himself to comic history, or will he, changing his medium of expression, pass to a higher and more legitimate comedy? He must do one or the other.[52]

A year later, following criticism of films like *A Woman* (1915), in which Chaplin not only dresses in drag, but creates jokes around his pincushion bosom and flirts with a number of men, the *Motion Picture Magazine* reported that an announcement had been made by the National Board of Censorship:

the old Charlie Chaplin has seen that the very methods by which his personality achieved success now imperil his unprecedented reputation by alienating a great part of the American public.[53]

The result would be 'a new fame based on a more delicate art'.[54]

At first glance, it may seem as though Chaplin did, indeed, capitulate to the criticisms and demands with which he was faced. Already, in *The Tramp* (1915), he had introduced pathos, romance, and an ambiguous, bittersweet ending. And in 1916 he made *The Vagabond*, a film which, as described by David Robinson, is replete with genteel and narrative values:

Charlie is a street musician. . . . Out in the country, he rescues a little blonde drudge from villainous gypsies. Their life together in a stolen caravan is a (very chaste) idyll until a handsome young artist chances along and wins the heart of the girl. The artist's portrait of her is exhibited and recognized (thanks to the inevitable birthmark) by her long-lost mother. The girl is whisked off to a new life, leaving Charlie alone and disconsolate, unable even to manage the usual recuperative flip of the heels.[55]

As Robinson himself points out, *The Vagabond*, as 'a well-turned miniature drama' in which Charlie adopts a friendless girl, 'anticipates *The Circus*, *Modern Times*, *City Lights* and *Limelight*'.[56] But in the meantime, Chaplin continued to make slapstick shorts, like *The Floorwalker* (1916) and *Pay Day* (1922), and he continued to get into trouble with 'respectable' opinion (notably over *The Pilgrim* (1923) and *Monsieur Verdoux* (1947), but also over scenes like the one in *The Kid* in which he improvises a toilet, for the boy he has befriended, from a chair with a hole in the seat and a cuspidor placed underneath). Even in the most apparently genteel and sentimental of the story films, and 'well-turned' dramas, neither the gags nor the vulgarity were ever fully abandoned – *City Lights*, for instance, contains a gag about shit, in the sequence in which the tramp is trying to earn some money as a road-sweeper: he cleans up the droppings left by a string of donkeys, but walks off in the opposite direction when a group of elephants pass by. Thus if Chaplin did indeed find 'new fame based on a more delicate art', its delicacy did not lie in the unequivocal adoption of genteel and story-based values. But nor, on the other hand, did it lie in any of the strategies of combination, motivation, and integration adopted by Lloyd and by Keaton.

Chaplin's solution was very much his own. It consisted not of blending, or seeking to blend, genteel and slapstick components, but of playing the one off against the other in order to highlight their differences. As David Robinson has pointed out, one of the commonest forms this strategy takes is that of using slapstick elements to undermine, or cut across, the genteel ones. This form is evident as early as *The Vagabond* itself (almost as early, in other words, as genteel components begin to appear):

> Chaplin's sentiment is invariably saved from mawkishness by comedy and the belligerence that always underlies his despair. His jealousy as he watches the girl dancing with the artist is not entirely impotent: he maliciously flicks a fly in the man's direction, and later manages to drop an egg in his shoes. After the girl's elegant mother condescendingly shakes hands with him, he suspiciously sniffs the perfume left on his fingers. He uses his favourite trick of deflating his own dramatic despair with farce: in *The Vagabond* the anguish of a lover rejected is quite eclipsed by the agonies of the same man accidentally sitting on a stove.[57]

Similar moments occur in *City Lights*, as for instance

when the Tramp first meets the blind Flower Girl with whom he instantly falls in love. He stops to gaze at her adoringly; she – unwittingly – throws a container of water over him. But *City Lights* illustrates particularly well that moments like this are part of a wider strategy.

Having met the Flower Girl, the Tramp is determined to help her. He makes the acquaintance of a millionaire by saving him from suicide in a moment of drunken depression. When drunk, the millionaire is friendly to the Tramp – he pays for flowers which the Tramp gives to the Girl, and allows him to borrow a limousine, thus enabling the Tramp to present himself to the Girl as a rich and eligible benefactor. When sober, however, the millionaire has no recollection of the Tramp. He leaves for a holiday just at the point when the Tramp discovers that the Girl's sight may be cured if he can find the money to pay for an operation. He tries various methods – including street-cleaning and prize-fighting – all without success. But then he meets the millionaire again. The millionaire gives him the money in another moment of drunken generosity. But the gift coincides with a burglary at his home. Now sober, he can remember neither his gift nor his friend. Having given the money to the Girl, the Tramp is arrested and jailed.

Up to this point, *City Lights* is marked by a number of divisions. Apart from setting up thematic oppositions (rich versus poor, blindness versus sight, powerlessness versus power, and so on), it has also established a principle of alternation, moving between sequences which feature the Tramp and the Girl, on the one hand, and sequences which feature the Tramp and the millionaire, or the Tramp trying unsuccessfully to earn some money, on the other. This alternation serves to articulate the double plot structure required of a classical feature film. There is a romance plot involving the Tramp and the Girl, which is predominant, and a plot whose goal is the gaining of money, which is subsidiary. The two plots are structurally interlinked, as is conventional. But the principle of alternation serves to stress the extent to which they are different. Moreover, if the plot about money is conditional upon the romance, the romance is conditional upon the Girl's ignorance of, and separation from, the scenes of which the plot about money consists.

The romance, of course, is the film's major genteel component. However, although most of the slapstick sequences occur in scenes which feature work or the millionaire, there is no clear-cut structural division here corresponding to the two kinds of plot. Indeed, as in the gag with the water referred to above, slapstick constantly interrupts and cuts across the sequences of genteel romance, thus displacing their sentimental tone. Inasmuch as this is the case, however, a further opposition is constructed, an opposition involving Chaplin's performance, persona, and role. Slapstick occurs in the romance scenes because the romance involves the figures of the Tramp, and because the Tramp is played by Chaplin. The romance itself, however, is only sustained because the Girl is unaware of the identity of her benefactor (and of the gags that go on around her), and because the Tramp is able to pose as somebody else.

Having thus constructed, indeed insisted upon, this opposition between genteel and slapstick components, and having thus both acknowledged and marked the extent to which the Chaplin persona is linked to the latter, the problem, for this film as for all Chaplin's features, is how to provide a suitable ending. In *The Circus* (1928), the tramp retains his identity, but at the cost of losing his love. In *The Gold Rush*, he refinds his love, but at the cost of losing his identity and becoming a millionaire. Both endings acknowledge that the opposition cannot be resolved. The ending of *City Lights* is a variation on the ending of *The Gold Rush*. The Tramp, released from jail, is now a shabby vagrant. While disconsolately wandering the streets he catches sight of the Girl, her vision now restored, working in a flower shop. She laughs at him initially, not knowing who he is, but finally recognizes him when she touches his hand while giving him a flower and some money. This ending is by no means unequivocal.

There is no way of knowing whether the romance will be conventionally fulfilled. What is important, though, of course, is the act of recognition. It is this act that rounds off the story and its themes, and it is of a kind entirely consonant with genteel values. It takes place, however, at a cost. For the figure now recognized by the Girl is no longer the spirited, mischievous centre of all the gags. Just as the condition of existence of the romance plot itself is that the tramp is a rich young man, so the condition of the plot's resolution is that the Tramp is simply a tramp.

All three of the films discussed above show the extent to which slapstick no longer existed in anything like its original form or context by the mid–1920s (except in shorts and cartoons). They also, therefore, show the extent to which the feature films made by Chaplin, Keaton, and Lloyd represent not so much the final flowering of an authentic slapstick tradition as the point at which it came either to be hybridized, combined with other components, or else industrially and institutionally marginalized.

7
The comedy of the sexes

In this chapter we shall consider what is perhaps the dominant form of situational comedy in film, the romantic comedy, focusing in particular upon issues of desire, ideology, comedy, and narrative. Of course, love stories are commonplace in Hollywood cinema. David Bordwell has noted how the 'classical' entertainment film tends to operate two lines of action – the ostensible 'generic' story (such as the commission or detection of a crime, the western adventure), and a heterosexual love story.[1] This latter tends to be of secondary importance in the 'male-oriented' genres (oriented, that is, not just around male figures but towards a fantasy matrix which is specified culturally as 'masculine' and involves patterns of action, adventure, and violent conflict). In such cases the woman tends to be situated as 'love interest', a term which implies that her narrative function is subsidiary to that of the hero and that she will ultimately be matched with him as a reward for the successful completion of his 'quest' or adventure. In some war films, westerns, and gangster films, the heterosexual love story can, as Brain Henderson suggests, be dispensed with altogether, its place occupied by a drama of masculine identity and male bonding.[2] The love story tends to be much more prominent in musicals, 'women's picture' melodramas, and, of course, in the romantic comedy, the latter a staple product of the classical Holly-wood cinema between 1934 and 1942. In such genres, women and their desires tend to be integral to the fiction rather than constrained by it, and they are moreover gener-ally seen as having a specific appeal to female audiences.

One of the points which has already arisen at several junctures in this study, and which will be a recurring issue in this chapter, is the relationship between comedy and melodrama. One of the prime features of the romantic comedy is the negotiation between female desire and the places 'offered' to women in patriarchal society, especially in terms of marriage and the family. As much recent criti-cal work has shown, this is fundamental also to the 'women's picture' melodramas which issued from Holly-wood in the 1930s and 1940s.[3] Indeed, we shall argue below that the romantic comedy in many ways offers a different perspective on the problems and issues which mark the discursive field of certain 'women's picture' melodramas. In order to make this clear and to highlight the factors involved in the translation of a dramatic (or 'serious') issue into the terms of comic pleasurability, we will begin with a brief account of the 'romantic melodrama'.

Love and desire in the romantic melodrama

> One should always be in love. That is the reason one should never marry. (Oscar Wilde)

By 'romantic melodrama' we are here referring to those 'women's pictures' which have at their centre a heterosex-ual romance, the fulfilment of which is, for one reason or another, problematic. The nature of the obstruction varies, but these films tend most often to represent a conflict for the female protagonist between her 'duty as a woman' and her desires. The latter are constituted in such films as deviations from the norm of marriage and the family. As is common in such nineteenth-century novels as *Madame Bovary* and *Anna Karenina*, romance is represented as a revolt against convention, but at the same time it has its own conventional trajectories. The romance, in fact, tends to be intensified when fulfilment is blocked: by various external obstacles, through the heroine's self-sacrificial choice, as in *Now, Voyager* (1942), or by the death of the woman, as in *Camille* (1936), *Waterloo Bridge* (1940), and *Letter From an Unknown Woman* (1948). It is in this respect, of course, that romantic melodrama most obviously deviates from romantic comedy and, in order to introduce our consideration of the latter, we will here sketch in certain of the strategies of these melodramas in regard to their representation of female desire, heterosexual relations, and the institution of marriage.

The romantic fantasies found in these melodramas often posit love as a glorious and transcendant emotional experience, as the apotheosis of female desire and identity – no matter what the final consequences may be. The romance is not only opposed to marriage, but it is also distinguished from (genital) sexuality, for the latter poses the danger of the subjugation of female desire, making not so much the culmination as the destruction of the romantic fantasy. Maria LaPlace has considered the implications of this in regard to *Now, Voyager*:

> The impossibility of the heroine's marriage to the hero in the woman's film is not necessarily a renunciation of sexuality on the woman's part; rather it is the prolongation of passion and desire. Emotional intensity is substituted for genital sexuality. The woman is neither fully possessed by the man nor taken for granted; she must continually be wooed and courted; romantic love is kept outside the mundanity of the everyday.[4]

Furthermore, the emotional intensity has a marked narcissistic basis – indicated, for example, in the way that the loved one functions as a romanticized projection of the woman's desire. The male, as LaPlace notes, 'must abandon his position of masculine control, aggressiveness and dominance and take up a position of equality to the woman'.[5] Figures like Jerry (Paul Henreid), in *Now, Voyager*, stand in contrast to such heroes as Rochester in

Jane Eyre who embody a dominating masculine power (although it is significant that *Jane Eyre* concludes, like *Seventh Heaven* (1928), with the hero blinded and thus dependent upon the heroine).

The fantasy of romance which is articulated in these melodramas can be seen, then, to eschew physical, inter-personal sex for a narcissistic eroticism. In Max Ophuls' *Letter From an Unknown Woman*, for example, the love of Lisa (Joan Fontaine) for Stefan (Louis Jourdan) feeds off his repeated failure to recognize her. As in *Only Yesterday* (1933), which has a similar story, intercourse between the hero and heroine is marginalized – what is important in each case is that sex does not lead to the union of the hero and heroine as a couple, but it results in a boy-child whom the woman can constitute as the controllable 'substitute' for the absent father (who in each case remains ignorant of the child's existence until it is 'too late' for the couple to be united). Such examples suggest the complex circuitry of desire which operates in the romantic melo-drama – how, for instance, the ending of *Letter From an Unknown Woman* while ostensibly detailing the *failure* of the union allows the triumph of Lisa's narcissistic roman-tic trajectory. The narrative mode of such melodramas tends to be characterized by missed meetings, marked coincidences, seemingly arbitrary reversals, and external obstructions – all of which frustrate the union and inten-sify the romance, but which ascribe the final renunciation to forces outside the control of the heroine. One is left with a sense, then, of the 'love that could have been' rather than a love which has been 'besmirched' by the mundanities of marriage and family.

The union which fails tends to be more common than that which succeeds. In this context, a film like *Seventh Heaven* (1927) is of interest because of the way in which its 'happy ending' is able to retain a sense of unsullied romantic grandeur, for the love between Diane (Janet Gaynor) and Chico (Charles Farrell) is able to transcend worldliness: the reunion of the couple occurs after both Diane and the spectator have accepted the fact of Chico's

death, and his consequent reappearance takes on connotations of the 'miraculous'. Indeed, when such romantic
melodramas actually allow the fulfilment of union, it tends
to be marked as 'impossible, incredible or fantasy'.[6] On
the other hand, when the union is blocked, the articulated
wish is not destroyed. Rather, its resolution is *postponed*.
What both tendencies suggest, then, is that these melodramas involve a triumph of fantasy over the conventional
restrictions which are involved in 'realist' narrative closure, where desire is in some way *fixed*.[7] The conventional
significance of the heterosexual union is that it represents
the subjugation of the heroine's desire both to the desire
of a man and to the patriarchal order and its institutions
of marriage and the family. As Maria LaPlace notes, the
marriages in *Now, Voyager*, for example – Jerry and the
diegetically absent Isabelle, the potential match between
Charlotte and the worthy but dull Bostonian Elliot Livingstone – are characterized as passionless and repressive.[8]
The same is true of *Letter From an Unknown Woman*,
both in the officially sanctioned courtship of Lisa and the
young lieutenant in Linz, and in her later marriage of
convenience to Colonel Stauffer. In *Seventh Heaven*, also,
there is an emphatic distinction between the Church-sanc-
tioned norm of marriage and the transcendental qualities
of the private union of Diane and Chico.

Love and marriage in the romantic comedy

We shall be concerned here largely with the romantic
comedies of the 1930s and early 1940s, with the period
regarded by many critics as the 'classic' age of Hollywood
sound comedy.[9] First, however, there is the problem of
defining just what is meant by the term romantic (or
sexual) comedy – a category which has also received attention under such designations as 'sophisticated' comedy,
'screwball' comedy, or the 'comedy of remarriage'. The
problem is exacerbated by the hybrid nature of much
Hollywood situational comedy, for an individual film can
include sophisticated, witty dialogue, examples of 'screw-

ball' eccentricity, farce, slapstick pratfalls, and so on (films such as *The Awful Truth* (1937) being exemplary in this respect).

Because of the prevalence of elements of romance and comedy in the majority of Hollywood films, Brian Henderson raises doubts about the viability of isolating the romantic comedy as a distinct film category:

> A workable subset 'romantic comedy' might refer to those films in which romance and comedy are the primary components or those without other such components as crime, detection of crime, Western adventure, war, etc. But what is 'primary' in any given case, is difficult to determine where romance and comedy are pervasive. Moreover, even if crime, western, war, etc, films are eliminated, the remainder is vast and its modes of conjoining romance and comedy myriad.[10]

Henderson fails to consider here the different functioning of elements of comedy or romance in various genres. It is not the mere presence of elements which is significant, but how they are deployed. Romance in a western, for example, is a different proposition to romance in a melodrama, as we have already indicated. Furthermore, crime is not specific to crime films, nor songs to musicals; similarly, a comedy may indeed contain elements of drama and action – and most do – but these do not invalidate its status as a comedy, just as a western does not cease to be such if it contains romance and comedy. In other words, it is not elements in themselves which count, but *processes*. Henderson's conception of generic specificity is too rigid, for no film is 100 per cent western, mystery, or comedy. It is more useful to conceive of genres as '*forms* of textual codification . . . as *systems* of orientations, expectations and conventions that circulate between industry, text and subject'.[11] In this sense, the romantic comedy does indeed have a definite prominence as a category recognized by the film industry, subsidiary media (the trade press, reviews, fan magazines, and so on), and audiences. It is also, of course, a category which is not restricted to film, having longstanding and various historical predecessors, stretching back to the classical traditions represented by Terence, Plautus, and Menander. To generalize to this extent, however, would be to risk stripping the 'screwball' comedy of both its cultural contexts and its *specific* uses of timeworn conventions and strategies – although it is important to stress how the very *familiarity* of the comic plot mechanisms contributes to the structuring of the spectator's attitude (in the expectation, for example, of the happy ending).

Henderson is quite right, of course, to suggest that there are difficulties in providing any precise definition. The films labelled romantic or 'screwball' comedies tend to vary considerably in regard to the narrative prominence of the romantic (courtship) plot. For example, in *The Talk of the Town* (1942), *My Man Godfrey* (1936), and *Mr Deeds Goes to Town*, the romance itself is subsidiary to a 'social' problematic: issues of law and justice in the first example, and issues of class and (social) responsibility in the latter two. Whatever the centrality of the heterosexual romance to the narrative, however, their representation of courtship – or, in such comedies of old love as *The Awful Truth* and *The Philadelphia Story*, the secondary courtship – has to address questions of sexual difference (of male desire in relation to female desire) and of individual desire in relation to its permissible forms and expressions (such as the viability of the institution of marriage in regard to individual desire and identity). This is the terrain of what is identified as the genre of melodrama, but in the comedies the particular negotiation of the contradictions which these questions suggest is subject to different representational pressures and imperatives, and to different formal requirements of narrative articulation and resolution.

In the romantic melodrama, as we have suggested, love often tends to be pitched against marriage, or frustrated by it, or both. The romantic comedy, however, leads inevitably towards (marital) union, even if the path of courtship is rocky. The narcissistic eroticism represented by such films as *Letter From an Unknown Woman* and *Now,*

Voyager becomes one of the obstacles which has to be overcome, as illustrated by such films as *Tom, Dick and Harry* (1941) and the more recent *Starting Over* (1979). Whereas much of the energy of the melodrama is directed against union, the romantic comedy attempts to counter the obstacles which stand in its way. Particular films may toy with the progress towards the 'happy ending', but it remains a firm structural expectation, which the path of courtship leads towards. Furthermore, whereas the romantic melodrama focuses upon a central female protagonist, her desires, and her renunciations, the romantic comedy – by adhering to a courtship plot – is concerned with a woman *and* a man. And whereas romantic melodrama vests its pleasures in a circuitry of desire necessitated by the mediation between desire and its cultural restrictions, the romantic comedy is concerned with the desires of the heroine insofar as they relate to heterosexual union. Although conflicting tendencies in the desire of the woman are addressed, these are made meaningful in regard to her eventual, and inevitable, *integration* within heterosexual monogamy.

One of the principal ways in which this is made acceptable is by the force given to the specialness of the couple *as a couple*. The compatibility of the man and the woman is asserted especially by contrasting them – individually, but especially together – with subsidiary characters who function, as Brian Henderson terms it, as an 'exemplar and exaggeration of conventional morality'.[12] Henderson discusses, for instance, how the characters played by Ralph Bellamy – as alternative suitor to/potential choice for the heroine in both *The Awful Truth* and *His Girl Friday* (1940) – function in this way, as

> both a character norm, against which to contrast the eccentricities of the leads, and a social norm, against which the film directs its satire. (These functions are not always embodied in a single character.) The main characters are screwballs in relation to him, but this is not mere madness, for it exemplifies the value of spontaneity, which reigns supreme in 'thirties romantic comedy, where it stands for

and includes wit, intelligence, genuine feeling vs. conventional response, adaptable moral response, vitality, life. In films without a Bellamy type, less prominent background figurés such as policemen, judges, storekeepers, relatives perform one or both functions.[13]

Romantic comedies celebrate the union of special individuals (their status as such resulting from personal qualities, of course, rather than privilege – *vide* the attack on the liberty of the spoiled rich in *It Happened One Night* (1934) and *My Man Godfrey*).

Nevertheless, in their resolutions these comedies have, if only implicitly, to reconcile the vitality and compatibility of the couple with marriage as an institution. The more successful of these films manage to suggest, however, that it is not so much a question of marriage sanctioning the union as the reverse. Thus, for example, Molly Haskell can find 'some thirties' comedies and musicals coy and unbearable, and others sublime', valuing such films as *The Awful Truth* and *His Girl Friday*, which 'celebrate difficult and anarchic love rather than security and the suburban dream'.[14] In these films Haskell identifies 'an equalization of obstacles and a matching of temperaments' and also a playful mutual eroticism where:

> A man and a woman seem to prickle and blossom at each other's touch, seem to rub each other with and against the grain simultaneously, and, in the friction, in the light in each other's eyes, to know themselves for the first time.[15]

Hence, in such cases marriage becomes a 'natural' extension of the matching of the two protagonists – the relationship is self-sanctioning. In both *The Thin Man* (1934 – a combination of marital comedy and mystery film) and *The Awful Truth*, for example, the marriage is represented as fun for both participants, as – in Ted Sennett's words – a 'reasonable relationship between two often unreasonable people'.[16]

That marriage, any marriage, is not automatically condoned can be seen in the frequency with which these comedies situate the 'ideal' marriage in contrast to examples of wrongful marriages – between, for example, Ellie (Claudette Colbert) and playboy King Westley (Jameson Thomas) in *It Happened One Night* – and potential marriages – between David (Cary Grant) and the prim, proper, unexciting Miss Swallow (Virginia Walker) in *Bringing Up Baby*, between Eve (Claudette Colbert) and rich, handsome wastrel Jacques Picot in *Midnight* (1939), between Lucy (Irene Dunne) and Dan (Ralph Bellamy) in *The Awful Truth*, and Hildy (Rosalind Russell) and Bruce (Ralph Bellamy) in *His Girl Friday*. These are all marked as examples of failed rapport, as wrongful, misguided matches from which the heroine has to be rescued (*Bringing Up Baby* reverses the sexual polarity).

For the spectator, one of the key factors in establishing the expectation of the (marital) union is the familiarity of the form of the romantic comedy – as well, of course, as the use of such stars as Grant, Colbert, Carole Lombard, Ginger Rogers, Irene Dunne, and Katherine Hepburn (performers who appeared also in melodramas at this time). Typically, the films will stress the compatibility of the couple while simultaneously placing in their path obstacles which keep them apart and prevent their mutual recognition of this compatibility: misunderstandings, misrecognition of each other's characters, misguided impressions of their attachments to others, the 'mistaken belief' that the correct path to happiness excludes love. As spectators we have a privileged insight into the 'truth' of the situation, knowing for example that A really does love B despite the circumstances which suggest to them the contrary. The appeal of the romantic comedy, as Ian Jarvie has noted, derives from the structural similarities between the vicissitudes of the romance in the films and those in the real world – the crucial differences being not only that in the films everything is more perfectly worked out, but that the spectator is, of course, not personally implicated and is thus certain that all will be resolved in the end.[17] The narratives progress via the jostling of complications towards that point where all is made known to the characters about their feelings for each other, and where the obstacles and doubts are overcome – although it must again be noted that the comparative liberty of comedy *vis-à-vis* drama does allow a certain play with the completeness of such resolutions (as in the case with *The Lady Eve*, considered in chapter 2). Unlike the spectator, of course, the characters operate without the security of knowledge that the union is inevitable – and unlike the comedian they are more overtly subject to the narrative process.

Initially the man and the woman are antagonistic towards each other, their desires marked as oppositional. The courtship takes the form of a negotiation of terms and positions, and it involves a transformation of those desires which are posited as barriers to the union. There tends, however, to be a marked imbalance, in the majority of the films, between the status accorded the desires of the man and the woman. Although there are such exceptions as *The Lady Eve* and *Bringing Up Baby* – which invert the standard trajectory of the romantic comedy and the cultural norm of male-dominated courtship patterns – most of these films locate the desires of the woman as the major obstruction to union, and hence as the principal object of the comic transformation.

This, of course, does not take the form of the sadistic interrogation of female desire found in the thrillers identified as *film noir*, for the aim of the romantic comedy is the woman's willing acceptance of the man, of union. Hence the necessity in these films of structuring a *perspective* on female fantasy – the *mise en scène* of desire – which is significantly different from that found in such romantic melodramas as *Now, Voyager* and *Letter From an Unknown Woman*. In these latter films the 'emotional' identification with the desiring character is intensified by suspense, by the play with relative levels of knowledge, but in the comedies such processes are deployed to disengage the spectator from the trajectory of the character's wish. This can be illustrated with a characteristic example from *Tom, Dick and Harry*. Telephonist Janie (Ginger Rogers) daydreams perpetually of marrying a millionaire – a wish which, like that of the heroine of *Stella Dallas*

(1937), is initially articulated via a scene at the cinema. Waiting at a bus stop, she sees the first star of the evening and makes a wish – desiring to meet the celebrity millionaire Richard Madison, whom she has just overheard on the telephone. At that moment a car which belongs to Madison pulls up. Believing that her wish is being magically realized, a stunned Janie steps into the car, to the pleasant surprise of the driver (Burgess Meredith). He drives her home and arranges a date, and Janie enters the house dumbstruck. However, as the car pulls away, *we* see, but she does not, that coupled to the rear is a motorbike and trailer, bearing a placard for 'Slatter's Garage'. Burgess Meredith is *not* playing the millionaire Dick but the garage mechanic Harry! Janie's misapprehension is continued for a few further scenes, and despite evidence about the reality of Harry's situation – he himself being unaware of her misapprehension – Janie persists in believing him to be a millionaire. When realization strikes her (he reveals that he has only $1.80 in his pockets) Janie slaps his face. She is punishing him for her own misapprehension, but the joke remains *on her*. The play with levels of knowledge, then, serves to distance the spectator from Janie's wish, and the whole of this sequence is an example of a relatively contained mini-narrative – a gag – for which Janie's wish functions as the 'set-up'. The 'screwball' comedies abound in such examples of 'magical' wish-fulfilment where the woman's desires for riches and the luxury life are set up to be countered: a number of the films, for example, not only represent a rags-to-riches Cinderella fantasy, but they blatantly refer to it *as* a fantasy (examples include *The Good Fairy* (1935) and *Midnight*). It seems to be a feature of narrative comedy in general – of the way in which comedy uses narrative – that there is such a play with the ways in which (melo)drama is generally organized according to scenarios of wish fulfilment. In comparison with a film like *Now, Voyager*, for example, one can see how in such films as *Tom, Dick and Harry* the fantasy is abbreviated and contained – and the joke against Janie is but one of the many which mark her conversion from a narcissistic determination to get what is best for her to an acceptance of a more conventional marriage for love.

The process of negotiation involved in such romantic comedies is not, then, simply a question of a 'battle of wills' between the woman and the man, but of narrational discrepancies between the discourses pertaining to each. What is most at stake is the *conversion* of the woman, even though there is a (lesser) degree of modification of the hero's views and values.

The imbalance between male and female 'perspectives' – between the 'truth-value' ascribed to each – is especially marked in the expository articulation of their oppositional desires. Frequently, there is a discussion between the man and the woman concerning what she 'should' want and what she says she actually *does* want: examples include the recurring debates between 'proletarian' reporter Peter Warne (Clark Gable) and runaway heiress Ellie in *It Happened One Night*, between the similarly down to earth Czerny(Don Ameche) and 'gold-digging' Eve in *Midnight*, and between Harry-the-mechanic and Janie-the-dreamer in *Tom, Dick and Harry*. In each case the male is situated as more on the side of the 'correct values' endorsed by the narration – to use Catherine Johnson's terms, he tends to be situated as the ideological 'first voice'.[18] Whether the woman is already rich and has become frustrated and spoiled as a result (as in *It Happened One Night* and *My Man Godfrey*) or whether she desires the rich life rather than conventional marriage (as in *Midnight* and *Tom, Dick and Harry*) the process of conversion represents a progression of the woman towards the position articulated and represented by the hero. The principle methods of this conversion tend to be the reversals represented by such gag sequences as that quoted above from *Tom, Dick and Harry*, and also the assertion of an ideology of 'true love'.

Bosley Crowther has remarked of the resolutions of such comedies that

> the blissful and buoyant realization the girl finally gets through her head is that these things [desire for wealth,

luxury, independence] can be well abandoned for the greater satisfaction of true love.[19]

Although the films may start out as overtly 'discursive' –
with the direct articulation of the opposed views of the
man and the woman – 'love' often makes an appearance
at the last moment as a *deus ex machina*, the genre's
equivalent of the 7th Cavalry. Heterosexual romantic love
figures as a 'magic' force, for it defies rationality and
cannot be argued with; it functions like fate in the 1940s
films noirs, as a 'supernatural' means by which narrative
resolution may be achieved in the face of at times overwhelming odds. We implied above that the field of heterosexual romance describes but a fraction of the complex
vicissitudes of desire with which the romantic melodrama
is concerned; rather, these melodramas frequently allow a
siphoning of desire away not just from marriage but from
the restrictions of romance in itself, opening onto a narcissistic economy of desire. With the comedies, however,
heterosexual love is staunchly reasserted as not just the
acceptable but also the 'natural' channelling of female
desire.

   What is important is not just the nature of the resolution
(which in a number of these films, as in such predecessors
as Shakespeare's romances, is *markedly* conventional and
'artificial') but how it is prepared for, how the 'ideology
of love' is structured throughout the films as the correct
path for the woman, how her comically 'aberrant' desires
are situated as such in relation to this ideology. We shall
return once more to *Tom, Dick and Harry* to illustrate
certain dominant, recurring tendencies in how these films
work through their discourses of love, marriage, and
female desire. Although Janie sets her sights – like the
heroines of *Midnight* and *Hands Across the Table* (1935)
– on marrying a millionaire, she is actually presented with
a choice between three suitors: the go-getting salesman
Tom (George Murphy), millionaire Dick (Alan Marshal),
and mechanic Harry. These three men represent three
potential marriages, three different paths her life could

take. This is highlighted by the stylized dream sequences which follow each proposal. In the first, she marries Tom but becomes largely a satellite to his ambition. While Tom is continually promoted, eventually becoming President of the United States, Janie spends her life at home, catering to their three children and congratulating her husband. In the second, her dream marriage to the idealist Harry – the polar opposite to Tom – is overtly pronounced by the justice of the peace to be a 'big mistake', and the stylized absurdity of the dream represents for her a life of domestic and maternal drudgery, while an idling, kiss-happy Harry is uninterested even in claiming the gift-horse of a $1 million radio prize. In the third option she marries Dick Madison, and there is a striking contrast between this dream and the former two. Here, Janie becomes a celebrity in her own right, the wedding making the front pages of the papers ('Janie Gets Married'), and she herself becoming the much-photographed toast of the town. Her home in this dream is an opulent mansion, where servants wait on her hand and foot, and throughout the dream, both the children and the husband, who are omnipresent in the first two dream marriages, appear hardly at all; the latter's major function being to proclaim 'You are the most beautiful woman here. You are the most beautiful woman anywhere.'

The third dream represents a fantasy which, Harry informs her, only ever has a minimal chance of being realized, with girls like her being meant for ordinary working men such as him. This 'common-sense voice' is echoed in the stylized way in which the dream sequences are represented, which particularly distances the fantasy of the third. Arguing against Harry's statement of her ordinariness, Janie declares that: 'It's just as natural for a girl to want to make a good marriage as it is for a fella to get ahead'. But even when she is articulating her views, it is not just that Harry's counter-arguments have a familiar 'common-sense' logic to them – because he represents 'love for its own sake' – but the very setting of the disputation mitigates against her case. Janie expresses her fantasy of the high life against the backdrop of ordinary, unpretentious Americans. Harry's date with her, on the cheap, is the direct antithesis of the giddy whirl she desires, and it demonstrates the setting within which she 'really fits'.

With her desires structured explicitly as 'erroneous', the actual turning point in the conversion of Janie occurs when she kisses Harry, and the sound of (extra-diegetic) bells rings in their ears (a kiss, then, with 'magical' properties). Although clearly responding to the kiss, Janie attempts to resist its implications and actively seeks out Dick Madison when the opportunity is presented to her. The film moves towards a scene in which Janie has to decide between her three suitors. She attempts to forestall this choice by imagining, in a fourth dream sequence, that she is married to all three men – a solution she accepts quite happily until her three spouses prepare for bed, at which point she cries out 'Just a minute. This is ridiculous', and the dream ends. She subsequently decides upon Dick, choosing the path of her fantasy, but there is a last-minute reversal which brings about the expected ideologically correct resolution. On kissing Harry goodbye, she once more hears the 'magic' bells, and then she impulsively rides off with him on his motorcycle. The kiss, then, comes to the rescue, triumphant where disputation failed, 'proving' to the heroine that – as Regi Allen (Carole Lombard) comes to realize in *Hands Across the Table* – 'You can't run away from love'. Such last-minute reversals are common in the romantic comedy – Ted Sennett cites *The Gilded Lily* (1935) and *The Bride Comes Home* (1935)[20] – and are characteristic of the 'comic forepleasure' of the cycle.

Tom, Dick and Harry, then, illustrates the importance of the woman's *choice* in the discursive manoeuvres of such films, although it is a 'choice' which is highly constrained and regulated. As we have suggested, the path of 'true love' is not subject to any in-depth questioning, but furthermore, the choice is represented in terms of deciding between three different *men*, the polygamous fourth dream sequence rendered as grotesque and unrealizable, and the possibilities of a non-marital alternative never being raised. The debate conducted between Janie and Harry, then, although it ostensibly seeks to raise the subject of what the woman wants, is highly trammelled. Not only does the articulation of the opposed desires of the man and the woman serve to mark out the latter as the central narrative *problem*, but the modification of the hero's views and behaviour – for example, of the headstrong rectitude of such heroes as Peter Warne in *It Happened One Night* and Czerny in *Midnight* – tends to be a secondary factor, both throughout the films and in the final manipulations of the resolution. In the majority of films, the union itself marks the culmination of the male's trajectory, achieved at the price of the conversion of the woman, and prepared for via such gag reversals as that quoted above from *Tom, Dick and Harry* where a 'conspiracy of knowledge' between the film's narration and the spectator detaches the latter from the woman's desires.

Brian Henderson makes a claim for the progressiveness of 1930s romantic comedy in comparison with its counterparts in the 1970s, claiming that it 'posited men and women willing to meet on a common ground and to engage all their faculties and capacities in the sexual dialectic'.[21] However, the 'common ground' tends in films like *Tom, Dick and Harry* to be much closer to the territory of the male – and this is stressed particularly in numerous scenes throughout the 'screwball' comedy of the period where the man acts as teacher of the 'correct values' to the woman (as in *It Happened One Night*, *My Man Godfrey*, *Once Upon a Honeymoon* (1942), and *Midnight*). 1930s romantic comedy is not *inherently* more progressive, then, but it is worth noting again the point made by Molly Haskell, that in some films the relationship between the protagonists has a vitality which exceeds the conventions, where compatibility overcomes 'plot artifice'. In the following two sections of this chapter we shall examine in more detail how this sense of the compatibility of the couple is often structured through instances of *play* between the man and the woman, and we shall situate this in regard to the centrality of play to comedy in general.

Comedy, play, and responsibility

Comedy tends to be aligned with 'fun', 'play', and 'entertainment'. Whereas drama deals 'seriously' with serious issues, comedy is felt to be funny because, as Catherine Johnson claims, 'it *lightly* violates serious codes' (our italics).[22] By providing a site for the *allowable* disruption of both cultural and fictional rules, comedy represents an alternative fictional mode to the dramatic genres – to melodrama, as the dominant *serious* mode of Hollywood cinema. Whereas (melo)drama relies upon the spectator's engagement with the fictional articulation of a set of narrative problems – an engagement based upon identification with one or very few desiring characters – the process of comedy more acutely involves a *play* between identification and distantiation. This difference is, indeed, most clear in the cinema situation: one watches a drama largely in silence, enrapt in attention, whereas with comedy laughter 'disrupts' the 'passively consumed' dramatic illusionism and one is pulled away from the world represented on screen and is united with other spectators as part of an *audience*. And as comedy frequently calls attention to its status as fiction the spectator is more aware that he/she is watching a *film* rather than looking in to a 'realistically' constructed world.

Comedy, as has already been noted, is precisely a game played with transgression and familiarity: it sets up deviations from 'rules' and 'norms' in order to re-place them. Particular problems, issues, and scenes are geared to a comic rather than dramatic elaboration, although, of course, certain subjects are regarded as 'unfitting' for a comic treatment, for a 'light' approach. For the play of comedy to function there has to be some consensual boundary between the 'light' and the 'serious' – which once crossed, as in a film like *To Be Or Not To Be* (1942), can be discomforting. Comedy has to handle its transgressions in particular ways, to disarm them: as precisely a game played with transgression and familiarity, comedy is characterized by mechanisms which cushion the impact of the former (which allow the transgression to be developed 'only so far'). In a drama, for example, the comic moment serves often as a 'cutting-off point', a means of sidestepping certain ramifications which would be *too* serious: a good example being the curiously hybrid Leo McCarey melodrama *Make Way for Tomorrow* (1937), a film which concludes with the final separation of an old married couple but, through a shift into light comedy on their last afternoon together, where their separation is transformed into a victory of the human potential for fun.

The 1959 sex/romantic comedy *It Started With a Kiss* contains a gag which is directed at the spectator rather than the characters and is worth examining in the light of the above comments. Joe (Glenn Ford), an ordinary soldier, is pursuing Maggie (Debbie Reynolds), who, in characteristic fashion, is determined to marry rich, even though she 'melts' when Joe kisses her. After their first kiss, in a nightclub, she is unsteady, stunned, out of breath, and – like Janie in *Tom, Dick and Harry* – she responds by kissing the male repeatedly. Smoke begins to waft upwards into the image, and a blurring and subsequent refocusing reveals the camera panning across a bedroom floor strewn with discarded clothing. The camera moves up to the bed and fixes upon two hands on the sheets, a woman's enveloped in a man's. What is implied by the juxtaposition of these two sequences is a chain of consequences: the suggestion is, of course, of *pre-marital* sex. However, once this possibility of an 'unsanctioned' sexual relationship is encouraged, it is rapidly disproved: the man's hand withdraws from that of the woman, to reveal a wedding ring on her finger. The joke is that the elision of the wedding scene has provoked for the spectator a 'false' expectation of transgression. The climax of the gag – the exposure of the ring – is that moment when this expectation is confronted, and the spectator reviews and corrects it. The pleasure of such gags is intrinsically linked to the resetting of boundaries: sex outside marriage is quickly converted into sex within marriage. The transgression is 'refamiliarized' (to use Mick Eaton's terms again).[23]

This kind of play with registers of meaning is one of the dominant characteristics of comedy. As we have already argued, comedy plays with the rules of language and behaviour that are structured both in the conventions of film representation (for example, in the genre system, or in the 'rules' of narrative motivation) and in culture more generally (for both fields involve notions of decorum, of propriety, of adherence to a norm or norms). In situational comedies, as distinct from comedian comedies, the comic 'rule play' tends to be closely integrated into and articulated within the conventionalized narrative process rather than pitched against it. The narrative is much less concerned with setting up opportunities for performance skills and self-contained gags, functioning rather as a vehicle for articulating and ordering comic transformations. The gags, similarly, tend to 'evolve' from the narrative, arising from, and neutralizing contradictions within, the discursive play.

The 'screwball' comedies have been valued by some critics as 'satires' of conventional courtship. They emphasize unconventional behaviour, and they play with both the norms of conduct and propriety and the conventions of the dramatic/serious representation of love. Not only do they set up such deviations from conventional courtship as the 'exceptional forwardness' of women in *Bringing Up Baby*, *The Lady Eve*, *My Man Godfrey*, and *Woman Chases Man* (1937), but the conduct of the courtship is frequently void of sentimentality. Indeed, it is often overtly combative, with sentiment replaced by competition and conflict: examples include the verbal sparring of Lily Garland (Carole Lombard) and Oscar Jaffe (John Barrymore) in *Twentieth Century* (1934), and the punches thrown between Hazel Flagg (Lombard) and Wally Cook (Fredric March) in *Nothing Sacred* (1937). The comic plotting of misunderstandings, impersonations, and the manipulation of circumstances serves to place the protagonists into extraordinary, compromised positions where standard expectations of behaviour are contravened, and licence motivated.

In this context it is worth examining some of the ramifications of the much-remarked use of 'eccentricity' or 'screwball' behaviour. Donald McCaffrey has claimed that the leading man and woman in these films tend to be freed from certain conventional restrictions: 'The heroes and heroines often do almost anything they wish. Even minor situations allow the individual to engage in a caprice shunned by respectable and proper people.'[24] This kind of deviation from accepted, respectable behaviour can be seen in much 1930s comedy, especially the films of W. C. Fields, Mae West, and the Marx brothers. In romantic comedy it tends to be represented as either a positive liberation from the norms (as in *Bringing Up Baby*) or as a danger to the normal (as in the social irresponsibility of the rich women in *My Man Godfrey*). Although examples of eccentric men and, especially, eccentric families recur in this period – the rich family in *My Man Godfrey*, the poor family in *You Can't Take It With You*, the mad family in *Arsenic and Old Lace* – we would suggest that romantic comedy tends to centre upon 'eccentric' women. And this 'deviance' from the norm, while a source of attraction, can represent a challenge to the men. In both *It Happened One Night* and *My Man Godfrey*, the eccentricity of the heroine is specified in relation to her high-class status. Ellie's removal from the norms of behaviour results from her millionaire father's attempt to protect her from the outside world: she is a 'poor little rich girl' whose eyes are opened onto the world of 'ordinary' lower-class America via her involvement with the idealistic, 'proletarian' reporter, Peter Warne, and her immersion in the *déclassé* milieux of Depression America (on a crowded bus, in the auto-camps, and so on). Her ignorance of the 'normal' is signalled by such details as her inability to dunk a doughnut properly, her lack of awareness of the importance of money, her false expectation of privileged treatment on the bus. In this film, the lower-class male 'saves' the woman from her shallow and over-privileged luxury lifestyle through a process of education into the standards and benefits of the 'ordinary' American middle classes.

The social idealism of *It Happened One Night* and its critique of the excessive liberty of the rich also marks *My Man Godfrey*: the family into which Godfrey (William Powell) enters as a butler is dominated by rich and spoiled women who squander the wealth generated by the hard-pressed father Bullock (Eugene Pallette). In *My Man Godfrey*, the women – Bullock's wife Angelica (Alice Brady), and her two daughters Irene (Carole Lombard) and Cornelia (Gail Patrick) – overturn traditional standards, in terms of familial and social order, and also (especially relevant here) in terms of the norms of heterosexual romance. The Bullock household is marked by a general inversion of patriarchal order: Bullock is displaced as head of the family, and the strong male figure, Godfrey – a voice of reason and social responsibility – is placed as a *servant*. The inversion of order is represented especially in a role-reversal seduction attempt, where Irene attempts to take advantage of her position as Godfrey's 'mistress'. Without any sign of encouragement on his part, she kisses Godfrey on the lips. He stiffens, leaves in silence, and retires to his bedroom, but Irene pursues him there, refusing to take heed of his embarrassment. She is 'comically' annoyed by his resistance – 'Don't you think it's rather indecent of you to order me out after you kissed me?' – and he then proceeds to chastise her (his words stressed by the film as 'serious'): 'Hasn't anyone ever told you about – certain proprieties? . . . that some things are proper and some things are not?'

Irene's wealth and privilege have resulted, as is the case with Ellie, in her insulation from the acceptable norms of conduct, and she similarly undergoes a 'conversion' under the guidance of a male in possession of the 'correct' values. Godfrey, unlike Peter in *It Happened One Night*, is not of the lower classes, although he initially poses as a 'forgotten man'. Rather, he is a 'Boston blueblood' whose past rejection by a woman of his class has led to a realization that the wealthy are out of touch with the 'real' world. He poses as a hobo to receive an 'education in life', and he henceforth sets out to educate and convert the Bullock family. Whereas in these two films the courtship results in the movement of the woman away from her high-class status, other comedies like *Midnight* mark the woman's desires in terms of 'gold-digging' aspirations or a 'Cinderella fantasy',[25] the impetus being towards the woman's renunciation of her desire for such status. Thus in both tendencies love is associated with an embracing of 'normal' middle-class marriage/union, with, especially, an acceptance of the authority of the male and a rejection of the woman's economic independence. Although the union represents a masking of differences, an idealized homogeneity, this particularly involves *placing* the desires of the woman in regard to the authority of the hero.

The 1930s romantic comedies, then, tend to hinge upon the dangers to the patriarchal order posed by the (potential) economic and social independence of women. In films like *Midnight* it is acknowledged that the woman can use her desirability for the sake of her own advancement – at the expense of conventional marriage – and this transgression and its countering occupy centre stage in the discursive play. One can see that this ideological project has a particular applicability in regard to the social-historical context: it represents a means of addressing and 'familiarizing' the challenges to the traditional values of patriarchal ordering of monogamy occasioned by the economic crisis of the late 1920s and early 1930s. *My Man Godfrey* makes this explicit, in its unification of a broad-based socio-economic recovery and the recovery of a disrupted *sexual* order. The 'screwball' comedy serves in general as a vehicle for resetting the positions of sexual-economic order. For example, whereas in the fantasy of the woman – as in *Midnight*, *Tom, Dick and Harry*, *The Gilded Lily* – the upper class represents an ideal of sexual and economic independence, the films' narration, complicit with such 'ideologically correct' heroes as Peter Warne, Godfrey, and Harry, present a critique of the values and lifestyles of the wealthy (although, it must be stressed, this critique is highly regulated). *Fifth Avenue Girl* (1939), by Gregory La Cava, director of *My Man Godfrey*, presents another negatively eccentric rich family, but it also features a Communist chauffeur whose values are discredited. The films are not concerned with any radical challenge to the upper classes so much as articulating a case for women to abandon 'self-seeking' desires. What is at issue is the reassertion of *male* authority as the norm in both the economic and the sexual spheres: in both *Godfrey* and *Fifth Avenue Girl* it is not predominantly the capitalist classes as such who are criticized, but rather the disorder provoked by the *women's* displacement of the father-figure as head of the family. *My Man Godfrey* relates the disorder in the Bullock family to the national economic disorder, and its resolution posits the re-establishment of the entrepreneurial power of Godfrey and Bullock. Godfrey transforms the city dump into a combination of enterprise and welfare project, redeeming the 'forgotten men' (who start out as the object of the rich women's scavenger hunt). However, it is worth stressing that the principal agent of this reassertion of order is from the upper classes (although Godfrey has 'seen the light' in terms of his social responsibilities) and that the enterprise project is in fact a *nightclub*. Economic reform in *My Man Godfrey*, then, involves transforming the leisure pursuits of the rich from 'female anarchy' to 'male business', and there is no attempt to challenge the *status quo* in regard to the class hierarchy: all that the 'forgotten men' want, and are given, is an 'honest job'.

It is misguided, then, to describe these films as 'satires' because of elements of unconventional behaviour in love. Rather, one must note how such 'eccentricity' functions in regard to the 'comic' narrative process – how deviations are 'set up' in order to be countered. As Wes Gehring has observed, despite the screwball comedy's 'frequent Looney Tune activities, its comedy is inherently conservative. . . . Granted, it is an unorthodox courtship, even a satire of the traditional romance, but it is still a courtship.'[26] The romantic comedy is concerned with the play between 'eccentricity' and convention in the field of love and marriage, but it moves towards the reassertion of the latter. Tensions, of course, are most likely to manifest themselves towards the endings of particular films for, as Gehring claims, 'they often bridge ninety previous minutes of largely comic differences'.[27] The resolution marks the cutting-off point for both the comic play with the rules in general terms and the 'deviant' or eccentric conduct of the courtship: it is the moment of integration, of ordering, when an 'adult' position of responsibility is conventionally accepted.

In many romantic comedies, however, there is a tendency towards stressing the artificial or formal nature of the conventional resolution, and by so doing to play down the 'serious' or 'adult' implications of (marital) union. Of course, for the spectator much of the pleasure of these films is derived from the deviations from convention, and just as a comedian/comedy like Bob Hope's *The Paleface* can in its resolution celebrate the licence of the comedian at the expense of integration,[28] so too the romantic comedies can comically produce resolutions which are sudden and 'magical' enough to preserve the sense of play, and thus disavow the restrictions of responsibility ('We have to end like this, but . . .'). Preston Sturges' *The Palm Beach Story*(1942) contains a particularly blatant example of a resolutely playful, absurdly 'magical' resolution, involving the last-minute introduction of identical twins for both Tom (Joel McCrea) and Gerry (Claudette Colbert) so that the remaining narrative complications can be rapidly ceded to a conventional multiple marriage.

The game of love

> When love congeals it soon reveals
> A faint aroma of performing seals
> (Lorenz Hart, 'I Wish I Were In Love Again')[29]

Catherine Johnson suggests that 'the content of comedy and drama can be identical, it is the attitude towards it that differs'.[30] However, this is not strictly the case, for although comedy may deal with the same sets of issues and problems, it is not solely a question of a difference in 'attitude' but also of how this relates to a particular 'shaping' of the content. One should concentrate not only upon what is overtly required to bring about the comic transformations but also upon what aspects of content are barred from the narrative activity of a comedy, or have to be 'played down' for the comic play to be possible. In the romantic comedy, for example, certain problematic issues integral to the romantic melodrama have to be forestalled. The complexity of emotional interrelationships is narrowed to a stress upon 'the couple', whereas melodramas often set up a conflict of emotional allegiances – for example, between heterosexual relations and maternal love (*Stella Dallas*; *Mildred Pierce* (1945)), or between allegiances to the nuclear family and the obligations of the extended family (*Make Way for Tomorrow*). In the romantic comedy such potentially problematic areas of emotional complication have frequently to be excluded, neutralized, or disavowed. *The Awful Truth* provides an interesting example of this. When Lucy (Irene Dunne) and Jerry Warriner (Cary Grant) divorce, the possible emotional complexity of the breakup is simplified because of the lack of children. However, the film makes comic play with this lack, a play which suggests the very fact of the absence: for the couple go to court to debate custody not of a child but of 'Mr Smith', the dog which brought them together (played by Asta, the 'surrogate child' of Nick and Nora Charles in *The Thin Man*). The film thus makes overt the lack of a complication which would shift it into the direction of melodrama. The courtroom sequence simultaneously both suggests and denies the lack of children, rendering the problem (through the substitution of the dog for a child) comic rather than melodramatic. A similar substitution occurs in Cecil B. DeMille's *Why Change Your Wife?* (1920) (where the dog tends to be associated with the husband) and in the grotesquery of the Duchess' pig-baby in *Alice's Adventures in Wonderland*.

Bachelor Mother (1939), in similar fashion, flirts with and disavows the emotional problematic familiar from the 'unwed mother' melodrama. Polly Parrish (Ginger Rogers), a salesgirl at Merlin's department store, is lumbered with a deserted baby she finds on a doorstep. Much of the comedy derives from the fact that nobody will believe that the baby is not actually hers. In the eyes of the other characters, Polly *is* the mother, and her actual treatment of the child, leaving it with strangers while she is out dancing, for example, seems notably deficient in maternal values. Our foreknowledge of the truth of the situation allows us, of course, a privileged reading of the erroneous assumptions of the other characters, but we are still forced to read Polly both as 'not mother' and 'mother' as we follow the logic of their misapprehensions. As with the example of the dog in *The Awful Truth*, the comedy here depends upon operating a potential double-reading, with the 'serious' implications both stated and disavowed – or, rather, stated through disavowal. Both are examples of how narrative comedy often deals with serious issues through mechanisms of relative knowledge or irony. We *know* that Polly is *not* the child's mother, but *what if* she were? This is one of the principal mechanisms of the displacement of the 'serious' in situational comedy. It is interesting that *Bachelor Mother* – like *The Lady Eve* – does not end with everything made known to the principal characters. Not only has Polly actually grown attached to the baby, but when David Merlin (David Niven) finally proposes to her he still thinks that she is the actual mother, Polly herself not choosing to deny the fact. This 'destigmatization' of unwed motherhood would, of course, be much more problematic in a melodrama.[31]

Stanley Cavell, in his book *Pursuits of Happiness*, suggests another area where the romantic comedy tends to 'repress' emotional/melodramatic complication: in the frequent elision of *maternal* relationships.[32] This generally absent area of emotional bonding tends to be replaced by father-daughter relations (*The Philadelphia Story, It Happened One Night*) or father-son relations (*The Lady*

Eve, and even *Bachelor Mother*, where David's mother is never mentioned and the only maternal figure is the 'pretend mother' Polly). Cavell stresses one implication of the frequent absence of the mother: it 'continues the idea that the creation of the woman is the business of men'.[33] This can be more easily achieved because the heroine is denied a 'maternal history' within which to situate her desires: the 'choices' offered to her tend almost exclusively to be in relation to men and what they desire of her. The exceptions tend to bear this out: for example, in *My Man Godfrey*, Irene's mother Angelica has an important function in that she corroborates the equation women + wealth = disorder. The Bullock household is totally under the sway of Angelica and her two daughters, and she even keeps an 'emasculated' male pet, her 'in-house' gigolo Carlo (Mischa Auer), who is reduced to absurd gorilla impressions to keep her amused. Godfrey staunchly resists the Carlo role in relation to Irene – who overtly regards him as her 'property' – and through his 'masculine' economic dealing he is ultimately able to restore order within the family: setting power back into the hands of Bullock, and ejecting the 'inverted' maternal rule represented by Angelica. (For a melodramatic treatment of the 'perversely' dominant mother, see Josef von Sternberg's *The Shanghai Gesture* (1941).)

Cavell's point about the 'creation' of women by men is clearly illustrated by *It Happened One Night*: Ellie is initially under the control of her rich father Alexander Andrews (Walter Connolly) and rebels against him by choosing a marital partner of whom he does not approve, the playboy King Westley. However, Peter Warne takes over Andrews' paternal role in relation to her – indeed Andrews is shown welcoming Peter as a prospective husband for his daughter. It is interesting that in such romantic melodramas as *Now, Voyager* and *Letter From an Unknown Woman*, it is the heroine's *father* who is absent, with her desire for the hero structured as an attempt to fill this lack. It is also worth stressing that the conclusion of *Now, Voyager* provides an idealized fantasy of motherhood, with Charlotte as 'good mother' to Jerry's daughter Tina, in the process replacing *her own* 'bad mother' as well: it is a relationship in which the male remains peripheral. This, then, is one area of emotional satisfaction which the romantic comedies, in their general elision of the woman's mother and the woman-as-mother, attempt to exclude.

Stanley Cavell not only notes a general tendency to elide mother-child relations to emphasize the courtship, but he further suggests that

> these films allow the principal pair to express the wish to be children again, or perhaps to be children together. In part this is a wish to make room for playfulness within the gravity of adulthood, in part it is a wish to be cared for first, and unconditionally (e.g. without sexual demands, though doubtless not without sexual favours).[34]

This is not a question merely of instances of regression – as in such Howard Hawks comedies as *Bringing Up Baby* and *Monkey Business* – but it further demonstrates a particular tendency in the representation of the *compatibility* of the couple. The romantic comedy asserts that the couple that can play together, as children, can stay together. This is especially clear in *The Awful Truth*, where the charismatic 'rightness' of Lucy and Jerry is figured forth in the way they 'spark' off each other – to come back to Molly Haskell's point – and the way in which their conflicts are marked by playful wit and irony, the vitality of which contrasts totally with the scenes between Lucy and her alternative partner, Dan (Ralph Bellamy). As we have suggested, the relationship between Dan and Lucy is an example of failed rapport, its stiffness stressed notably when they dance at a nightclub – with their bodies markedly mismatched in rhythm – and also in the contrast between her trained voice and Dan's 'downhome growling' when they sing 'Home on the Range'. Lucy cannot play with Dan, and she cannot be her natural, playful self (which she is with Jerry, even in dispute). Life with Dan is solid and serious whereas life with Jerry is 'fun and

games': even their initial breakup becomes a to-and-fro
game of dissimulation and exposure.

Just before Jerry and Lucy are reunited – sexually – at
the end of the film, they spend a restless night in adjoining
rooms, each desiring to make love to the other but neither
feeling secure enough to make the first move. The impasse
is broken by the convenient and repeated opening of the
connecting door, blown by the wind, an action which
prompts them to speak to each other. The dialogue runs
as follows:

Jerry: 'In a half an hour we'll no longer be Mr and Mrs.
        Funny, isn't it?'
Lucy: 'Yes, it's funny that everything is the way it is on
        account of the way you feel.'
Jerry: 'Huh?'
Lucy: 'Well, I mean, if you didn't feel the way you do,
        things wouldn't be the way they are, would they?
        I mean, things could be the same if things were
        different.'
Jerry: 'Things are the way you made them.'
Lucy: 'Oh no, things are the way you think I made
        them. I didn't make them that way at all. Things
        are just the same as they always were – but, only,
        you're the same as you were too – so I guess
        things will never be the same again.'

                    *   *   *

Lucy: 'You're all confused, aren't you?'
Jerry: 'Aren't you?'
Lucy: 'No.'
Jerry: 'Well, you should be, because you're wrong about
        things being different because they're not the
        same. Things are different, except in a different
        way. You're still the same, only I've been a fool.
        But I'm not now. So long as I'm different, well,
        don't you think that, well, maybe things could be
        the same again, only a little different, huh?'

The joke here is, of course, that in this explanation scene
the literal meaning of their words is redundant; what really
matters is that the couple are brought back to a state of
intimacy. It is another example of a comic play with mean-

ing, of a 'deliteralization' of meaning: Lucy and Jerry are re-established as playing *together* at the expense of logic, of ordered meaning. The sense of play is carried through on a narrational level in the final shot, with the 'metaphor' of the male and female clock figurines moving into the same hatch together substituting, playfully, for the sexual union of the couple (which is legitimized in terms of the Hays Code (Hollywood's system of self-censorship) as Jerry and Lucy are still – just – married).

The ending of *The Awful Truth*, then, as well as re-establishing the playful intimacy of the couple, also illustrates how in 1930s film sexual union is represented (displaced) as play. It is easy to overstress here the influence of the Hays Code in the determination of such displacements of the sexual act. Brian Henderson falls into this trap:

> The sexual question always circulates in romantic comedy, it is its utterance that is forbidden. On this prohibition romantic comedy stands. Indeed one can see the entire spectrum of romantic comedy as so many variations on this unuttered question. In comedies of old love, the unspoken question is 'Why did we stop fucking?' In comedies of new love, it is 'Why don't we fuck now?'[35]

True, the sophisticated verbal intercourse of such films as *The Awful Truth* and *The Philadelphia Story* testifies to a displacement of physical sexuality into language, but this is not merely a question of the 'repressions' of institutional censorship. For such displacements also characterize the way in which courtship and seduction are conducted in real life, as a means of overcoming the social and interpersonal restrictions bearing upon the expression of and acceptance of sexual 'proposals'. There are cultural 'rules' for the conduct of relations between sexually 'interested' individuals, rules internalized by individuals: desire is mediated through – by no means uncontradictory – standards of speech and decorum. Another factor which needs stressing here is that courtship is *not* simply a question of seduction (although the 'sex comedies' of the 1950s and

1960s often represent it as such). Henderson further neglects to take account of the *place* of fucking within 1930s romantic comedies, for they are concerned with a level of compatability exceeding sexual intercourse. Sex has its place, of course, but it signifies that a more extensive level of compatibility has been reached – it is not the end in itself. So it is not, then, a question of simply 'repressing' physical sexuality between a man and a woman, but of situating it in relation to a broader concept of heterosexual union.

Hence the couple, as Cavell suggests, are unified together 'as children' in their play, which is in itself a displacement from the divisions represented by the 'adult' and the 'serious'. Rather, the perfect matching of the couple articulates a fantasy of dyadic fusion, an overcoming of the differences between them. In his paper, 'Creative writers and daydreaming', Sigmund Freud related play to fantasy: he considered the fantasies constructed through adult daydreaming, for example, as a continuation of and a substitute for the play of childhood.[36] Both were viewed by him as means of 'translating reality' in accordance with the pleasure principle, in regard to what the subject *wishes* reality to be rather than what it actually is.[37] The romantic comedy represents an *idealization* of heterosexual romance, an idealization which has to be detached (as we have indicated) from certain issues which would problematize it. These films harbour 'a vision which they know cannot be fully domesticated, inhabited in the world we know. They are romances.'[38] The playing together of the couple – which, of course, is not just verbal, as the hunts for the bone, the dog, and the leopard illustrate in *Bringing Up Baby* – not only marks them out from the confinements of 'the everyday', but also marks a contrast both with the 'eccentric' play of the comedian (who plays *alone* – *vide* the end of *The Paleface* where Jane Russell is literally pulled out of the film to provide Hope with the final gag),[39] and with the 'homo-erotic' play of such male comedy duos as Laurel and Hardy, Martin and Lewis, and Morecambe and Wise. The play of the heterosexual couple also, of course, rejects the fantasy gratifications of the romantic melodramas we have discussed: in films like *Midnight* and *Once Upon a Honeymoon*, an initial narcissistic fantasy on behalf of the woman is transformed into 'play' with a man. Whereas the emotional circuitry and the fantasy displacements of the 'women's picture' melodrama can be seen to be motivated by the real-world restrictions bearing upon women in terms of marriage and the family, the romantic comedy functions to affirm heterosexual union and consequently, by ideological 'sleight of hand', marriage.

With union represented in terms of 'play' rather than 'duty', some romantic comedies represent heroines who oppose their own 'best interests' by resisting the playful/-sexual side of their 'nature' (this, in *Bringing Up Baby*, is turned around, so that it is the man who represses his playful, natural side). In *Once Upon a Honeymoon*, for example, Katie O'Hara (Ginger Rogers) is in danger of being stifled beneath the ossifying pretensions and studied inflexions of her chosen identity 'Katherine Butte-Smith', fiancée to an Austrian baron (Walter Slezak). She has to be rescued from this fate by the efforts and example of male reporter-figure O'Toole (Cary Grant). The comedy directed at European class pretensions is characteristic of the director, Leo McCarey (cf. *Ruggles of Red Gap* (1935), *Duck Soup*, and the 'gigolo' Armand Duvalle in *The Awful Truth*). In this film, the importance of the capacity to play to the conversion of Katie coexists with the importance of social responsibility, the two being somewhat deliriously combined at the end where Katie and O'Toole and even a ship's captain allow her hated Nazi baron, von Lube, to drown, while pretending that they must do something about it. The scene which most clearly establishes Katie's initial repression of playfulness (and, in the terms the film suggests, of her 'true' self, and her 'true' sexuality) occurs when O'Toole poses as her dresser. While this impersonation allows him physical contact with her body, Katie remains unaware of its sexual connotations as long as she believes that his motives are professional. At one point he sets her off in a giggling fit where her 'true self' breaks through the stiff, formal attempts at self-control ('See here, my man', she reproaches O'Toole haughtily). This is similar to the situation in Ernst Lubitsch's *Ninotchka* (1939), where Leon (Melvyn Douglas) attempts to seduce Soviet special envoy Ninotchka (Greta Garbo) away from her drab, 'unfeminine' rigour into embracing both love and the pleasures of capitalism. Ninotchka resists his attempts to 'break her down', describing love as 'a romantic designation for a most ordinary biological or – shall we say – chemical process. A lot of nonsense is talked and written about it.' He attempts to convince her of the error of her ways in conventional fashion, with a kiss, but it does not totally break through her formality, and he is more affected by it than she. However, the winning of Ninotchka occurs later: seeking to prevent her from taking life too seriously, he cracks a few jokes to get her to smile, almost failing until he accidentally falls off his chair. Ninotchka bursts out laughing, and from that moment on she is converted: love, laughter, and play are unified!

Cavell sees these films as representing a search for childhood and innocence, whereas marriage of course represents 'adult' responsibility and the continuation of the cultural order. These two propositions are, on the face of it, contradictory. This is perhaps why so many romantic comedies stop short of following the trajectory of the romance into marriage, and end with the point of union itself. *Tom, Dick and Harry*, for example, does not attempt to explore whether Janie's doubts about her marriage to Harry (in the dream) will actually be realized or not, but ends with the resolution of the complications preventing union. The consequences are rarely followed up, and even marital comedies like *The Awful Truth*, *The Philadelphia Story*, and the peculiar *Two-Faced Woman* (1942) are pressured by the inevitability of *re*union.

The blockages to union, or the obstacles which intervene between the married couple, tend also to be marked by 'comic disavowal'. This happens in the exaggeratedly playful revelation of infidelity which sparks off the divorce proceedings in *The Awful Truth*. As Ian Jarvie suggests (of 1950s and 1960s romance/sex comedies), 'in reality romance flounders on far more involved and irritating matters which are not in the comedies'.[40] In the romantic comedy, the obstructions to or disruptions of romantic love/marriage are streamlined to the requirements of a process of conventionally ordered narrative transformation. This is, of course, highly *familiar*, not just in the nature of the 'happy ending' itself but throughout, in the patterning of impersonations, misapprehensions, and comic reversals. The films, then, are able to play down the 'serious', 'adult', or 'responsible' connotations of marriage. As the marriage itself is more often implied than actualized, we can see that the point we raised earlier holds force in a literal fashion – the nature of the resolution of the romantic comedy *necessitates* (because of the structuring of the plot towards the point of union or reunion) the romance sanctioning the marriage, rather than vice versa.

The battle of the sexes

The particular ideological character of the 'screwball' comedies can be seen by comparing them with their predecessors and successors in the genre of romantic comedy. The many situational comedies of the 1920s have been somewhat overshadowed in histories of film comedy by a focus upon the feature films of Chaplin, Keaton, Lloyd, and Langdon, but what evidence there is suggests an intriguing and voluminous strain of romantic and marital comedy, with such generically suggestive titles as *So This is Marriage* (1924), *An Exchange of Wives* (1925), *The Waning Sex* (1926), *The Demi-Bride* (1926), and *Tea for Three* (1927). These comedies of contemporary sexual mores appear to have been ushered in by Cecil B. DeMille's marital comedies and dramas, films which addressed the challenges to 'the cultural patterns of Victorian patriarchal sensibility'[41] in the postwar period. Such films as *Old Wives for New* (1918), *Don't Change Your Husband* (1919), *Why Change Your Wife?*, and *Forbidden*

Fruit (1921) posited that the conflict between the patriarchal keystone of marriage and the postwar transformations in the cultural profile of sexuality – what Richard
Maltby refers to as the consumerist 'revaluation of the
cultural place of the erotic'[42] – could be resolved by the
'sexualization' of one or both partners. In *Why Change
Your Wife?*, for example, the marriage breaks up as a
result of Beth's (Gloria Swanson's) rigidity in conceiving
of marriage as 'duty' rather than 'fun'. Her reunion with
Robert (Thomas Meighan) is attendant upon her sexual
'self-discovery', through a glamorous change of appearance and her embracing the pleasures of consumerism.
The film attempts to strike a balance between the old and
the new, between 'duty' and 'fun', for the transformation
undergone by Beth is not embraced in isolation from traditional marital responsibilities – hence the film's rejection
of Robert's second wife, the frivolous playgirl Sally Clark
(Bebe Daniels).[43]

In these films the salvation of marriage takes the form,
primarily, of making *oneself* more desirable for one's partner, a process of self-fetishization reliant upon a panoply
of 'sex-aids' (fashion, phonograph records, art-deco trap-
pings, and so forth). In the 'screwball' comedies, however,
there is a reversal of this pattern, for not only is it the
union rather than the individual which is made desirable,
but there is also a marked attempt to detach sex or
romance from wealth. The upper-bourgeois milieu cele-
brated by DeMille tends, in the 'screwball' comedies, to
be situated as the fantasy world which the heroine has
ultimately to reject. The representation of woman as fet-
ishized spectacle, common in the 1920s, was rendered
especially problematic after the crash of 1929; hence one
can see the 'screwball' comedy's obsession with addressing
and rechannelling the challenging desires of women in
terms of a general attempt to reaffirm traditional sex roles.
Whereas in the 1920s, then, marriage is shown to benefit
from the spice of luxury, in the 'screwball' comedies the
association between the desirability of women and econ-
omic/social advancement is highly problematic. This is

highlighted, as we have indicated, in both *It Happened One Night* and *My Man Godfrey*, where the stress is upon the reform of both general economic priorities and the disrupted sexual/familial order. Similarly, one can note the prevalence of the 'gold-digger' figure and the 'Cinderella fantasy' as objects of comic transformation. Each option represents a means by which women can escape the conventional restrictions of marital and economic subservience and is, accordingly, ideologically discredited and willingly abandoned by the 'screwball' heroines.

Ted Sennett furthermore suggests that the appearance of these comedies around 1934 represented a deliberate shift away from an early 1930s cycle of 'sex-and-sin' melodramas[44] (what Richard Maltby and Lea Jacobs refer to, respectively, as the 'kept woman' or 'fallen woman' cycle.[45]) Films such as *Baby Face* (1933) and *Red-Headed Woman* (1932) – Anita Loos' script for the latter being an unusual *comic* treatment of the subject[46] – featured women who aggressively sought the high life, using their sexuality for their own advancement. these films lacked the marital rationale of DeMille's films. In their focus upon the heroine's 'single-minded drive for wealth and excitement'[47] they aroused agitation among moral groups (who had grown especially powerful since the economic collapse) and consequently among film censors.[48] As a result of this pressure, it seems that the subject of such 'transgressive' female desire shifts from melodrama to comedy – a form of comedy, moreover, in which the overt stress upon 'eccentricity' enshrines a deintensification, a refusal to treat problems 'seriously'. The attitude of the 'screwball' comedy is summarized by Sennett as 'Why not confront life's problems – a broken love affair, a crumbling marriage, a murder – with cheerful impudence and occasionally a wild streak of lunacy?'[49] Considering the economic and cultural climate of the period it is worth noting how a prime concern in these films is with the deproblematizing of the woman's transgressive desires, accounting for her ambitions in terms of a 'natural' female eccentricity rather than, say, as deriving from mercenary, ruthless motivations (as is the case in the early 1930s melodramas and also with the *femmes fatales* of 1940s *films noirs*).

By the 1940s, the sexual and class divisions which had provided the context of motivation for the 'screwball' comedy had been superseded by what Dana Polan refers to as 'an ideology of commitment and community'.[50] The 1930s-style romantic comedy ceased to be such a staple feature of Hollywood production, and in the early wartime years in particular there are indications of a reaction against validating romance as all-important. Such films as *Arise, My Love* (1940), *Once Upon a Honeymoon*, and *Talk of the Town*, for example, are much more emphatic combinations of romantic comedy and weighty drama. Both the wartime and postwar periods in America were characterized by complex discursive reorientations which strongly affected Hollywood production policies and the generic standardization of the 1930s. The problematic of the woman who desires wealth and independence shifted, as we have suggested, into the realm of the *film noir* thriller/melodrama, the fetishization of the *femme fatale* provoking a paranoia masked in DeMille's controlled eroticism. Sennett, however, notes the persistence into the late 1940s of the 'boss-lady' comedies,[51] a spin-off from the romantic comedy in which the woman's aspirations for a career are countered when she falls for a man who can 'open up her heart' to reveal her 'repressed' femininity.

When the romantic comedy makes an explicit comeback in the 1950s – with a number of the key 'screwball' comedies remodelled to fit both the ideological climate and the new parameters of Hollywood film style – one finds that romance and courtship become increasingly displaced by an emphasis upon sex and seduction. Increasingly during the 1950s and 1960s – and under pressure from the cultural impact of post-Kinsey sexology, with its mechanistic detailing of sexual response, sexual frequency, and so forth – the comedy becomes broader as the emphasis upon physical sexuality intensifies. This results in an increased level of innuendo, often with the males as bearers of sexualized jokes at the expense of women (and especially those women who seek to define themselves in non-sexual terms, like the professional heroines of *Pillow Talk* (1959), *Sex and the Single Girl* (1964), and *A Very Special Favour* (1965)). There is also an emphatic reliance upon 'physical' comedy, especially as a means of 'pulling off' the resolution. Many of the films conclude with either broad bedroom farce (as in *It Started With a Kiss*) or manic, extended chase sequences (as in *That Touch of Mink* (1962), *Sex and the Single Girl*, and *What's New Pussycat?* (1965)), often at the expense of the patterned, witty dialogue of the 'screwball' comedies. In such cases, indeed, the union seems more blatantly forced than 'developed' through mutual play, and as a corollary the element of sexual conflict is intensified.

In many of the sex comedies of the 1950s and 1960s, the hero's prime aim is to break down the woman's sexual resistance and take her to bed. The 'conversion' required in the 1930s is no longer so wide-ranging, and in such a 'battle of the sexes' the stakes narrow down to a question of her virginity and his virility. This is emphatic in such films as *Sex and the Single Girl* and *Pillow Talk* where the hero is attracted to the woman precisely because she is one of the few actually to resist him. There is also a marked ambivalence concerning marriage, exemplified in the very title of *The Tender Trap* (1955).[52] As Stanley Ford (Jack Lemmon) comments in *How to Murder Your Wife* (1964), 'Marriage is not a basic fact of nature, it's an invention . . . it exists only because the women say so'.[53] Marriage represents an end to the male fantasy of unbridled sexual liberty, to the 'playboy fantasy' common in these films which posits an idealized state of phallic omnipotence. Films like *That Touch of Monk*, *The Tender Trap*, *Pillow Talk*, and *It Started With a Kiss* abound in scenarios of male sexual frustration, where marriage figures as a castrating restriction. Marriage becomes a compromise for the male, and in a turnaround from the 'screwball' comedies it is the *hero* who now has to be convinced that marriage is worthwhile, that it is worth renouncing his freedom for. In *Pillow Talk*, for example, Brad Allen (Rock Hudson) compares the single man to a tree standing tall in a forest, with marriage as equivalent to being chopped down to size and transformed into furniture for the home. The onus in films like *Pillow Talk* and *What's New Pussycat?* is upon finding a woman for whom, as Brad is told, 'you look forward to having your branches cut off'. It is quite characteristic of the period that female dissatisfaction with marriage or heterosexual union is much more rarely voiced, and when it is the woman tends to be characterized as either repressed (as in Natalie Wood's sex-researcher heroine in *Sex and the Single Girl*) or perverse (as with the sexually resistant wife Maggie, in *It Started With a Kiss*).

Return to romance?

As we have shown with the example of the 'screwball' comedies, the comedy of the sexes seeks both to address cultural transformations in heterosexual relations and marriage and also to hold these transformations in place. Although marriage is often acknowledged as necessitating self-sacrifice or compromise, it still functions to symbolize a union which is lasting. By the 1960s this had become problematic under the brunt of the decade's cultural fixation upon 'sex as individual liberation', and the romantic/sexual comedies of succeeding years have in general sought to come to terms with the legacy of these wide ranging changes. Brian Henderson, for example, sees in films like *Semi-Tough* (1977) a withdrawal of both men and women from engagement in the 'game of love': 'It seems like when the new self pulls itself together, it is away from the ground of full sexual dialectic. To argue this is to argue the death of romantic comedy.'[54] In the light of the romantic comedies of the late 1970s and early 1980s, however, this comment seems unnecessarily apocalyptic, for these films can perhaps most aptly be described by Woody Allen's phrase in *Annie Hall*, the 'nervous romance'.[55] This term suggests the tension in such films: there is a reluctance about commitment to a heterosexual union in an age where divorce and marital disruption are prevalent, but there is also a contrary pull which is strongly marked by fantasy, hearkening for an 'old-fashioned' security in heterosexual romance (rather than sex). Allen's *Manhattan* (1979) and Alan J. Pakula's *Starting Over* (1979) are exemplary in this respect. The protagonist of each film, a male, is facing emotional flak from a disrupted marriage, and oscillates between insecurity and potency in regard, respectively, to his ex-wife (*Manhattan*'s 'independently minded' lesbian caricature Jill (Meryl Streep), *Starting Over*'s self-centred singer-songwriter Jessie (Candice Bergen)) and to a woman with whom he can remain dominant (the doting schoolage girlfriend Tracy (Mariel Hemingway) in *Manhattan*, and the neurotic post–30 Marilyn (Jill Clayburgh) in *Starting Over*). Both films imply that the contemporary breakdown of monogamy represents a particular challenge to the male, and that it is the 'post-feminist' woman who is largely to blame (her desire for independence rendered as an inflated narcissism).

The current revival of romantic comedies – such 1987 films as *Blind Date*, *Who's That Girl?*, *Roxanne*, *Moonstruck*, *Made in Heaven*, and *Broadcast News* – intensify this desire to 'return' to heterosexual romance in the contemporary era of sexual revisionism. Twenty years after the peak of the 'sexual revolution', the concept of 'the couple' is being reinvoked as a safeguard not merely against the divisions of modern life but also against the post-AIDS danger of 'illicit' sexuality (that which is outside the 'norm' of heterosexual monogamy). In these comedies, the notion of charismatic individuals who are 'made for each other' and 'ought to be united' is forcefully reminiscent of the 'screwball' films: *Moonstruck*, for example, has a characteristic 'magical' resolution. James Brooks, writer and co-producer of *Starting Over*, which makes the point clearly, suggests how his highly successful comedy *Broadcast News* is marked by the desire to return, nostalgically, to pre–1950s conceptions of romance:

But the strange thing for me was that we worked very hard to catch everything *true*. . . . I cared very much about it being different from other pictures. And then when the whole thing was finished it was amazing to see we were still in the tradition of romantic comedy. It really did amaze me, even though in some way that was the goal. We spent so much time pushing away from that, that the fact that we ended up being there surprised me.[56]

Section 3

8
Comedy, television, and variety

Comedy in the world of television

The term 'television' can imply or refer to a number of distinct things, each of them indicative of important aspects of television as an institutionalized apparatus of representation. The term 'television' can, for instance, refer to the television set – an item of domestic furniture, something we can rent or buy and take home with us. The term in this sense is indicative of the centrality of the home, the family, and domesticity both to television and to its audience. It is indicative also of a crucial aspect of television as a technology: the television set is a receiver; it cannot normally transmit sounds and images, despite the fact that it was initially invented as a means of two-way communication. The technology of television is used overwhelmingly to broadcast sounds and images from a centralized, institutional source to a mass audience via receivers located in the home. A further technological feature of television is the nature of its sounds and images and the way they are produced and transmitted. As John Ellis has pointed out, in comparison with cinema, the images and sounds of broadcast television are of poor definition and quality; the image is smaller and hence less suited to spectacle. It tends to occupy a secondary position with respect to sound, which acts as an anchor point in viewing, and mostly carries both essential information and subordinate detail.[1] The sounds and images of television are produced and transmitted electronically. Unlike cinema, their production and reception can to all intents and purposes be simultaneous: television can be broadcast 'live'. Partly for this reason, the sounds and images of broadcast television, no matter how they are organized, and no matter what the precise temporal relation between the moment of production and the moment of reception may actually be, tend to convey an overwhelming impression of directness and of the present as opposed to the pastness of events represented in the cinema.[2]

These technological and institutional characteristics have, in turn, a distinct bearing on TV aesthetics, on the way the images, sounds, and forms of television are organized, scheduled, and presented. The presence and immediacy of the images and sounds, together with the constant presence of the TV set in the corner of the room, give rise to the perpetual availability of television (and hence the need to ensure that availability through the transmission of images and sounds for long periods of time throughout each day, each week, each month, and each year), as well as to its capacity (and propensity) for direct address. As Raymond Williams points out, we as viewers tend to experience television not just as a discrete set of individual programmes, but as units within larger, sequential blocks of time: an evening's viewing, a week's viewing, a month's viewing and so on.[3] These blocks are composed of units which are organized according to principles of repetition and temporal regularity: in any one evening, children's programmes will be broadcast at a certain point early in the evening, the news will be on at about 6 o'clock and again at 9 o'clock or 10; across the week, films will be shown at regular times on regular days, as will episodes of soap operas, documentary and current affairs, prestige drama, and so on; and across each year, there will be seasons, where the balance of scheduling may change slightly, where new programmes (regularly scheduled) will be broadcast.

Both within and between the programmes themselves, the viewer will be regularly addressed by link people, announcers, newsreaders, chat-show hosts, compères, and presenters. What John Ellis has called the 'timeless now' of television, the constant and immediate availability of its world, and the present tense of its images and sounds, allows, indeed in part demands, a marking of the co-presence of TV and viewer, the function precisely performed by these mediating figures, each permitted, in various ways, to look into camera and speak to us.[4]

Both the organizational forms of broadcast units of images and sounds across the blocks of time composing the schedule, and the capacity of television for various types of direct address, have considerable bearing upon the forms of comedy that are prevalent on TV. According to John Ellis, the basic unit of television is not the programme, but the segment: 'small, sequential unities of images and sounds whose maximum duration seems to be about five minutes'.[5] Segments are organized into groups. These groups are either 'simply cumulative, like news broadcast items and advertisements, or have some kind of repetitive or sequential connection, like the groups of segments that make up the serial or series'.[6] Segments are organized into programmes or items, and these in turn are programmed 'vertically', across the evening or day, and 'horizontally', across the week, the month, and the season. The segments are thus various, but all have an element of regularity – both of type and of a position within the schedule. On the one hand, there is a variety (of types and positions, together with the uniqueness of every segment), and, on the other, there is repetition (of type, of form of organization, of place, of a slot within the schedule). In combination with the demands of continuity, and with the characteristic of a 'timeless now', these conventions give rise to one of the major forms of broadcast programming, the serial or series, and hence to one of the major forms of broadcast comedy, the sit-com. As with all series or serials, we can switch on at the same time each week and update ourselves on the lives and situations of what often become very familiar characters. In the case of serials, like *Blot on the Landscape* or *The Beiderbecke Affair*, we can also update ourselves on the progress of a plot. (In a series – like *M*A*S*H* or *Terry and June* – plots and stories rarely extend beyond each episode.) The presence of a narrative, whether confined to episodes or not, means that the segmental units of broadcast television are here developmental rather than just sequential. This in turn tends to entail forms of indirect address. Sequential segmentation and direct address tend much more to mark the variety formats that comprise the other major site of comedy on broadcast TV.

Television itself, with its separate segments, slots, and schedules, and its different genres and types of programme, can be considered a variety form. It is thus hardly surprising that programmes of variety entertainment, sequentially presented acts and forms whose unity lies solely in a time span, a distinctive structure, or in the recurrence of a particular performer or performers across otherwise separate acts and items, tend to be much more prevalent on television than in the cinema. Like the forms and institutions of theatrical variety from which they derive, the forms and types of television variety all differ slightly in structure, in the degree to which comedy is prevalent, and in the ways in which the four major forms of variety comedy – the comic song, the monologue, the double-act, and the sketch – are combined in a programme.

Thus a show like *Sunday Night at the London Palladium* will include comedy as only one among a number of different kinds of entertainment – singing, dancing, juggling, magic, and so on. A particular act or performer will appear only once. Continuity is provided by a compère (Bruce Forsythe and Norman Vaughan in the 1960s, Jimmy Tarbuck more recently). The compère is himself a comic performer. He will introduce the show with a monologue and intersperse jokes among the patter introducing each act. The precise balance between monologues, songs, and double-acts will depend upon the nature and speciality of the performers featured each week – though sketch-acts tend to be rare. The structure of *Friday Night Live* is similar in that a variety of acts are presented by a resident compère (Ben Elton). The acts are different in style (the programme is aimed at a younger, Channel–4-watching audience), and they are more restricted in kind (almost exclusively comedy acts and music). Moreover, certain acts and performers are regulars: they will appear each week, usually at specific and regular points within the programme (Harry Enfield's 'Stavros' monologue always occurs after Ben Elton's opening introduction), and often, like some of the guest bands, more than once. (Thus in a number of respects, *Friday Night Live* is a modern amalgam of variety and revue.)

By contrast, shows like *The Two Ronnies*, *The Dave Allen Show*, and *Alas Smith and Jones* may feature a number of individual items and forms, but they will be predominantly – or exclusively – comic. The only other type of act presented with any regularity will be a music act – either by a guest artist who changes each week, or by a resident (like Loudon Wainwright III in the most recent of the Jasper Carrott series). The style of comedy, and the precise balance between the types of comic item, will depend entirely upon the nature of the performer or performers around whom the shows and series are built. Those built around individual comics like Jasper Carrott or Dave Allen will include a number of lengthy monologues, sometimes lasting more than six minutes. These will be interspersed with sketches, either singly, in the case of Jasper Carrott, or in thematically-linked sequences of three or four, in the case of Dave Allen. Double-acts are less likely to feature monologues (Ronnie Corbett's regular joke-telling routine in *The Two Ronnies* is something of an exception). Much more prevalent are sketches and sequences of 'cross-talk' (in which the comic duo engage in joke-swapping, banter, and comic discussion). As with the first of the two basic kinds of TV variety, there is thus a fundamental similarity of item, structure, and format between all the individual shows and series. Difference is provided by performance style and speciality (a point to which we shall return in a moment), and by the establishment of a regular, specific, and distinctive order of items. *The Two Ronnies* always begin with a 'newsreading' sequence, which will always be followed by a sketch. Towards the end of the show, there will be a comic-song-cum-production number, followed and concluded by a further (and shorter) item of newsreading. *Carrott Confidential* always begins with a pre-credit sequence involving Carrott on his way to the studio stage. This will always be followed by a monologue. *Morecambe and Wise* begin each show with an item of cross-talk. And so on. To the general predictability of the basic variety format is added the specific predictability of each individual series.

Individual style and speciality have been mentioned a number of times. They are important not least because they provide another level of specificity, novelty, and difference, and, if the performer is well-known, another level of predictability and repetition. Thus where Dave Allen performs lengthy and conversationally delivered monologues, Bob Hope delivers a rapid stream of one-off verbal gags. Ben Elton wears a distinctive show-biz suit, more formal and stagey than Jasper Carrott's open-necked shirt and jacket, less eccentric than the dress of Freddie Davies or Jimmy Cricket. Little and Large tend to specialize in cross-talk. In this respect they are similar to Morecambe and Wise and Cannon and Ball, but different from the Two Ronnies, who rarely engage in cross-talk outside the specific and fictionalized parameters of character and situation provided by the format of the sketch. And so on.

At this level, individuality can be seen as the product of distinct and systematic variations on the form (as well as the content) of the basic routines and components of variety: the sketch, the double-act, and the monologue, which we now consider in more depth.

The sketch, the double-act, and the monologue

Although it is possible to trace the origins of the sketch and the double-act to the routines of Renaissance *commedia dell'arte*, and to medieval flyting and farce, the forms as we know them today have their immediate origins in the institutions of nineteenth- and twentieth-century theatrical variety: music hall, vaudeville, pantomime, the circus, the minstrel show, the medicine show, the fairground attraction, and American burlesque. More specifically, it would seem that the stand-up or solo comic monologue has its origins in America in the verbal style of circus clowning prevalent in the 1830s and 1840s (prior to the advent of Barnum), in the minstrel show stump speech, and in the sales pitch of the fairground barker and medicine show salesman.[7] The double-act (and cross-talk) have their origins in the banter developed between the clown and master of ceremonies in the circus, and between the 'Interlocutor' and 'Endmen' (Tambo and Bones) in the opening section of the minstrel show.[8] The sketch, meanwhile, has its origins in the various types of afterpiece prevalent in all forms of nineteenth-century theatre, and again in the minstrel show.

The essence of the monologue lies in the fact that a solo performer speaks directly to an audience. (On television, a comic monologue is usually addressed directly to a studio audience and indirectly to the audience of the television programme in which it occurs, though the latter may well be acknowledged directly as well.) There are various types of monologue and various styles of solo performance. Prevalent in the nineteenth century in America, and in the early twentieth century in England (following the lifting of regulations about speech on the variety stage, and the bringing together of all forms of theatre under the jurisdiction of the Lord Chamberlain, in 1912), was a style in which jokes and funny lines were heavily motivated. They would be linked by a developed narrative or grounded in the relatively elaborate description of a comic situation, or else arise as a consequence of parody (hence of deviations from well-known forms of oratory like election speeches or Shakespearian soliloquies). And they would be delivered by a performer whose persona was markedly 'fictional': the comic performer would be playing a 'character' or 'type' – the country bumpkin, the wily or vacuous politician, Hamlet, or Lady Macbeth – complete with theatrical costume, and adopted accent and attitude. As an example, here is an extract from a routine by the American comic, Joe Welch, in the character of the naïve or ignorant immigrant (a very popular type in nineteenth-century American comedy):

> 'De oder day I vent to de Grand Central depot and I lay me a fife-dollar bill on the shelf and say, "I vant a ticket for Yonkers." He say, "Excursion?" I say, "No funeral." Ven I got to Yonkers, I vent to de cemetary to visit my brother's dead grave. I kneel down on de grave and I pray and cry for two hours. Den I look at de name on de grave and I see me de mistake. I was crying for two hours for nothing. When I find de right grave I shall cry all over again. I vent to de janitor of de cemetery and I ask him, "Vere is my brother buried?" He say, "How long has he been dead?" I say, "Six months." He say, "Vat is his name?" I say, "Nathan Jacobson". He say, "Vat did he look like?" I say, "He is de picture of me." He say, "Impossible! Anybody that look like you ought to be dead longer than six months."[9]

Aside from Harry Enfield (with characters like Stavros, Loadsamoney and the others), contemporary examples of this kind of act are hard to find in a pure form. Jimmy Cricket and Ben Elton might be cited, though both their acts contain modifications based on subsequent, and very different, solo styles. Thus Jimmy Cricket wears the stage costume, and adopts the accent and persona, of the stereo-typical Irishman. But his act rarely consists of lengthy stories. It tends instead to comprise loosely linked, one-off jokes. Ben Elton, on the other hand, retains the narrative format. His routines often consist of lengthy stories in specific and detailed situations and settings (Intercity trains are a favourite). But the stories are personalized – presented as what happened not to some clearly constructed persona, character, or type, but instead as what happened to Elton himself. The persona – the 'I' – of the character is merged with the persona – the 'I' – of the performer. (The two are not clearly separate as they are with a performer like Enfield.) Hence the following (delivered in the characteristic tone of mounting hysteria, with increasing staccato and speed):

> 'I did a degree actually. I was at Manchester University . . . I'd be in there – first year, 6 o'clock – in the Students Union bar sipping a glass of white wine to myself, humming a Leonard Cohen ditty to myself . . . suddenly, the door would get smashed down . . . in they'd come – twenty-four mud-stained wallies, rugby balls under their arms. They'd throw-up on the floor just so they could skid across it 'stead of walk, pirouette into the middle of the room – they'd see me. They'd say, "He's reading a play at University. He must be queer. He should be pouring beer over his head and intimidating women. He must be queer. He must be gay. . . .'

And so on.

The use of unlinked – or loosely linked – jokes, on the one hand, and of a 'personal' persona, on the other, are stylistic variations on the comic monologue which, according to Roger Wilmut, date in England from the late 1920s:

> today the expression 'stand-up comic' suggests a man who comes on-stage – usually wearing a smart suit – and tells a string of unrelated jokes. In the early 1920s both the expression and the style were unknown.[10]

Wilmut attributes the introduction of the stand-up style to Dickie Henderson Sr and Ted Ray. It fed into television from the stage, and from variety on radio. It can be exemplified today by the work of TV comics like Jim Davidson (though Davidson does also tell stories) and, in particular, Tom O'Connor, Bob Monkhouse, and Jimmy Tarbuck. It is no coincidence that O'Connor, Monkhouse, and Tarbuck have all featured heavily on television, not only as performers of stand-up spots, but also as presenters, hosts, and compères, for two of the primary features of the stand-up style are particularly consonant with these roles. The first is the use of direct and *personalized* address, the cultivation of an air of genial familiarity enabling the performer to address guests, contestants, and performers alike with professional ease. (One of the prime exponents of the stand-up style in America, Bob Hope, has specialized, among other things, in hosting events like the Oscar ceremonies, a role requiring similar skills in the use of direct address.) The other main feature of the stand-up style – the use of rapid, one-off jokes shorn of any elaborate or elaborated context – is also highly-suited to the role of host or compère. Jokes of this kind can be quickly inserted into the flow of an introductory discourse, or a session of questions and answers, without interrupting their progress or disturbing their primary purpose to any great extent.

The temporal and structural differences between the stand-up style and the style of the elaborated monologue can best be illustrated by looking briefly at the way Ronnie Corbett's solo spots in *The Two Ronnies* shows are put together. For what is formally distinctive about these spots is the way they use elements of both styles, and, more than that, the way the differences between them are exploited for structural purposes. The spots are usually written by Spike Mullins. The diminutive Corbett is seated informally in a large leather chair facing the studio audience. The camera is positioned such as to approximate the view of the studio audience (it is slightly below Corbett's eye level), but from much closer in. (As ever, the television viewer is positioned as a *privileged* member of the audience.) There are occasional cutaways to a side-on view (presumably to cover an edit on the soundtrack). Corbett begins by announcing that he is going to tell a funny story – a story in the style of the elaborated monologue. This story is eventually unravelled, complete with description and embellishment, and capped with a final punchline. It usually focuses not on Corbett himself – not on the 'I' of the performer – but on a third (clearly fictional) person.

Thus one of the spots begins: 'Here's a rather unusual item about an octopus.'

The story turns out to concern a man who works in a zoo, and who is given the job of cleaning out a tank containing an octopus. However – and this is the stylistic hallmark of the spot – the story is continually interrupted for the purposes of further self-contained quips and anecdotes, usually of a shorter and more personalized kind, a kind that does feature the 'I' of Ronnie Corbett. Thus the octopus story, in this particular case, is immediately interrupted for the sake both of jokes about Corbett's size and of a further story purporting to be an account of an incident in Corbett's childhood. Only after this is the octopus story resumed. Once again, though, it is immediately abandoned for the sake of asides, and yet another personalized story:

> 'But I digress, and back to the story of the octopus, which concerns a chap who got himself a job in a zoo. And the first morning, the man in charge said to him, "This morning I'd like you to clean out the octopus." And the chap said "Uh, uh . . . how do I do that." [In an accent of exaggerated stupidity.] "Uh, uh, how do I do that." Actually, I'll tell you why the crew are laughing. Because that voice is a very lifelike impersonation of our new producer on the show. . . . I don't know why I'm laughing. If I'm not very careful the unemployment population would have risen on Monday to one million, two hundred thousand and a half.
>
> Anyway, I must be fair and say that this one, this new producer, is better than the other chap – you know, the other fellow. He had to go, you know. He drank as well, you know. This man doesn't drink half as much. He spills most of it. I actually heard this joke at the other producer's farewell party. A very quiet affair to be honest. Actually, as good times go it would rate about the same as being trapped in a lift.'

There are more jokes about the party, and the difficulty of getting a drink. There is a joke about being shown a home movie. The punchline is used as a transition back to the story about the octopus. Its arbitrariness, however, is as self-consciously and knowingly marked as the comment 'But I digress', which is used in nearly all these spots. It serves to stress both the principle of incremental interruption used to structure the monologue and the foundation of that principle in a deliberate clash of solo styles:

> 'then the Head of Light Entertainment showed us the home movie of his divorce. No, it's rather a sad story actually. She was a German girl and they met during the War. They could never agree about how to bring up the children. He wanted them to go into show business. And she wanted them to invade Poland.
>
> Which rather luckily reminds me of the joke I was telling you, about the chap with the Polish octopus. Remember the one? I suppose that sounds a bit contrived does it? But you've got to admire the style haven't you – haven't you? I know you're out there. I can hear you breathing. So the zoo keeper said to the man. . . .'

And we are back finally for the end of the story.

Roger Wilmut traces the antecedents of the double-act in, among other things, the master and servant dialogues of classical and Shakespearian comedy:

> This pattern of a serious or 'straight' man trying to cope with the vagaries of a comic servant set the pattern of the principal type of double-act as it flourished in the first half of this century.[11]

The dialogue of master and servant thus gave rise to the ' "cross-talk" type of double-act – which often took the form of the straight man attempting to perform seriously and being interrupted by the comic'.[12] Many of Morecambe and Wise's routines took this form: Wise would be speaking to the audience, perhaps introducing the show or one of its guests, and Morecambe would interrupt either directly ('Can I ask you something?') or indirectly, by doing something that disturbs or distracts his partner:

> Wise: 'Here we are again lads and lassies, yes, here we are again ready to dip into the fun barrel

	for yet another 45 minutes to three quarters of an hour of fun, laughter, joy – and what are you doing?'
Morecambe:	'Oh, I'm sorry . . . forgive me. I wasn't listening. Sing it again, it's one of your best songs that.'
Wise:	'I wasn't singing. What were those funny movements you were doing there?'
Morecambe:	'I was looking down, you see, thinking to myself, what a beautiful piece of mechanism legs are. As I walked on I said to myself, "Eric, you are walking on two of nature's miracles." '

And so on.

With Morecambe and Wise, the principle of interruption, a principle which, as we have seen in chapter 3, is fundamental to comedy and to its jokes, gags, and comic moments, is highly conventional. It is the necessary causal factor that sets the routine in motion. Conventional, too, is the absence not only of a fictionalized setting but of any apparent context of rehearsed performance or professional activity. The routines are constructed as spontaneous conversations between people who, but for the interruptions, would be introducing guest artistes, singing songs, acting in sketches, and so on. One of the effects of this convention is to personalize the personae of the performers. They are not playing characters in sketches. They are not performing rehearsed routines. They are not even adopting professional roles as hosts and compères. They have not yet got round to that. They are simply themselves – all the more so because these interruptions to the performance of genuinely fictional characters and proper professional roles are marked as the consequence of *personal* foibles and traits.

Of course, these foibles and traits – Eric Morecambe's mischievousness, for instance, and Ernie Wise's vanity – are, like the routines themselves, constructed fictions. They serve as motivation for jokes, lines, and gags, and very often also as a principle of structural cohesion. Eric will

use the occasion to play on Ernie's sense of self-import-
ance. And where this is the case, there is a variation on
the roles of comic and straight man built into routines
of this kind. Where conventionally the straight man is
practised, professional, and in a position of knowledge,
and where conventionally the comic is bumbling and
ignorant, here the roles are reversed, while the guise of
convention is maintained. In other words, Wise is the
straight man, and Morecambe the comic. But Morecambe
knowingly exploits the conventions of his position to put
one over on Wise. He can do so because Wise's vanity
(his sense that he is the straight man, if you like, with the
straight man's conventional attributes) allows him, in fact,
to be duped. It is Wise who is really ignorant, who is
constantly made fun of, who becomes the butt of the jokes,
and Morecambe who makes fun of him, either directly, as
when he tells his partner that his body is so beautifully
built he should consider becoming a model ('Sometimes I
go too far'), or indirectly, as when the routine quoted
above continues, to reveal Wise's ignorance of maths. As
Eric completes his line about legs and nature's miracles,
Ernie continues:

> 'I know that.'
>
> Morecambe: 'You know that because you are an educated
> man. That's why you know. How many A
> levels have you got?'
>
> Wise: 'Twenty-three.'
>
> Morecambe: 'Twenty-three A levels, ladies and gentle-
> men, this boy – in mathematics, am I right?'
>
> Wise: 'Well seventeen A levels in mathematics and
> another two making twenty-three.'

It is interesting to compare Morecambe and Wise in this
respect with the more recent act of Mel Smith and Griff
Rhys Jones. Where in the case of Morecambe and Wise
the personae and positions of relative knowledge are consistent across their individual routines, with Smith and
Jones they vary: sometimes the former is crass, or ignorant, or boorish, sometimes the latter. On the studio stage,

performing direct to an audience, it is Smith who frequently plays the boorish comic to Jones' straight man, as in this routine, where Jones appears initially to be speaking both personally and seriously, outside any performance context whatsoever. Smith is seated beside him:

> Jones: 'I just want to be serious for just a minute here –
> if I may, just for a moment. We don't, obviously,
> want to use this programme as a platform. We're
> television people. But we know we couldn't
> operate without the incredible back-up of the
> arts in Britain today generally.'

Smith speaks in agreement, helping Jones to continue (rather than interrupting to digress, or to interpolate a difference of view):

> 'Right, right.'
> Jones: 'Both of us have been outraged by the present
> cuts, and we both believe that this government
> is the most uncultured this century.'

Smith agrees again. But this time his tone, and in particular the words that he uses, clash comically with the tenor of Jones' speech, marking the emergence of an 'uncultured' persona whose later comments on the opera constitute a genuine interruption. The divergence of opinion that ensues sets the cultured earnestness of Jones off against the ignorant vulgarity of Smith, thus producing the familiar positions of straight man and comic:

> Smith: 'Too bloody right.'
> Jones: 'And we think it's important that we should
> demand that the government give adequate
> funding to all the arts as much as it can in the
> near future.'
> Smith: 'Yes, yes – all the arts, you say? Not opera,
> obviously.'
> Jones: 'Well, yes, opera. We can't be discrimating
> about these things.'
> Smith: 'Opera's a bag of steaming old pooh-poohs, to
> be honest.'
> Jones: 'Well *you* may not like it, Mel. '

Smith: 'Well – you know – all those great Italian blub-
         berinos poncing around in fancy dress – you
         know. Pathetic really.'
Jones: 'I know it's not to your taste, Mel. '
Smith: 'It's tosh. Let's face it. It's tosh – foreign tosh,
         for the most part, as well.'

In their face-to-face routines, on the other hand, the
roles are reversed. Both men are, at times, incredibly
stupid. But Jones is consistently more stupid than Smith.
It is thus Smith who is the straight man here, and Jones
the ignorant comic:

Smith: 'I've been going through a very miserable and
         expensive time.'
Jones: 'You've renewed your Arsenal season ticket
         again.'
Smith: 'Me divorce. Me divorce has come through,
         innit. I tell you – divorce – it's a horrible thing
         to happen to anybody. I don't care who they are
         – young or old, male or female. . . .
Jones: 'Married or single.'
Smith: 'It's the kids I feel sorry for. '
Jones: 'Me too – they shouldn't let them get married
         in the first place.'

Smith and Jones' head-to-head routines occupy a middle
ground between the double-act and the sketch. In double-
act routines of the kind cited earlier, the performers appear
as personalized professionals: they appear as 'themselves',
as people whose profession is comic performing. The audience is acknowledged and often directly addressed. The
context of the routines – their motivating framework – is
the performance situation itself. The routines take place
here, now, 'live', in front of the studio audience, and in
front of the audience watching at home. In the head-to-
head routines, Smith and Jones are shot not frontally but
in profile, as they talk to one another across a table. The
presence of an audience is never acknowledged. There is
thus already a difference in presentation and address: we
look on as unobserved observers at something happening
elsewhere (outside our presence) and at a time which is

unspecified – but which need not be here and now – just as we would while watching a full-blown sketch, or indeed a narrative fiction. The performers wear open-necked shirts in contrast to the suits they wear in other double-act routines presented direct to the audience on stage. They thus wear costumes, albeit of a rudimentary kind. In addition their personae are fictionalized. The parts played by Smith and Jones in these routines are given traits and biographies (or biographical details) of a kind as to mark them, not as performers with personae, but as characters. All they lack are fictional names. (Significantly, though, they never call one another Mel and Griff, as they do in other kinds of routine.) Finally, there is a prop – the table – and hence the beginnings of a diegetic space and of a fully fictional situation. All that is missing is a detailed set, a specified fictional time and/or place, and a narrative event to motivate the cross-talk and turn it from cross-talk into dialogue.

Characters, fictional settings (a specified 'elsewhere'), dialogue, and some kind of causal event to set a conversation or an action in motion, are the differentiating hallmarks of the sketch. For example, one of the sketches in *Victoria Wood As Seen on TV* is set in a department store. There are two performers, as in a double-act, but they play specified fictional roles, that of a shop assistant and a customer. The lines they speak are lines of dialogue: the exchanges between them take the form of a specified type of conversation – a sales pitch and a response – which is justified by all aspects of the setting. The conversation begins because the customer enters the shop, and because the assistant, in fulfilling her role, tries to sell her some cosmetics. The comedy comes from the deviations from what we would conventionally expect an assistant in a shop to do and say, and from the consequent humiliation of the customer:

> Assistant   'Good morning, madam. May I interest you in our skin-care range, though I have to admit that from here your skin looks flawless?'

Customer:	'Thank you.'
Assistant:	'But then again, I failed my driving test because I couldn't read the number plate. *Do* you have spots?'
Customer:	'No.'
Assistant:	'Would you like some? I'll just do a quick check on the computer. Colour of eyes?'
Customer:	'Blue.'
Assistant:	'Grey. Hair?'
Customer:	'Blonde.'
Assistant:	'Mousey. Condition of pores: open, closed?'
Customer:	'They're sort of ajar.'
Assistant:	'Let's see. Dear me. To we in the trade, that's not so much of a complexion – more of a doily.'
Customer:	'Don't you sell a product that would close them up a bit?'
Assistant:	'Well, we do an astringent, but really, with pores that big, you'd be better off with a darning needle and some pink wool. . . .'

The sketch ends with the final humiliation of the customer and the end of the conversation as another customer is hailed by the assistant:

Customer:	'Well, it sounds like I'm so ugly, nothing's going to be any use.'
Assistant:	'Oh, I don't know, madam. There's our special formula lipstick.'
Customer:	'What good's that?'
Assistant:	'It's six foot high, you can stand behind it. Can I help you madam?'

This sketch is typical of all sketches in tracing the effect, or effects, of a single cause: the conversation, complete with multiple insults, each directed against the body of the customer, is initiated by the entry of the customer into the store in close proximity to this particular assistant. (An additional level of motivation – not causal, but veri-similitudinous – is provided by the fact that the customer is female rather than male: in our culture, women are 'naturally' expected to be concerned, and worried, about their physical appearance, and thus likely to be drawn into conversation with a sales assistant selling beauty products in a department store.) The cause here, then, is a physical event. Most causes in sketches are causes of this kind, though sometimes they are stated verbally rather than directly represented. Thus one of the sketches in *Not the 9 O'clock News* consists of a television interview with a highly intelligent, talking gorilla and his master: the TV interview format allows the interviewer to state in his introductory remarks that the gorilla has been taught to speak English. The sketch can follow from there, with the gorilla quoting Aristotle, citing his preference in music for the songs of Johnny Mathis, and, in particular, exhibiting and illustrating the difficulties in his relationship with his master.

A number of *Two Ronnies* sketches are interesting in this connection, particularly those written, or co-written, by Gerald Wiley. In these sketches a cause is established with a particular formal premise – usually linguistic – which is used to structure the sketch as a whole and to act as the site and vehicle for funny lines and comic effects. One sketch, for instance, is set at a convention for writers of limericks. One of the writers introduces himself. The ensuing conversation takes limerick form:

Arnold: 'How do you do?'
Algernon: 'How do you do?'
Arnold: 'My name's Dear, Arnold Dear. I come here every year.'
Algernon: 'My name's Algernon Crust. You write limericks, I trust?'
Arnold: 'No, I'm only here for the beer. Just a joke. Just a rhyme and a joke. I can't help it I'm that sort of bloke. Just a joke and a rhyme and a jolly good time. What I really came for was a . . .'
Algernon: 'Smoke?'

In another sketch, set in a railway carriage, the dialogue is spoken to the rhythm of the train on the track. In another, a conversation between a barman and a customer in a pub is formally structured, both as a conversation and as a series of funny moments, around points at which the customer searches for a word to finish his sentence, which the barman tries to supply:

Bert: 'Evening, Harry.'
Harry: 'Hello, Bert. What are you gonna have?'
Bert: 'Very kind of you. I think I'll have a pint of, er . . .'
Harry: 'What light?'
Bert: 'No.'
Harry: 'Brown?'
Bert: 'No.'
Harry: 'Mild?'
Bert: 'No.'
Harry: 'Bitter?'
Bert: 'Bitter. Pint of bitter.'
Harry: 'Pint of bitter. How are you then, alright?'
Bert: 'Mustn't grumble. Mustn't grumble. Just been up the . . .'
Harry: 'Club?'
Bert: 'No.'
Harry: 'What, dogs?'
Bert: 'No.'
Harry: 'Fish shop?'
Bert: 'No.'
Harry: 'Doctor's?'
Bert: 'Doctor's. Yes, I've just been up the doctor's. Only I've been having a bit of trouble with my . . .'
Harry: 'Chest?'
Bert: 'No.'
Harry: 'Ears?'
Bert: 'No.'
Harry: 'Waterworks?'
Bert: 'No . . . wife.'

And so on.

Monty Python

As is well known, many of the most formally innovative television sketches were featured in *Monty Python's Flying Circus*, which was initially broadcast in the late 1960s and early 1970s (the first series was broadcast in 1969). *Monty Python*, in fact, introduced innovations, not only in the format of the sketch, one of the basic building blocks of the TV variety show, but also in the structure of the variety show as a whole. For this reason, and because apart from a chapter in Roger Wilmut's book, *From Fringe to Flying Circus*,[13] there has been little detailed analysis of the *Python* sketches and programmes (and perhaps rather too much unreflective celebration), we conclude this chapter by looking closely at the overall structure and shape of one particular programme, as well as at some of the items within it.

The show we discuss is one of the programmes in the second of the four *Python* series. It was originally broadcast on BBC1 in the autumn of 1970. It is twenty-five minutes long, and, like all variety shows, is segmental in nature and structure, comprising in addition to title sequences at the beginning and end some twenty-three items. Three of these are animated sequences, twelve are sketches, and eight are linking segments of one kind or another (announcements, voice-overs, titles, and so on). These numbers and categories, although reflecting the programme's segmental nature and the general range of its items (there are, for instance, no stand-up solo spots, or items of traditional stand-up cross-talk), are nevertheless necessarily approximate. This is because the structure of the individual items, and the way they are articulated one with another across the span of the programme as a whole, make it difficult to decide where some of the items begin and end, and to determine their function and type.

For instance, the programme begins with a number of Gumbies filmed facing the camera in an exterior location in front of an office block. (A Gumby is defined by Roger Wilmut as 'a brainless sub-human with rolled-up trousers, braces, steel-rimmed spectacles, a small moustache, and a handkerchief with the corners knotted as a headpiece'.)[14] The Gumbies announce 'The Architect's Sketch'. The function of this sequence is at this point clear and unambiguous: it is a linking segment. However, the Gumbies make their announcement a number of times. Finally, they point upwards out of frame. The camera begins to pan up the building behind them, and to close in on one of the windows. Cut to an interior. 'The Architect's Sketch' begins with Graham Chapman in a business suit speaking to two other businessmen (played by Terry Jones and Michael Palin): 'Gentlemen, we have two basic designs for this . . .'.

But as he is speaking, the Gumbies are still audible outside through the window. He tries again. Still they can be heard. He goes over to the window and tells them to shut up. He starts again. Again the Gumbies continue to speak. Chapman grabs a pail of water, opens the window, and empties the contents. Muffled cries from outside. Cut back to the exterior. The Gumbies are now soaking wet. Cut back finally to the office interior. Chapman can now continue uninterrupted.

Here the function of the Gumbies has changed. In a more conventionally structured variety show, linking sequences and introductory segments would clearly be separate from the sketches that follow them. Although one of their basic functions is to provide continuity, another is to mark off items one from another and to signal quite clearly their basic nature and type. Normally, of course, links and introductions are provided by hosts and compères. If these hosts and compères are themselves comic performers, and if they are the stars of the show in question (like Morecambe and Wise, or Cannon and Ball), they themselves may appear in a sketch. But there would be no confusion as to their respective functions and roles, and the function and nature of the sequences themselves. Here, though, elements of the linking segment and the sketch overlap with one another, eventually to generate what is in effect a hybrid mini-sketch, one which begins with the

Gumbies' interruptions, and ends with the bucket of water. One of the elements of overlap – the continuing presence of the Gumbies' voices on the soundtrack – takes the form of intrusive interruption. But it is not just a vocal intrusion; it is an intrusion of one functional segment (the linking segment) into another (the sketch). The vocal overlap is justified, in turn, by an overlap of diegetic space. The pointing of the Gumbies as they make their announcement, the words they speak ('Up there! Up there!'), and, finally, the nature of the movement of the camera, cue the existence of a single diegetic space that encompasses both the exterior setting of the link and the interior setting of the sketch. This generation of a single, overall space prepares the way both for the vocal interruptions and for the gag with the bucket of water. The gag itself both finally cements the link between the two spaces, and caps the transformation in the role of the Gumbies. This mini-sketch complete, the interruptions over, the sketch as announced can, at last, begin.

The principles of diegetic and functional overlap, on the one hand, and of interruption and intrusion, on the other, continue to structure the rest of the show. Thus The Architect's Sketch continues with two prospective designers for a block of flats outlining their plans to the businessmen funding the project. The plans of the first – a specialist in abattoirs who suggests, among other things, a set of rotating knives at the end of an interior conveyor belt ('The last twenty feet of the corridor are heavily soundproofed.') – are rejected as unsuitable ('I'm sorry. We want a block of flats, not an abattoir'). The architect is surprised at first ('I hadn't fully divined your attitude towards the tenants'), then angry, mainly, it turns out, because he wants to become a freemason:

'Sod the abattoir, that's not important. But if you could put in a word for me I'd love to be a mason. Masonry opens doors. I'd be very quiet, I was a bit on edge just now but if I were a mason I'd sit at the back and not get in anyone's way.'

He is still rejected. A second architect comes in. As he explains his plans, the model he is using as demonstration falls apart, catches fire, and eventually explodes. His plans, nevertheless, are accepted. The agreement is sealed with an extraordinary masonic handshake. The first of the architects opens the door, and speaks, in close-up, to camera: 'It opens doors, I'm telling you.'

A voiceover intervenes: 'Let's see that handshake again in slow-motion.' There is a BBC action replay of the hand-shake, and the voiceover continues, telling us how to spot a mason as we watch a filmed exterior sequence of men in pinstripe suits bouncing down the road and shaking hands in various complicated ways. Thus a topic – free-masonry – which initially appears halfway through a sketch is reintroduced at the end, not only to cap it with an unexpected punchline, but also to motivate a transition to a sequence which takes up the theme of masons as its primary element. This sequence in turn blends into another. We see a naked, antlered mason standing in a queue at a bus stop. Next, he appears in cutout form in an animated sequence as a voiceover and explains how masons can be cured of their addiction to masonry through the use of aversion therapy (in the form of a large and animated boot).

Throughout this particular part of the programme, there is more overlap than interruption: the architect's diatribe, for instance, and his plea for masonry membership occur within the conventional parameters of a sketch. If the diegetic integrity of individual items is disturbed, it is in the interests of continuity rather than disruption. The natural boundaries between the items are smoothed over (rather than stressed) by the use of thematic and formal links. The theme of masonry extends across three of the items, as does the use of voiceover. The sequence of masons in the street and the animated segment both adopt a quasi-documentary mode of address, and so on. A little later, though, interruptions are much more marked. A Chemist's Sketch is interrupted by a BBC apology ('for the poor quality of the writing'), then for the use of a prohibited word ('Semprini': a policeman comes on to arrest the chemist who uses it). After each interruption, we shift location to a different shop (run in each case by a different and 'less naughty' chemist). Once the sketch finally gets under way, when a man comes in wanting aftershave smelling of fish, there are further gaps and delays as the chemist goes off in search of the product. The first of these gaps is filled by an address to camera by the actor playing the customer (or rather, by Eric Idle playing the actor playing the customer). The second is filled by a vox-pop sequence in which various people are asked to name their favourite aftershave (the answers range from 'a body rub called halitosis' to 'rancid polecat').

Two other major formal hallmarks of *Python* programmes are strongly evident in this particular sequence. The first of these is the use of repetition (or repetition and variation). For example, the sketch itself is repeatedly interrupted (in a number of different and ingenious ways). The apology that constitutes the first of these interruptions is one of four apologies scattered across the programme as a whole: the very first item, the Gumby announcement discussed above, is preceded by an apology ('The BBC would like to apologize for the following announcement'). A little later the BBC apologizes 'for the amount of repetition in this show' (an apology that is then itself immediately repeated). Repetition of a different kind is evident in the use of figures and characters who recur, not just across the span of this particular programme, but across the span of the series of programmes as a whole. Thus one of the figures interviewed in the vox-pop sequence is a Gumby. Another is the cardinal from a sketch about the Spanish Inquisition, which featured in an earlier show in the series. The function of interruption is constantly performed by policemen arresting the characters in The Chemist's Sketch and the vox-pop sequence. And so on. Here, in particular, repetition serves an integrating function, providing links across a sequence in a programme, across the programme as a whole, and across the series of which the programme is a part.

The other major hallmark, perhaps the one for which the *Python* shows are best known, is the use of *ostranenie* for comic effect: laying bare the conventional device, drawing attention to the artifice inherent in conventional forms of representation, in order both to produce comic implausibility, and to expose the arbitrary absurdities and limits inherent in these forms and their uses. Roger Wilmut has discussed this aspect of the *Python* style under the rubric of what he calls the 'format sketch':

> The idea of taking a basic premise and reversing it is older than Python ... but a particularly Python development is to take the format of something like a television quiz programme or discussion – or indeed anything with a strong and recognizable style of presentation – and then empty the content out of it, replacing it with something ludicrous. The most suitable term for this would be a *format sketch*.[15]

In the particular sequence under discussion, the vox-pop segment and the BBC apology would constitute good examples. Characteristically, they are both examples of the formats of institutionalized, broadcast TV. Elsewhere in the programme there are examples of other kinds of undermined format (notably a parody of the credit sequence of early 1960s British thrillers in a sketch which features 'The Bishop'). However, as Wilmut has noted apropos of the first *Python* series, the use of TV techniques and formats as the basis for sketches and segments is especially common:

> There seems to be something of an obsession with television presentation, and the programmes regularly parody the use of captions and the then current BBC–1 'trade mark' (which shows a revolving globe).[16]

One of the effects of using TV formats, and in particular the formats of announcement and apology, is to produce a markedly 'self-reflexive' style. Coupled with the uses of repetition and diegetic overlap, the sense is created not only of a distinctive and extensive comic world, but of a world that pertains to TV. The other effect is not just to expose the limits of conventional TV formats but to link their absurd arbitrariness to institutions and representatives of institutional power. There is a mocking of that power and of the authority it assumes in the relentless use of presenters and announcers who appear out of context (seated at desks in fields and the like). This mocking of the powers of the broadcasting institutions (a mocking which nevertheless recognizes that these powers are real) is especially evident wherever issues of censorship are raised, whenever 'the BBC' intervenes to protest at a sketch, or to stop it halfway through (as when the announcer intervenes in The Chemist's Sketch to apologize for the use of terms like 'bum').

In all these cases, parody is perhaps too weak and restricted a term to describe the techniques involved and the effects they produce. One of these effects is to inscribe the world of *Monty Python* firmly within the familiar world of television while also marking it as at one step removed from that world. In this respect – in making strange the familiar, in rendering unfamiliar the conventions to which the medium of which it is a part is normally subject – *Monty Python* performs what is in fact, for all its inventiveness, a very conventional comic role. However, this role is rendered more complex – and the style even more 'self-reflexive' – by *Python*'s use of some of the conventions and forms of variety comedy as the basis of a number of its 'format' sketches.

Among the formats involved here, the most consistently used, and undermined, is that of the 'well-made' sketch: the sketch that sets out consistent diegetic parameters, introduces a cause or premise, and develops to end in a climax and punchline. One of the means used to mock and to undermine this format is to stop a sketch in mid-progress, thus preventing the use of a punchline (at least in its traditional form). As with The Chemist's Sketch, a particularly favoured device is that of censorious interruption by a figure of authority (a BBC spokesman, for instance, or an army officer, or a policeman). In one of the shows in the third series, the principles of censorious interruption and punchline abandonment are rendered explicit. One of the reasons offered for the interruption is precisely the lack of a punchline. The means of interruption is identified at which point it is, of course, used once again, this time to interrupt the interrupter:

First Policeman: 'Right – I'm arresting this entire show on three counts; one – acts of self-conscious behaviour contrary to the 'Not In Front Of The Children Act'; two – always saying 'It's so-and-so of the Yard' every time the fuzz arrives; and three – and this is the cruncher – offences against the 'Getting Out Of Sketches Without Using A Proper Punch Line Act', namely, simply ending every bleeding sketch by just having a policeman come in and . . . wait a minute . . .'

Second Policeman: (entering and placing a hand on the first policeman's shoulder): 'Hold it.'

First Policeman: 'It's a fair cop!'
(A large hand appears through the door and places itself on the second policeman's shoulder. Blackout.)

Although the abandonment of punchlines and the technique of stopping a sketch halfway through are constant *Python* traits, it should be noted, as Wilmut points out, that by no means all the *Python* sketches are structured this way. Some (like The Architect's Sketch) make use of a conventional 'hard' punchline; others merely a 'soft' one (their conventional shape otherwise remaining fairly intact). It should also be pointed out that the technique of censorious interruption, in particular, can itself provide, or function as, a punchline. What happens here is that a sketch is simply capped, not from the inside but from outside. Whether or not interventions function in this way, most function not simply as interruptions that bring the sketch to a final halt, but also as a means of providing continuity: they link one item to the next (or to other parts of the programme as a whole), thus minimizing the effects of definitive closure that a punchline or a conventional climax would normally produce. A similar function is performed by what one might call 'the divided sketch' where, although setting and/or characters remain a constant, the sketch appears to change direction, or to peter out and turn into another, different, sketch. Thus, in The Chemist's Sketch, when the chemist himself finally returns to the shop, having gone out in search of the aftershave, it is only to announce that the branch down the road has also run out. At this point another customer enters (two, in fact: one man is concealed inside the coat of another), and steals an item from the counter. A policeman is called. He then proceeds to arrest an innocent customer (the one who wanted the aftershave) and generally to behave in a manner that by no means conforms to our conventional cultural image of what a 'proper' policeman should be like. Thus the sketch about the aftershave becomes a sketch about a loony policeman, but with the continuity provided by the setting of the shop and the characters of the salesman and the customer seeking the aftershave. Thus there are elements of the general structural principle of disturbance and interruption, but elements, too, of the principle of overlap.

Undermining some of the traditional conventions of the sketch is not the only means by which an awareness of these conventions is brought to the fore. Another, used extensively throughout this particular programme, is to call attention to them through the use of captions and labels, or other verbal means. A sketch in an insurance office features a crooked insurance agent and a man who wants insurance for his car. The latter is captioned 'A Straight Man'. Another man comes in ('Another Straight Man'). He begins to complain that his insurance claim has not been paid. The first man interrupts:

'Excuse me. Do I have any more
lines?'

Insurance agent: 'I'll have a look in the script. Are
you 'Man'?'

Man: 'Yes.'

Insurance agent: 'No . . . no, you've finished.'

Man: 'Well, I'll be off then.'

A similar reference to the basic conventions of sketches
(indeed all dramatic fictions) is made by the customer in
The Chemist's Sketch. He turns to camera while the chemist goes off in search of the aftershave:

'Sorry about this. Normally we try and avoid these little
pauses . . . longeurs. Only dramatically he's gone to the
basement, you see. Of course, there isn't really a basement.
But he's just gone off and [he gets slightly embarrassed],
and we just pretend. Actually what happens is that he just
goes off there, off camera and just waits there so it looks
as though he's gone down to the basement. Actually, I
think he's rather overdoing it. . . . Ah.'

Cut to a shot of the actor playing the chemist, standing
next to a camera. He rushes back on set, and the sketch
continues.

The *Python* programmes, then, combine a comic foregrounding of the conventions of television, with a comic
foregrounding of the conventions of comic forms themselves. It is this *combination* that produces the particular
density of construction and self-reference that constitutes
the hallmark of their style. This style, and the techniques
and concerns that produce it, did not, of course, spring
from nowhere. Roger Wilmut has traced its seeds and
antecedents in *The Goon Show* on radio, in Spike Milligan's *Q. . .* series on TV (the first, apparently, to abandon
the use of the punch-line),[17] and more generally in the
comedy produced by a specific generation of writers and
performers (including the Pythons themselves) who began
their careers in the late 1950s and early 1960s writing and
performing in revues at Oxford and Cambridge. (*Beyond
the Fringe* is an important early product.) These writers

and performers constitute, for Wilmut, a third generation of twentieth-century variety comedy in Britain. They follow the music-hall styles and performers of the first half of the century, and the generation he labels the 'NAAFI comedians' which includes those like Tony Hancock, Spike Milligan, Peter Sellers, and Harry Secombe who began their careers entertaining the armed forces during the war.[18] Rather than go over this ground again in detail, however, we would like to stress two particular features of this third generation which help to account for the *Python* style and type of humour.

The third generation as a whole began writing and performing at a point in the late 1950s when conventional music hall was virtually dead, and when television was becoming established as the primary form of mass entertainment (and, hence, popular comedy). It is thus not surprising that there should be a general mocking or abandonment of traditional variety forms and format, as well as an awareness of the forms and formats of TV. The NAAFI generation had already begun deconstructing and reworking some of the conventions of variety – and of the sketch and solo performance. This process was continued by *Beyond the Fringe*, and by TV shows like *That Was The Week That Was*, *Not So Much a Programme*, and *Not Only But Also*. Where the forms were not abandoned or undercut, they were renewed or extended through the injection of contemporary subject matter (hence their reputation for satire), or through the adoption of new kinds of comic absurdity. (Peter Cook's monologues as E. L. Wisty, and his dialogues with Dudley Moore in *Not Only But Also*, stand as important examples of the latter.) At the same time, this generation grew up and began writing and performing at a time when, after the introduction of commercial television into Britain in the mid–1950s, the conventions and formats of broadcast TV were themselves either being reworked or established for the first time.

The educational and intellectual formation of this third generation is also worth noting. An Oxbridge education guarantees neither comic novelty nor an acute awareness of form. However, a certain kind of education is necessary to feature the names of western philosophers in jokes, sketches, and songs (of which there are a number, from an Alan Bennett sketch in *Beyond the Fringe* to Monty Python's 'Philosopher's Song', scattered throughout the work of the Oxbridge generation), or to write a format sketch in which the object of a local talent contest is to summarize Proust's *A La Recherche du Temps Perdu* ('once in a swimsuit, and once in evening dress'), as Monty Python have done. Just as important, a certain kind of education is needed to understand or appreciate these sketches and jokes; one has at least to have heard of Proust, or Sartre, or Hegel for these jokes or sketches or songs to make some kind of sense. It is no accident that the comedy produced by the Oxbridge generation succeeded in capturing audiences throughout the 1960s and early 1970s, at a time when education in general, and higher education in particular, was rapidly expanding in Britain. Nor is it an accident that the audience was a cult audience in many cases, and relatively young. It was an audience that shared the culture (and the attitudes to that culture) of the writers and performers themselves. Moreover, like these writers and performers, that culture included not only philosophy but television. It was an audience that, for the first time, grew up with television, that was just as aware as the writers and performers of its massive expansion, of its provenance, and of its developing conventions and forms.

In more general historical terms, then, the renovation of variety comedy brought about by the Oxbridge generation – and hence, at its peak, the innovations of *Monty Python* (with respect both to variety and to television) – were the product of a particular set of circumstances, influences, and events. These included the demise of traditional theatrical variety, the rise of television, and the absurdist influence of the Goons and, in particular, Spike Milligan. They included what was regarded at the time as a moribund political culture. (Hence the force of much of the satire.) And they also, importantly, included a rela-

tively liberal governing and programming regime at the
BBC, a regime which, for all its ambivalence towards some
of the programmes produced by the Oxbridge generation,
was far more open to experiment and controversy than
the one in power today.[19] Within this context, the moribund forms and conventions of variety were renewed,
extended, or deconstructed in an encounter with the culture of a group of young writers and performers at
Oxbridge. That culture included both the cinema and, in
particular, television. It was through television that the
group found a large and consistent audience, an audience
which shared its culture and concerns, and which was
therefore able to understand (and prepared to enjoy and
encourage) the innovations it introduced. Nowhere was
this more the case than when (as supremely with *Python*)
those innovations bore simultaneously upon the variety
forms that television had helped to displace and render
moribund within their original theatrical context, and the
forms and conventions of television itself.

9
Broadcast comedy and sit-com

Broadcast television is largely a form of variety entertainment. However, like radio before it, television differs from earlier forms in that it functions not as a 'special event' – although it can create its own sense of event, from royal weddings to 'Live Aid' – but is rather accepted as a staple feature of home life. Television is markedly 'commonplace', whereas the cinema has from its earliest days invested in the extraordinary, with a proclivity towards spectacle and fantasy. As John Ellis has noted, the purchase of a cinema ticket gives one the right not only to view a particular film but also to participate in the cinema *experience*,[1] a specific mode of engagement by sounds, images, and narrative in a 'theatrical' context. Although nowadays this experience is quite clearly structured around the single feature film, this has not always been the case; in the 'classical' era of the 1930s and 1940s, the feature film was the culmination of a 'package' of entertainments, preceded by cartoons, shorts, a serial, a newsreel, a supporting feature, and even live acts. Cinemagoers of the period 'experienced cinema as an integrated succession of entertainments that went far beyond the simple experience of viewing a film together in a more or less anonymous crowd'.[2] In this sense, of course, the mainstream cinema was following in the path of other commercial entertainments in which the notion of '*a performance*' was central, but particularly the variety form of vaudeville and music hall.

The organization of the film industry, of its modes of production, distribution, and exhibition, and also the organization of its 'product specifications' (especially the standardized parameters of similarity and difference such as the star system and the genre system) were developed in accordance with specific conceptions of the cinema as a mode of entertainment. Just as the cinema adapted pre-existing forms and genres of popular entertainment, so too did television, but in the case of the latter there was already a major home-based broadcast medium – radio – which provided a model for its programme formats and its scheduling policies. In many ways, and despite the obvious differences between the two media, broadcast television is an extension of broadcast radio. They are historically part of the same process, the 'domesticizing' of leisure and entertainment (a process continued with home video, and cable and direct-broadcast satellite transmissions). The character of these two media does not result from any *inherent* qualities they may share – radio technology in particular has had marked non-broadcast applications in communications and military intelligence – but rather from their institutional contexts. And it is not just a question of TV and radio sets being established features of the home, for the institutionalized address of the broadcasting media appeals to, and assumes as a norm, a family-based conception of the home. The address of TV is 'intimate and everyday, a part of home life',[3] and its scheduling policies hinge upon an image of the average or ideal viewer who watches as part of a middle-class nuclear family (peak time or prime time is 'family time'), whether the broadcasting organization is commercial, like the independent television companies, or a 'public service' like the British Broadcasting Corporation.

Not only is there a marked institutional continuity between the broadcasting organizations controlling both radio and television broadcasting – the BBC, and the networks NBC, CBS, and ABC in America – but the television industry, on its relaunch in the postwar period, closely modelled its function, programme formats, and scheduling policies upon those developed by the radio industry. Broadcast radio, when it was establishing itself during the 1920s, was in itself immediately in competition with a wide range of entertainment and information industries: vaudeville and music hall, the phonograph industry, newspapers and magazines, the 'pulp' periodicals, and cinema. Radio had to establish itself alongside these other media – which had in turn to differentiate themselves from radio – and in so doing it drew upon them and translated them for its own programme formats.

In this chapter we examine one aspect of this process of transformation – how radio adapted existing forms of comedy – and suggest how the innovations of radio programming were in turn taken up and adapted by television. First we consider the ways in which radio adapted variety forms in both America and Britain, and then we concentrate upon the ideological form of the sit-com on both radio and television.

Radio comedy – variety forms

The United States

In the classic years of American radio, from the early 1930s to the mid–1950s, comedy programmes were, in terms of their ratings and levels of sponsorship, among the most successful on the air. This was a period when broadcast radio in the United States was dominated by two major organizations, the National Broadcasting Company (NBC), which was formed in 1926 (and actually operated two network services, NBC 'Red' and NBC 'Blue') and the Columbia Broadcasting System (CBS), formed in 1927. A third network, the American Broadcasting Company (ABC), was formed in 1943 when the Federal Commission (FCC) forced NBC to divest itself of one of its services. Before the domination of the networks, broadcast comedy had taken a rather impromptu form. According to Arthur Wertheim, whose detailed study, *American Radio Comedy*, will be referred to extensively here, 'in its early years radio was primarily a cultural and educational medium broadcasting music and information'.[4] Between 1920, when the first commercially licensed station opened in Pittsburgh, and the formation of NBC in 1926, the comedy output largely comprised badinage and jokes between orchestra members and announcers, amateur and 'small-time' professional comedians, or such song-and-patter duos as the Happiness Boys.[5] Once established, the networks drew advertising agencies and sponsors on a large scale, attracting them with the extensive 'consumer penetration' made possible by networked broadcasting (in comparison not only with local radio but also with such other advertising media as newspapers and magazines). Once the receiver was bought the listener could receive 'free' entertainment, and radio thus had a distinct advantage over its rivals for advertising revenues – a factor which proved important during the Depression, when other forms of entertainment were hit badly but radio boomed (in 1929 one in three homes possessed a receiver).[6]

The networks made commercial arrangements between the advertising agencies representing the sponsors and the individual radio stations, but many of the decisions of programme-making were actually in the hands of the agencies themselves.[7] Jane Feuer has suggested that the subsequent innovation of broadcast TV in America was determined to a large degree by the desire to emulate the success of radio as 'a model for selling the family to advertisers'.[8] Howard Fink argues that it is because the networks sought to deliver as large an audience as possible to the sponsors that they began specifically to adapt pre-existing forms of popular culture and to transmute them into distinctive radio genres, advancing from the restricted formats of radio's early years.[9] For example, radio in America adapted newspaper comic strips in the form of serial adventures; newspaper-style reporting and commentary; and from the various genres of 'pulp' fiction were formed the genres of popular radio drama (mystery, adventure, suspense, western stories, and so forth).[10] Besides these, there were also sound adaptations of films – in the highly-rated *Lux Radio Theatre* show, for example – and also, of course, adaptations of theatrical variety shows.

Wertheim reports that the small-scale, regional organization of radio in the early 1920s meant that sufficient funds were not available to attract high-ranking vaudeville talent. Furthermore, vaudeville agents and producers advised their performers against – or even barred them from – appearing on the rival medium.[11] With the formation of NBC and CBS, however, the increase in sponsorship led to the regular weekly scheduling of large-budgeted, hour-long variety programmes 'modelled on vaudeville's bill of fare'.[12] Such shows are *The Eveready Hour* (1926), *Roxy and His Gang* (1927), and *The Chase and Sanborn Hour* (1931) which featured an assortment of music, song, and comedy 'spots' from 'big-time' vaudeville and Broadway talent.[13] However, problems arose from this initial reliance of radio entertainment upon performers and writers from theatrical variety. For example, vaudeville, revue, and talking-picture star Eddie Cantor, who hosted *The Chase and Sanborn Hour* in its early years, used jokes and routines lifted directly from vaudeville almanacs and also continued to use funny costumes and slapstick on the air.[14] Such 'visual' material proved a success with studio audiences but did not transfer well to the listener at home, and this problem was also faced by other contemporary vaudevilleans transferring to the medium such as Ed Wynn and Milton Berle. Whereas the theatrical variety performance allows a direct rapport between performer and audience, with radio the audience is invisible. The early–1930s innovation of the studio audience was a partial solution to this problem, helping performers to improve the timing of their routines and also, of course, serving to 'cue in' the laughter of the home audience (a practice which continues in TV comedies today, with either studio audiences or the American system of 'canned laughter', again first used on radio). Another obstacle made manifest in the early 1930s – and one to be duplicated with television later – was the fact that regular radio appearances for a potential mass audience necessitated far more material than was needed in vaudeville, and comedians like Cantor, Wynn, Jack Pearl, and Joe Penner were forced increasingly to rely upon writers rather than to retread their tried and tested routines.

The networks and the sponsors were seeking precisely to attract listeners on a regular basis, and the straight variety format – unlike the already established forms of the sit-com series and the serial – lacked firm principles of continuity. Thus in the mid–1930s there is a discernible shift away from the vaudeville-styled show (although it was by no means totally displaced) towards formats better suited not just to the sound medium but especially to the institutional imperatives of commercial broadcast radio. This trend was exemplified by the shows of Jack Benny, an ex-vaudevillean who, unlike Cantor, Wynn, and Berle, consciously attempted to develop a style more suited to the 'intimate' nature of radio. Fellow radio-comedy star Fred Allen, with whom Benny had a long-running mock-feud later imitated by Bob Hope and Bing Crosby, commented that:

> Practically all comedy shows on radio owe their structure to Benny's conceptions. He was the first to realise that the listener is not in a theater with a thousand people, but is in a small circle at home. The Benny show is like a 'One Man's Family' in slapstick. When they tune in to Benny, it's like tuning in to somebody else's home.[15]

The nature of the comedy in itself indicated the shift from the theatrical variety model: 'Benny's shows de-emphasised timeworn vaudeville routine by reducing the number of puns, he-she jokes, and "feed-lines" by the stooge'.[16] In his first two NBC radio series, for Canada Dry in 1932 and Chevrolet in 1933, Benny was gradually moving towards the format which characterized his highly-rated

The Jell-o Program (from 1934) and later *The Jack Benny Show* (which lasted on the air until 1955, also transferring successfully to television).[17]

Three major features which contributed to the success of Benny's shows were adapted by many of the major shows to follow in the 1930s and 1940s. The first is pinpointed by Sid Colin, creator of *The Army Game* for British Independent Television in the late 1950s:

> What was fascinating about Benny's show in particular was its *architecture*. We had nothing like it. We had variety, music-hall; the American shows were *entities*. Characters were invented and exploited. . . . But the important thing was that they were built like plays, with *plots*. (Our italics)[18]

Benny's thirty-minute shows came to develop a continuity lacking in the sixty-minute variety programme. They represented, in other words, a move towards the structuring principles of *situation* comedy. The song numbers (by Kenny Baker and later Dennis Day) and the commercials tended to be integrated: for example, in the show broadcast on 9 April 1950, Day's song, 'Dearie', is diegetically motivated in the opening diner scene as a number on the jukebox.[19] The commercials did not function as straightforward interruptions but were frequently incorporated as running gags between Benny and announcer Don Wilson. Continuity existed within and across shows, and also across and between series. Running gags, catchphrases and set-piece routines were also regularly occurring features, creating a sense of familiarity over a twenty-year time span. The sketches themselves were constructed around situations with which the audience could identify, not necessarily because they were 'true to life' but because of the familiarity with the Benny show itself. Furthermore, as Mary Livingstone, Hilliard Marks, and Marcia Borie comment in the comedian's biography:

> Jack's shows were never built around one-line gags or fast quips. Each programme began with a funny premise and the dialogue was written to fit it, instead of being contrived

in order to arrive at a pre-ordained joke. On Benny's shows, the jokes were never an end in themselves – they just naturally evolved from the basic situations.[20]

The second influential feature of the Benny show is related to the first and concerns character creation. Benny and his writers evolved a persona for the comedian which allowed the development of running gags and routines – jokes about his vanity, lying about his age, his stinginess, his bad movies, his bad violin-playing. Benny set himself up as a 'lovable fall-guy',[21] as the butt rather than the wielder of gags, and the same set of character predicates was able to fuel Benny's performances into the 1970s.

Although Benny's show was clearly organized around the (fictionalized) persona of the comedian, it differed from the more straightforward variety shows centred around a performer in that Benny's status as a comedian was important to the *situational* context. Moreover – and this is the third important innovation – the show featured a 'gang' or 'family' of regular performers, each with their own idiosyncratic characterizations, who were bonded together in a work context – which is, precisely, the presentation of *The Jack Benny Show*, with announcer Don Wilson, orchestra leader Phil Harris, (real life) wife Mary Livingstone, and 'manservant' Eddie 'Rochester' Anderson. As Benny himself commented: 'The use of situations involves comic characters who grow in value as they become more and more familiar to the audience.'[22] Benny's 'gang' was a family of co-workers, and in its own discourse concerning its 'creation' Benny's show represents itself as a 'family affair'. Thus, although Benny's radio persona carried over certain aspects of the problematic of 'comedian comedy' – in that the central figure is out of sync with the decorum of the everyday – his individuality is never a threat to the 'gang', and neither is he ever threatened with exclusion from it. Rather, Benny's aberrant personality quirks are made light of, subject to continual good-humoured putdowns which reiterate his status as part of the 'family' at the expense of his individualistic pretensions. No matter how Benny may try to assert his difference, he is always returned to the stability of the 'family' group.

The innovations we have described above were soon adopted as standard within American comedy shows which were similarly structured around comedians. *Town Hall Tonight* (1935), Fred Allen's successful show of the period, differed from Benny's in that he did not use regular characters, but continuity was instead provided by segments or 'spots' which recurred from show to show. Wertheim points out that *Town Hall Tonight* was a comedy 'magazine' programme, with the regularity of the format and Allen's comparatively abrasive satirical persona allowing space for a variety of situations. Writer-performer Allen remarked of his approach:

> Since the radio comedian really had to depend on the ears of the home audience for his purpose, I thought that a complete story told each week or a series of episodes and comedy situations might be a welcome change. . . . Hoping for longevity in the new medium, I planned a series of programmes using a different business background each week – a newspaper office, a department store, a bank, a detective agency etc. The comedy would involve the characters employed in, or indigenous to, the assorted locales.[23]

One significant aspect of this show was its parody of the conventions of radio reportage – the opening 'spot' on the show comprising 'news bulletins' about the citizens of the imaginary small town which provided the setting. Another regular item was a 'spot' entitled 'People You Didn't Expect To Meet', which consisted of interviews with people in real-life bizarre jobs.[24]

The Benny and Allen shows – like the sit-com format we shall consider below – represented the development of comedy formats which were more suited to commercial radio. The networks and the sponsors were seeking to draw listeners on a regular basis and the structures of these shows, with their firm principles of continuity, aided this purpose. Tuning in to a certain show on a certain network at a certain time of the week (both shows were in peak family listening slots) became a habitual way to use broadcast radio. The Benny and Allen shows, and those which adapted their structuring innovations, were part of a general *standardization* of radio as a commercial medium of entertainment. It was not just a question of the success of individual formats or shows or personalities, for regularity of scheduling exerted pressure towards the standardization of radio's output and listener habits: when a comedy series ended, for example, it would be replaced by another comedy show. Certain times of the week became associated with certain types of programme: Benny's show, for example, was on a Sunday evening slot for twenty-one years.

The large-scale shift of the radio industry to Hollywood in the latter half of the 1930s[25] elevated the status of radio entertainment, and established the practice, for example, of guest appearances by Hollywood stars. But Wertheim sees it as representing the end of radio comedy's period of innovation. The comedy shows broadcast from Hollywood were slick and professional, and resolutely standardized – 'a thoroughly commercial product packaged by advertising agencies for their client sponsor'.[26] This is suggested particularly by the longevity of the top radio comedians of the 1930s and the fact that a star like Benny could rely upon the same basic situations and running gags for so long. Wertheim sees this trend towards the slick, 'pre-packaged' shows as exemplified by Bob Hope's Pepsodent-sponsored programme (on NBC from 1938). As became the norm for post-Benny radio variety comedy, Hope's shows were written by a team of writers. The script was extensively pre-tested and then edited down for 'laugh-efficiency' so that by the time of the broadcast little could go wrong;[27] such shows became even more efficient after the widespread introduction of prerecording in the late 1940s.[28] Hope's show followed the Benny format in that it comprised three conventional sections punctuated by a song and commercials – an opening rapid-fire monologue by the comedian; a middle section featuring repartee between Hope, his regular cast, and guest stars; and a closing sketch.[29]

Even the long-running *Amos'n Andy* shows changed in 1943 from a fifteen-minute daily serial to a weekly thirty-minute show with a single comic situation, guest stars, and musical items.[30] Fred Allen's show of the 1940s, *Allen's Alley* (from 1942) was also thirty minutes long, and like Benny's show 'featured a permanent cast of character actors and actresses playing the same role every week'.[31] One of the major reasons for such conservatism is that, as was the case with network television later, the regular scheduling of a programme depended upon its achieving consistent ratings, which meant that new shows had immediately to compete with such top-rankers as Benny. There was thus strong pressure to adopt a tried and tested format. Another indication of this is the strategy of the 'spin-off', which is still familiar on television. This policy of generating a new programme from elements of an existing success (thus minimizing the time it takes for a new show to establish itself) derives from the American comedy shows of the 1940s: the sit-com *Fibber McGee and Molly* engendered *The Great Gildersleeve* and *Beulah*, and in 1946 the Benny show gave rise to two sit-com spin-offs featuring members of his 'gang' – *The Phil Harris-Alice Faye Show* and *A Day in the Life of Dennis Day*.[32] Indeed, another form of spin-off dominated the early years of American TV comedy, with a large number of popular radio shows transferring to the new medium – not just programmes featuring such stars as Benny, Hope, and George Burns and Gracie Allen, but particularly a high proportion of sit-coms.

Britain

The formation of the British Broadcasting Company from a consortium of radio-receiver manufacturers brought continuous, regular broadcasting to Britain in 1922; the company became, in 1926, a public corporation funded by the sale of licences.[33] In the United States commercial broadcast radio was subject to relatively little federal control, but the BBC was and still is much more accountable, with the principle of public service being institutionally enshrined in its charter.[34] As in America, radio faced initial hostility from various sources, in particular the newspaper industry and the variety profession. Although the BBC broadcast its first variety performance in 1923, agents, theatre managers, and performers resisted full-scale variety programming until well into the 1930s. Furthermore, there was for some time no adequate machinery within the corporation for the production of variety shows. It was only in 1930 that a separate revue and vaudeville section of the production department was created and initiated the first variety shows to be organized on a regular basis – such series as *Songs from the Shows* (1931) and the long-running *Music Hall* (1932).[35]

The BBC programmers were particularly inflexible about broadcasting entertainment, demonstrating a marked resistance to emulating the American commercial models. John Reith, the BBC's first Director-General, was exemplary in this respect, adhering to an ideology of 'quality' broadcasting which stressed its educational and informative role at the expense of entertainment. Even so, whereas the American networks sought to 'deliver' the family audience to advertising interests, the BBC had a similar commitment to middle-class family listeners: as Paul Alan Taylor has commented, the BBC's attitude towards entertainment was 'governed by the fact that broadcasting is part of the *domestic* life of the nation'.[36] Standards of 'taste' on BBC radio were more rigid and paternalistic than those operating in the music halls, although the latter also sought a middle-class family audience, and the corporation furthermore allocated very small budgets for variety programmes throughout the 1930s.[37] During this period radio entertainment still tended to be equated with song and music, and variety programmes were among the last to be scheduled on a regular basis.[38]

However, while the BBC was strongly biased in favour of light band music, there was direct competition from the early 1930s from two American-style commercial stations broadcasting to Britain from Europe, Radio Luxembourg and Radio Normandie. These stations broadcast dance music, record programmes, and variety shows featuring such well-known artists as Gracie Fields and George Formby.[39] According to Roger Wilmut, it was not until 1937 that this competition had some effect, and the BBC began to experiment with forms of entertainment more suited to the conditions of radio broadcasting than the studio variety shows and theatre broadcast.[40] In that year the first sit-com appeared on British radio, a series of fifteen-minute programmes entitled *Mr Muddlecombe, JP*, featuring Robb Wilton and based on his music-hall sketches.[41] There was also a magazine show on the air in that year – *Monday Night at Seven*. But most commentators agree that it was *Band Waggon*, first broadcast in January 1938, which proved to be of greater influence: 'For the first time, a Variety programme was placed on a regular day, at a more-or-less regular time, and with a regular comedian, Arthur Askey.'[42]

The magazine-style *Band Waggon* was a conscious attempt to emulate American-style comedy formats, a number of which could be heard in Britain via Radio Luxembourg.[43] The show differed from the variety models in that it was structured around the regular team of Askey and Richard Murdoch and represented a move towards a comedy of character and situation – with Askey and Murdoch supposedly living on the roof of Broadcasting House. As Barry Took has stressed, in this hour-long show the sketches featuring the two comedians occupied only ten minutes, with the rest being a standard mixture of variety and song 'spots'.[44] However, its regular scheduling allowed the development of running gags, catchphrases and comic business, and was also the first BBC variety show to use a regular writing team (Askey, Murdoch, and Vernon Harris).[45]

The popular success of *Band Waggon*, and the departure of Reith from the BBC in June 1938, made it possible for the corporation to attempt further comedy series/shows. As Asa Briggs has remarked of *Band Waggon*'s successor, the thirty-minute *ITMA* (*It's That Man Again*), 'the idea behind it was not only to capture the large audience of *Band Waggon* but for the first time deliberately to produce British programmes with American-style quick-fire patter'.[46] The show's star, Tommy Handley – an experienced radio and stage comedian – had a very 'American' 'rapid-fire speed in delivering a string of wisecracks',[47] and the initial format mooted for the show (later to be rejected) was a British transposition of the Burns-Allen format.[48] *ITMA* was comparable to the American shows in its multiple-character, ensemble format and in the use of running gags, recurring character 'turns', and catchphrases.[49] *ITMA*'s success was helped by the wartime restrictions on alternative forms of entertainment, and it also drew upon such topics as the intensified wartime and postwar state bureaucracy, with Handley playing at one point the Minister of Aggravation and Mysteries. There was a gradual progression in the long run of the show (1939–48) from what the scriptwriter Ted Kavanaugh referred to as a series of 'rather vague and disconnected adventures' towards a slicker format with an emphasis upon 'continuity of action by the same characters'.[50] Thus, although the plots were farfetched, they had a firm dramatic structuring, and in the show's bizarre characters and 'quickfire succession of short scenes and verbal non-sequiturs'[51] *ITMA* maintained a 'surreal' edge (like another contemporary programme, *Danger – Men at Work*). *ITMA* was not only an attempt, then, to move further from the prewar tradition of variety shows, but it can also be sharply distinguished from the domestic sit-coms which would come to dominate radio and television in later years. Whereas the latter appeal to conceptions of the familial and middle-class 'everyday', Kavanaugh has said that with *ITMA* he attempted 'to use sound for all it was worth, the sound of different voices and accents, the use of catchphrases, the impact of funny sounds in words, of grotesque effects to give atmosphere – every device to create the illusion of *rather crazy or inverted reality*' (our italics).[52]

In the wake of *ITMA*'s initial success, the BBC programmed other regular comedy series, ranging from such programmes as *Garrison Theatre* and *Happidrome*, which were basically old-style variety shows featuring regular comedians and sketches, to *Hi, Gang!*, which featured the American stars Bebe Daniels and Ben Lyon and were based upon the Benny-type model, featuring 'fast patter, comic sketches, "wisecracks", and lots of music and songs performed by the regulars and guests'.[53] Paul Alan Taylor notes a general shift in the war years away from the variety models and towards situation comedy: in Robb Wilton's show, for example,

> from 1939 on, the comic sketches of Mr Muddlecombe were becoming comic plots. It was not joke-telling but character comedy some distance removed from the punning style of *ITMA* or the extravagant surrealism of *Danger – Men at Work*.[54]

In 1942, the BBC began to broadcast recorded shows by Benny, Allen, Hope, and others, and in the same year John Watt, then Director of Variety, sent his assistant Pat Hillyard to America to acquire American comedy writers and stars.[55] Furthermore, the establishment of the 'Forces Programme' in 1941 (transmuted in the postwar period into the 'Light Programme') rebroadcast both British and American comedy shows and has been seen by Roger Wilmut as accelerating the regularity of radio scheduling.[56]

Just as the BBC standardized its scheduling and its programme formats much later than the American networks, so too the innovative period of British radio was 'delayed'. Between 1944 and 1955, before TV began to supplant radio as the dominant medium of home entertainment, there was a continuing search for new formats and the development of those already existing.[57] The war years produced a large number of writers and performers who had not previously worked in music halls and other variety contexts but who gained experience in troop entertainments, with some working on such radio shows as *Laughter Command*, *Navy Mixture*, and *Stand Easy*, which were produced for and by the armed services. One of the postwar products of this 'new generation' was the long-running *Take It From Here* (1947–58), a comedy sketch-show featuring a regular cast (Dick Bentley, Joy Nichols, and Jimmy Edwards, all transferring from *Navy Mixture*) and written by Frank Muir and Denis Norden, who were signed to Ted Kavanaugh's writing agency. From 1953 the show included a regular series of sketches featuring a gross 'working-class' family, 'The Glums', which Denis Norden has described as an attempt to satirize the 'cosy family serials and soap operas'[58] which prevailed in the period.

More characteristic of dominant trends in British radio comedy was *Ray's a Laugh* which starred wisecrack comedian Ted Ray and started out as an American-style three-'spot' show with songs and music. However, from 1952 the domestic sketches which had been a regular feature became the basis for the entire show, with Ray playing an 'average' family-man (rather than a performer).[59] Other domestic sit-coms of the period included *Meet the Huggetts*, *Life With the Lyons* (a development from *Hi, Gang!*), and *The Clitheroe Kid*, all of which transferred to television, as did the non-domestic sit-com *Hancock's Half-Hour*.

An alternative to this 'naturalistic' domestic comedy was represented by *The Goon Show* (1951–60), which starred Spike Milligan, Peter Sellers, Harry Secombe, and initially Michael Bentine, all of whom were ex-'Naafi' entertainers. The show extended the 'crazy', 'surreal' comedy which had marked both *ITMA* and certain music-hall artists like Bud Flanagan[60] and Billy Bennett (who specialized in 'madcap word associations and inverted logical reasoning').[61] The Goons exploited the capacity of radio for a non-naturalistic comedy of exaggerated voice impressions and sound effects, to create a sense of dislocated reality. The show precisely flaunted the nature of radio as a sound medium (Wilmut describes the style as 'radio comedy as pure radio')[62] representing a departure both from the sit-com and from the slick American personality shows with their cosy and predictable formats. The storylines, punctuated by musical items, tended to be fragmentary and overtly illogical, with a tendency towards situations and 'impossible' gags which resisted 'visualization'.

As a significant mass-entertainment variety medium, radio survived longer in Britain than in America. However, by the late 1950s television had become firmly established as the major broadcast medium and was able to attract writers and performers from radio and also to adapt the formats of radio shows. Barry Took sees *The Clitheroe Kid* (1958) as the last of the major domestic sit-coms on British radio, and he notes that one reason for this was the comparative cheapness of such alternative, non-scripted formats as panel shows and quiz games.[63] Another reason, of course, is that by this time the sit-com had already become one of the staple forms of television entertainment, so much so that it is often mistaken as a format developed by TV.[64] In the 1960s, indeed, it was common policy for the BBC to adapt successful TV shows to the radio, which suggests how much the comedy on the two media have in common. Such 1960s TV-radio adaptations as *Steptoe and Son* and *Dad's Army* reversed the radio-TV trend of the 1950s.

Because radio in Britain continued as a much more diversified medium than in America the BBC was able to develop forms of radio comedy distinct from those on television. *Beyond Our Ken* (1958) and *Round the Horne* (1964), for example, were revue-type sketch-shows featuring Kenneth Horne, a radio veteran of the wartime RAF show *Laughter Command* and its postwar successor *Much Binding in the Marsh*. Horne functioned, like Benny, Allen, and Handley before him, as a 'stooge' rather than a joke-wielder, frequently switching roles between announcer and in-sketch performer. The show's other regular characters were oddballs and it continued the *ITMA/ Goons* tradition of zaniness and exaggerated sound effects.

As discussed in the previous chapter, the next wave of comic performers in British broadcasting included Peter Cook, Dudley Moore, John Cleese, Graham Chapman, and Bill Oddie, all of whom moved from varsity revues to theatre, radio, film, and television work in the 1960s and 1970s. The most notable radio show featuring such comedians was *I'm Sorry I'll Read That Again*, described by Barry Took as 'a young person's *Round the Horne*, a kaleidoscope of funny voices, catchphrases and innuendo revolving at breakneck speed and with a complete disregard for logic'.[65]

Although radio comedy in Britain tends to be overshadowed by television, at least it still exists. The BBC's cultural monopoly over national radio has maintained diversified programming into the late 1980s (while still, on Radio 1, accommodating the comparatively low-cost DJ format to which US radio shifted almost exclusively in the 1960s and which characterizes the bulk of British commercial radio). Although the proportion of comedy shows on British radio today is not, of course, comparable with the heyday of the 1940s and 1950s, Radio 2, Radio 4, and the BBC World Service, still manage to broadcast diverse comedy programmes. In a typical week in 1988 one is able to tune in to panel shows featuring such established wits and performers as Frank Muir, Denis Norden, and the late Kenneth Williams (*My Word*; *Just a Minute*; *Quote, Unquote*); such topical comedy shows as *Saturday Night Fry* (featuring Stephen Fry and Hugh Laurie), *Radio-Active*, *Loose Ends*, and *Two Cheers For . . .* (the radio equivalent of *Spitting Image*); and such sit-coms as *King St. Junior* and *Flying the Flag*. Occasionally, radio shows like *The Hitch-Hiker's Guide to the Galaxy* or *After Henry* will make a significant impact and transfer to TV.

Broadcast situation comedy

The radio sit-com

We have considered above the ways in which broadcast radio adopted and transformed existing modes of variety comedy, moving from the modular 'programming' structures of vaudeville and music hall towards formats with firmer principles of continuity. As we suggested, the rationale for such developments was the desire of the broadcasting industry, both in the USA and Britain, to draw a mass, regular audience and to institutionalize habitual listening (both for the individual show and for radio in general). The other major form of radio comedy was the situation comedy which, because of its narrative basis and its series form, had quite firmly inscribed principles of continuity, as we shall consider below. We examine here how the sit-com – which in its familiar television form was largely 'inherited' from broadcast radio – functions as an 'ideological form', how it operates as a *stabilizing structure* which is particularly suited to the imperatives of the broadcast media.

Like many other characteristic broadcast forms, the sit-com was not born with radio but was instead adapted from pre-existing entertainment forms, not only from the vaudeville and music-hall sketches which are sometimes cited as predominant influences,[66] but also from other forms of repeatable narrative. For example, Jack Gladden has traced the roots of the domestic sit-com back to the sketches of domestic life printed in the American mass-circulation newspapers of the 1870s and 1890s.[67] Such sketches, he notes,

> appeared regularly (weekly) in a medium that was available to people of moderate means (the newspaper). The sketches were brief (governed by how much space they could be given in the columns of the paper) and each sketch was complete in itself. Each sketch centred around the same characters (a husband and a wife) and each involved a great deal of conflict and action. The plots were simple and the action usually took place in the home.[68]

It is not difficult to see here the prototype of such TV domestic sit-coms as *I Love Lucy*, *Terry and June*, and *No Place Like Home*. As with their TV and radio successors, these early forms sought to address and structure a conception of the 'everyday reality' of the targeted middle-

class family audience: 'the plots centred around situations
with which the average reader was familiar: houseclean-
ing, catching a train, illness, whitewashing the cellar or
fence, moving furniture, reducing the gas bill, quitting
smoking and dozens of purely domestic situations'.[69]

Gladden sees a direct line of progression in the development of the domestic sit-com from these sketches, through
the newspaper comic strips which largely replaced them
from the late 1890s (the most popular, such as 'The
Nebbs', 'Blondie', and 'Bringing Up Father', dealing with
domestic situations in a humorous way),[70] and thence to
radio and television.[71] Without having space to engage too
deeply with this history, we should note other precursors
of the domestic sit-com before we move on to broadcast
radio forms. For example, although they were largely displaced from newspapers, humorous sketches with a domestic setting continued to feature in such up-market periodicals as the *New Yorker* (James Thurber's 'Mr and Mrs
Monroe' series in 1928–9, for example). And, as we have
already noted, the comedy shorts produced by Hollywood
were often produced in a series format and moved increasingly towards situational comedy in the 1920s and 1930s.
Edgar Kennedy appeared in a long-running series of shorts
– 103 made by RKO between 1931 and 1948 – which
were initially billed as the *Average Man* series, with Kennedy regularly appearing as a middle-class husband
embroiled in scenarios of domestic frustration, seeking
and failing to assert himself as head of the household.[72]
Subjects of shorts featuring such stars as Leon Errol, Andy
Clyde, Charlie Chase, and Laurel and Hardy also frequently tended towards the increasingly standardized territory of domestic situations and marital frustration. Hollywood further aided the entrenchment of domestic situation
comedy in a series of B films based on the 'Blondie' comic
strip (which was later the basis for two TV sit-coms).

Not all sit-coms, however, are based around the home
and the bourgeois family. For example, the first widely
successful radio narrative comedy, written and performed
by Freeman Gosden and Charles Correll, centred around

two unmarried southern blacks who have moved to a northern city. Gosden and Correll developed the format which became *Sam and Henry* (1926) and later *Amos 'n'Andy* (1928) when they were asked to do a programme along the lines of a comic strip.[73] Both shows were broadcast in brief (ten- or fifteen-minute) episodes, five or six times a week, and the team moved quite quickly from a vaudeville/minstrel show double-act of loosely related gags towards a structured and cross-generic format. Arthur Wertheim describes these shows as 'slow moving, melodramatic and sentimental'.[74] Indeed, formally the shows deviated from the sit-com model to be dominant in later years in that they represented a hybrid between the episodic series and the serial, featuring 'continuous story lines centred upon regular characters',[75] with the storylines frequently running for two or three weeks.

Howard Fink ascribes the phenomenal success of *Amos 'n'Andy* in the early 1930s to the development of 'consistent characters, a persistent scene, and situations developed not for comedy alone, but along the lines of dramatic progression and conclusion'[76] – a description which could apply equally well to a contemporary soap opera like *Eastenders*. The regular, saturated broadcast of the shows, together with the continuing storylines, enabled a hitherto unknown 'rapport' between the listeners and the fictional characters and situations to develop. Furthermore, Gosden and Correll (who did all the vocal characterizations until the 1940s) achieved a particular feeling of 'intimacy' by broadcasting without a studio audience, the two men sitting alone together around a microphone.[77] This unpressured mode of performance contributed to the 'natural', 'homey' feel of the comedy and of the characters themselves, and the combination of comedy and sentiment produced a reassuringly cosy representation of both the effects of the Depression and the lives of urban blacks.[78]

More characteristic of the sit-coms produced during the 'classic' years of broadcast radio were those shows discussed by Wertheim which featured self-contained plots and a setting which was closer to the interests and aspir-

ations of the middle-class family. For example, *Easy Aces*
(1931–49) – broadcast at the height of its popularity in
thrice-weekly fifteen-minute episodes – was a prototype
of such husband-wife TV sit-coms as *I Love Lucy* and
Betwitched, and was the antithesis of *Amos'n'Andy* in that
the Aces 'were a prosperous white couple who lived in an
upper-class neighborhood in Manhattan'.[79] The writer-
performer Goodman Ace attempted a 'naturalistic' and
low-key form of comedy which eschewed the minstrel
show routines which were the roots of *Amos'n'Andy*; he
'did not aim for belly laughs, but for consistent character
humor'.[80] The dialogue was conversational, and the setting
was largely restricted to the Aces' home, with much of the
action centred around the 'scatterbrained' wife Jane Ace.
The George Burns-Gracie Allen Show of the 1940s was
another example of upper-middle-class sit-com. Burns and
Allen teamed up as a vaudeville act in 1923 and the
characters they developed – Gracie Allen as the archetypal
scatterbrained woman, George as a wry straight man –
were later transferred to film, radio, and television. Their
initial radio appearances were on such early–1930s variety
shows as *The Chase and Sanborn Hour*, and with their
own starring show they adopted the format pioneered by
Jack Benny, until a drop in its ratings led them to shift to
domestic sit-com.[81] However, both this radio show and its
successor on television were unusual examples of a sit-
com which incorporated vaudeville routines and took liberties with the 'naturalistic' mode of domestic sit-com
(especially in George's direct address to the camera).[82]

Fibber McGee and Molly (1935) and *Vic and Sade*
(1932) were sit-coms with a rural/small-town setting.
Whereas the former created much of its comedy from
eccentric small-town 'characters' and exaggerated incidents – foreshadowing later TV shows like *The Beverley
Hillbillies* and *Petticoat Junction* – the latter was more
firmly centred upon the family unit and followed the
approach of *Easy Aces* in aiming to create a sense of
'everyday family life': incidents were underplayed and created 'from the inconsequentialities of daily living and the

banalities of small-town life'.[83] Vic and Sade, the Cook family, were tagged as 'radio's home folks' and the fifteen-minute daily broadcasts took the form of conversations between the family members (with the couple later adopting an 11-year-old child to broaden its family appeal). Whereas initially the format of the show resembled that of the radio soap opera, it changed in the 1940s (when, as we have noted, radio programmes became increasingly standardized) to a weekly thirty-minute show with a live audience, and an increased number of characters and settings.[84]

Television began to supplant radio as the major home-based medium between 1948 and 1952 in America and after 1955 in Britain. In the postwar years there was intensified competition between the three American radio networks, indicated in particular by 'talent raids' during which, for example, ABC secured Bing Crosby, Abbott and Costello, and Groucho Marx, and CBS lured Gosden and Correll, Jack Benny, Burns and Allen, Red Skelton, and Edgar Bergen from NBC.[85] Such competition was not motivated solely by the desire to achieve an eminent position in the field of radio entertainment but also to secure top-rated talent for these networks' television services. During this period, network executives began to plough profits from radio into their TV departments, and the new medium proved highly popular with the sponsors (for example, up to 1950 there was actually a shortage of available sponsor-time on American network TV).[86] The radio-comedy stars were particularly in demand because of their long-term familiarity to audiences – the same audience sought for television – and after some resistance these stars began to appear on TV once its future was no longer in doubt. Television began increasingly to take over the function of radio as a medium of broadcast entertainment, and radio itself gradually began to be differentiated through the 1950s, spurred on not only by the dominance of TV but also by a shift in radio listening away from the home. The widespread innovation of car and portable radios resulted in a new conception of radio as entertain-

ment, and the format of the 'personality' disc jockey programme began to displace many of the characteristic radio
forms of the 1930s and 1940s (with even Gosden and
Correll switching to the DJ format in the 1950s).[87] The
number of radio comedy programmes declined substan-
tially – in January 1956, for example, the only major
programme on the air was *The Charlie McCarthy Show*.[88]

In its early years, TV bought in experienced radio
comedy stars and their formats, and introduced such new-
comers to broadcasting as Sid Caesar and Imogene Coca
(whose high-rated Saturday-night variety programme,
Your Show of Shows, included Neil Simon, Mel Brooks,
and Woody Allen among its writers). It also attracted
such ex-vaudevillians as Milton Berle and Ed Wynn whose
slapstick style had not transferred well to the sound
medium. However, the radio sit-com had a more significant and lasting impact on the forms of TV comedy.
Numerous sit-coms transferred from radio to TV, including *The Life of Riley*, *The Goldbergs*, and *Easy Aces* in
1949, *Beulah* in 1950, *Amos'n'Andy* in 1951, *The Adventures of Ozzie and Harriet* in 1952, *Father Knows Best* in
1954, *The Great Gildersleeve* in 1955, and *Fibber McGee
and Molly* in 1959. *I Love Lucy* (1951) was also partially
derived from Lucille Ball's radio sit-com *My Favorite Husband* (which also made a direct transition in 1953).[89] More
important, however, than the transfer of individual shows
was the incorporation of the sit-com as a major television
format, and one which inscribed a domestic conception of
the TV audience. Once established as the dominant form
of narrative television comedy, the sit-com soon developed
an independence from radio, and a high proportion of TV
sit-coms were based on successful feature films (a trend
which continued in later years with such shows as *The
Odd Couple* and *M*A*S*H*).

The sit-com was not the only format to make the transfer from radio to TV: others included the soap opera
serial, the drama series, panel shows, quiz games, and the
'personality'-hosted variety show. In the next section of
this chapter we pay particular attention to the functioning

of the sit-com as a form of TV series-narrative comedy, stressing how it is a format which is particularly suited to the general ideological aims of television as a medium of home-based entertainment.

The sit-com on television

The term 'sit-com' describes a short narrative-series comedy, generally between twenty-four and thirty minutes long, with regular characters and setting. The episodic series – of which the sit-com is a subset – is, with the continuing serial, a mode of repeatable narrative which is particularly suited to the institutional imperative of the broadcast media to draw and maintain a regular audience. In order to examine the ideological 'machinery' of the sit-com, we shall compare briefly the differential operations of the series and the serial, paying attention to their respective modalities of narrative transformation.

The continuing serial was, as we have noted, one of the earliest regularly programmed narrative formats on broadcast radio, associated from early on with the domestic dramas known as 'soap opera' and deriving formally from the serial modes of periodical fiction, comic strips, and such early film serials as *Fantomas* (1913) and *The Perils of Pauline* (1914). Temporal development is integral to the serial, of course, although in earlier forms there tended to be an end point to the narrative which the film serials, for example, both pushed towards and delayed. Whereas in the early years of radio there was some overlap between the modes of the serial and the series – *Amos 'n'Andy* being the prime example – the two soon became quite distinct and the soap opera as we know it today was differentiated. The form is characterized by multiple storylines, multiple characters, a regular community and/or family setting, and a quite crucial sense of events 'unfolding' without there being a definitive end to the narrative (in fact, through the sheer accumulation of detail and a sense of dynamic 'history' such an ending tends to be impossible).

As Jane Feuer has stressed, although it is quite common

to see the soap opera serial as a developmental mode in which 'both situations and characters grow organically',[90] narrative development tends in fact to be highly trammelled. Although a single episode may contain various storylines and situations, it is precisely part of the psychological-emotional 'realism' of the soap opera that characters repeatedly move through the same scenarios and keep making the same mistakes.[91] Not only does this insinuate an ideology of individual identity as powerlessness (for the characters' options are deterministically constrained), but it serves to create a significant predictability for the viewer as to the actions, choices, and future of the characters. Thus, to take a recent and controversial example, when Kath Beale (Gillian Taylforth) is raped by Wilmott-Brown (William Boyde) in the episode of *Eastenders* broadcast on 7 July 1988, this plot development is motivated by the fact that Kath was raped as a teenager – even though Wilmott-Brown acts 'against character' in forcing himself upon her. As Kath says in a later episode, 'There's something about me that asks for it. It's obvious – twice is not a coincidence'. It certainly is not! Being a generically hybrid mode, the soap opera has to hold in place often conflicting regimes of generic motivation, and the notion of 'character as destiny' can function as a safety-valve to conceal the extent to which events are determined by plot exigencies.

In the series mode there is a significantly different sense of time, history, and continuity, although like the soap opera the sit-com hinges around repetition and a forestalling of closure in terms of the series as a whole. Individual episodes have a 'classical' narrative structuring in that the narrative process is inaugurated by some disruption of or threat to a stable situation, necessitating the movement towards the reassertion of stability. However, whereas in the feature film narrative closure is marked by establishing an equilibrium which differs from that disrupted at the start, in the sit-com the end of the episode represents a *return* to the initial situation. What the sit-com pivots around is a 'refamiliarizing' of the recurring situation, protecting it and redefining it in the face of various disruptions and transgressions. In other words, the sit-com relies upon a different form of repetition from the soap opera serial – the situation is not allowed to *change* but is rather subjected to a recurring process of destabilization-restabilization in each episode. The sit-com's process of narrative transformation relies much more emphatically, then, upon circularity. Whereas soap operas painstakingly maintain a sense of ongoing temporal development, the sit-com encourages the viewer to 'forget' many of the events of preceding episodes. Not that the individual episodes are totally discrete, however: for example, Philip Drummond has considered the importance to the series mode in general of what he terms 'synchronizing motifs', that is, regularly occurring bits of business, repeated situations, and catchphrases (for example, Harold Steptoe's complaint that his father is a 'dirty old man'), and also 'the elaboration of a (more or less) continuous internal "mythology" and hermeneutic for the series as a whole'.[92]

In other words, the sit-com relies upon a trammelled play between continuity and 'forgetting', the key to which, as Mick Eaton has suggested, is maintaining the basic parameters of the situation:

> the demands of constant repetition in/of the series, needs to be one whose parameters are easily recognisable and which are returned to week after week. Nothing that has happened in the narrative of the previous week must destroy or complicate the way in which the situation is grounded.[93]

However, it is not uncommon for sit-coms to permit some modification of the basic situation – indeed, this may be necessary in the case of long-running programmes, to forestall stasis or broaden the generative nucleus of the situation. The domestic sit-coms *I Love Lucy* and *Bewitched* (1964) both start out as husband-wife shows but over several series the situation is expanded: they have children, the children grow up and go to school, and so on. Additional characters may thus be incorporated to stave off overfamiliarity.

A 1988 BBC1 *Network* examination of the sit-com included a comment by Jeremy Isaacs, former chief executive of Channel 4, that 'It is a form in which it is impossible to bring in new work. It is the most conventional form in British television.' However, some degree of differentiation is necessary for the long-term success of any sit-com: indeed the sit-com cannot totally escape the 'obligation' which marks television in general to address and incorporate changing cultural standards and a sense of its own 'development' as a medium. The charges of conservatism, excessive stereotyping of racial, class, sexual, and regional differences, and so on, which are often levelled at the sit-com seem to pinpoint not so much the total imperviousness of the form but rather the particular way in which it operates as a *site of negotiation* of cultural change and difference. As such, the sit-com cannot simply repeat itself but rather its structuring mechanisms serve as a means of reaffirming norms by *placing* that which is 'outside' or potentially threatening.

The term 'sit-com' tends not merely to describe the formal properties of the half-hour narrative TV comedy, but it also carries perjorative connotations. It tends to be associated with its most pervasive and obviously conventionalized type, the domestic or family sit-com. Thus, in their book, *Bring Me Laughter*, Bruce Crowther and Mike Pinfold write of *M*A*S*H*, a 'quality' sit-com with the serious setting of a Korean war hospital, that 'To describe [it] as a situation comedy is more than a mite inaccurate'.[94] Similarly, writer-producer James L. Brooks has remarked of *The Mary Tyler Moore Show* (1970): 'When somebody called *Mary* a sitcom, we'd be furious. We weren't doing sitcom. We were doing character comedy.'[95]

With the domestic sit-com entrenched so early in television history, and particularly suited, as we have suggested, to the priorities of the institution, one of the ways to produce a 'quality', differentiated show is to appeal to a sense of 'character realism' at the expense of the 'triviality' and formulaic nature of the domestic sit-com. Thus, for example, some episodes of *M*A*S*H* are intentially non-comic, and *The Mary Tyler Moore Show* and many of the quality sit-coms which followed it in the 1970s are not only set outside the conventional family household but are also marked by a mixture of comedy and 'liberal' sentiment (a combination referred to in the trade as 'warmedy').[96]

In the domestic sit-com itself the situation comprises what Mick Eaton refers to as an 'inside'[97] which is a highly recognizable conception of the middle-class nuclear-family unit. The disruptions which provide the motor for the individual plots come either from conflicts within the family – which tend to be trivialized and disavowed of serious repercussions – or from intrusions from the 'outside' which can easily be rejected. A few random examples will suggest the nature of such disruptions and how they are handled. In a 1988 episode of the BBC series *No Place Like Home*, the stability of the upper-middle-class family is threatened when the wife, Beryl Crabtree (Patricia Garwood), expresses the desire to go out to work. Furthermore, she applies for a job in the company for which her husband Arthur (William Gaunt) works. This represents a threat to the family order as it complicates the separation between home and work which such programmes generally maintain, and also (in a series which rigidly centres the husband as central protagonist) represents a threat to the domestic sexual hierarchy and division of labour. However, the episode resolutely sidesteps these areas of complication – which would nudge the show into the realm of domestic drama – by throwing up a plot twist: Beryl does not get the job because the manager employs his mistress instead. Both Arthur and Beryl are angry that she has been overlooked – that is, the problems which initially threatened to divide them have now been replaced by a conflict between them and the 'outside'. After several plot developments, the unfair appointment is exposed (by the neighbour Trevor, so Arthur is not forced into any problematic conflict with the company), and the episode

ends with an irritable Arthur impatiently hurrying Beryl
so they can both get to work on time. This would seem to
usher in a significantly altered situation, but in subsequent
episodes there is no mention of Beryl working at all, and
she is once more located firmly within the home. In other
words, certain developments are allowed to be carried
across episodes, while others are not.

In an episode of *Bless This House* entitled 'Get Me to
the Match on Time' (1972), the threat to family unity
comes from a choice which Sid Abbott (Sid James) faces
between attending the Cup Final (where with his neighbour Trevor he can indulge in a raucous masculine display
of team loyalty) or attending the wedding of his sister-in-
law (a plot very similar to that of Laurel and Hardy's *Sons
of the Desert* (1933)). His wife Jean (Diana Coupland)
tells him that he has to go to the wedding because 'You
are part of a family. . . . And one of us is getting married'.
But Sid schemes to escape, first pretending to have 'flu and
later that he has fallen downstairs. However, Jean returns
from the wedding sooner than expected, to find Sid dressed
in his football gear, and she drags him off to the reception.
Sid's behaviour testifies to a preference for an 'outside'
activity characterized by male bonding rather than the
'female' occasion, the wedding, where Sid is to be seen as
part of the family, has to dress in fancy clothes, and so
on. The final victory of the wife results in the family
occasion taking precedence; in the consolidation, that is,
of the 'inside'.

In another episode in the same series entitled 'Love Me,
Love My Tree' a row develops between the Abbotts and
their neighbours when Trevor cuts down Sid's cherry tree.
In this and other family sit-coms, the next-door neighbours
form a crucial part of the situation as an 'outer circle' of
the 'inside', mediating between the family as an insular
unit and the 'outside' world of social relations. As Jean
says before the row breaks, 'It is lovely to be home again.
. . . After all, we've got a lovely home, and lovely kids,
and lovely friends next door'. The row escalates in a exaggerated manner, with each household threatening to sell

up and move out of the neighbourhood. But the conflict is also deliberately trivialized – as Sid's son Mike says, 'I can't understand you, Dad – the world is full of trouble and you get hung up over a grotty little tree'. When all are reunited, Trevor delivers a little homily: 'Good neighbours are hard to find, aren't they?' The reconciliation thus returns the situation to normal, although – as is actually quite common in sit-coms – there is a concluding 'epilogue': the row flares up again when Trevor mentions the tree. Through the closing credits sequence both men are frantically re-erecting the 'For Sale' signs in front of their houses. This 'epilogue' does not, of course, dismantle the situation again so much as acting as a final *frisson* which can playfully undercut the sentimentality of the plot resolution. Such 'epilogues' provide a final, structurally segregated gag which is marked as 'not to be taken too seriously'. It is not so much, then, a return to instability as a testimony to the strength and 'obviousness' of that stability (for the row over the cherry tree represents no real long-lasting threat to the situation).

Programmes like *No Place Like Home* and *Bless This House* demonstrate clearly the investment of both the sit-com and television in general in the bourgeois nuclear family as a model of stability, of 'normality'.[98] Sit-coms are an integral component of prime-time programming, and even when the situation departs from the 'average family' setting, normative conceptions of the family operate as a framework within which to read the 'aberrant' situation – as in the variously disrupted families found in *Home to Roost*, *Miss Jones and Son*, *Me and My Girl*, *Kate and Allie*, and *Steptoe and Son*, all marked by the lack of one parent. The sit-coms produced by the MTM company in the 1970s are interesting in this respect for they tend to be situated outside the nuclear family, but principles of unity, allegiance, and obligation are structured in a 'surrogate' family network. *The Mary Tyler Moore Show* and programmes which followed in its wake, such as *M*A*S*H*, *Taxi*, *Cheers*, and the more recent *Throb*, are structured around a 'family of co-workers'. In terms of their often large casts and their concentration upon a wider range of emotional interrelationships, these sit-coms move closer to the territory of the soap opera. Jane Feuer sees such shows as a more 'realistic' mirror for their time (in that they acknowledge, if only implicitly, that 'the nuclear family was no longer the dominant form outside the texts') but also as utopian, 'in that love and work merged in an essentially harmonious universe that represented a throwback to a less corporate age'.[99] The recurring situation in such shows is that a 'family' member would come to realize that 'family unity represents a higher goal than personal ambition'.[100] In other words there is the same emphasis upon group unity as is found in the domestic sit-coms, but a different conceptualization of the group; the machinery of the sit-com form functions in each case to preserve the stability of the recurring situation and to protect the relationships it comprises from disruption. To illustrate further the ways in which these American sit-coms work, we shall draw briefly upon a few episodes from *Taxi*, a series made for ABC in 1978 by four ex-MTM producers, James L. Brooks, Ed Weinburger, Stan Daniels, and David Davis.

The show is set in the lower-class milieu of the Sunshine Taxi Company and features a large regular cast of taxi drivers. The generative nucleus of this show is thus quite broad, especially as many of the drivers hold down other jobs as well and represent mixed educational and social backgrounds – although there is only one regular woman, Elaine (Marilu Henner). The show continues the MTM-style 'warmedy', with a recurrent attention to friendship, emotional interdependency, and loyalty, and a similar utopian conception of work. For example, despite the playfully sadistic glee of the shift supervisor Louie De Palma (Danny DeVito) the taxi drivers form an egalitarian group, willing to accept and incorporate such misfits as the drug-scarred 1960s casualty 'Reverend' Jim Ignatowski (Christopher Lloyd) and the incompetent East European mechanic Latka Gravas (Andy Kauffman), each of whom is unsuited to life in the world outside.

A typical episode will posit a disruption to the unity of this group: for example, shaken after a mugging, Alex (Judd Hirsch), the principal character, decides to leave the garage for a safer and more lucrative job as a waiter; he eventually returns when he realizes that the good friends he has there provide the greater satisfaction and are worth taking the risk for. In another episode a row develops between Tony and Bobby when the latter neglects the goldfish whose care Tony has entrusted to him; the threat to the stability of group relations is overcome when Bobby realizes the responsibilities that come with friendship and Tony accepts Bobby for what he is. A further episode posits another type of threat common to the sit-com, when the diminutive and aggressive Louie attempts to reform his character, only to have his co-workers tricking him back to his old self (a similar plot is found in a 1956 episode of *The Phil Silvers Show*, 'Bilko Gets Some Sleep', when Bilko's character change threatens to destabilize the situation). The sentimental character of the resolutions to this show tend, as in the 'Love Me, Love My Tree' episode of *Bless This House* and many examples of *The Mary Tyler Moore Show*,[101] to be followed by a short comic 'epilogue' which playfully reaffirms the 'normality' of the character interrelationships: they do not dwell upon the emotional concatenations of the individual plot but 'get on with their lives'. The 'epilogue', then, tends to underline the self-contained nature of the individual episodes.

Thus in both the domestic sit-com and such 'surrogate family' shows, the regular setting and the regular characters are bonded together into a repeatable unity, with the structure of the sit-com representing an activity of 'communalization', reaffirming the stability of the group and the situation. As Francis Wheen has commented:

> The abiding rule, whether in *M*A*S*H* or a 'family' sitcom such as *The Dick Van Dyke Show*, is that a character must not face the world alone: she or he must experience the joys and tribulations of life as part of some larger social unit.[102]

In terms of its communalizing role, the sit-com can be regarded as a microcosm of broadcast TV in general, in that the medium attempts to inscribe the viewer as part of its own 'family'. Television is 'allowed into' the home, and it precisely makes itself 'at home', addressing itself in intimate terms to 'You, the viewer'. Both the sit-com and television in general are concerned with reaffirming cultural identity, with demarcating an 'inside', a community of interests and values, and localizing contrary or oppositional values as an 'outside' (which can, of course, be rendered comprehensible). The sit-com and TV in general seek to align the viewer with what Gillian Swanson has referred to as cultural 'systems of propriety, or norms of acceptability', and to 'provide a set of conventions which draw directly on an acknowledgement of a shared area of experience and cultural identity ... [which] presupposes certain inhibitions the transgression of which implies marginality, an identity outside the norm.'[103]

As we have noted, the activity of comedy tends to be integrally related to notions of conformity to and deviance from norms. The sit-com is important to television precisely because of its consolidatory function, not just in terms of the narratives as 'represented' but also for the ways in which these are made meaningful for the audience. The viewer is imbricated as 'part of' the scene rather than functioning as a separate 'audience' to be performed to/for, because 'naturalistic' comedy involves a more casual activity of 'eavesdropping'. In its communalizing activity the sit-com can be seen to extend the 'bonding activity' of joke-telling. For example, in his consideration of the generative processes of the 'smutty joke', Freud notes how the initial object of the joke – the sexual exposure of a woman – becomes transformed in the establishment of a 'joking relationship' between the teller and the audience.[104] As he puts it, the one who listens

> soon acquires the greatest importance in the development of the smut ... gradually, in the place of the woman, the onlooker, now the listener, becomes the person to whom

the smut is addressed, and owing to this transformation it
is already near to assuming the character of a joke.[105]

The telling of a joke – and this holds for any tendentious
joke, not just 'smut' – serves to establish a demarcation
between an 'inside' ('we who share the joke') and an
'outside' (in Freud's example, in the location of sexual
difference). Such jokes create a communal bonding
between the participants which establishes a relationship
of *power*, of inclusion and exclusion. Of course, the object
of such joking may not necessarily be a woman, for the
constitution of the 'outside' can include and marginalize
other forms of non-normative sexuality, or racial, class,
regional differences, and so on. Joke-telling in general
takes the form of a 'social contract': in announcing that
one is to tell a joke ('Have you heard the one about . . .')
one is promising the listeners a pleasure which is, as we
have suggested, integrally related to a sense of inclusion,
to the affirmation of communal bonds between joke-teller
and audience. The sit-com, then, represents an institution-
alizing of the pleasures and processes involved in such
joke-telling.

Of course, as Barry Curtis has observed, 'ignorance,
lack of sympathy with or enthusiasm for the transgressions
involved can fail to generate a comic response, and, in
that case, deny the "meaning" of the comedy'.[106] Hence it
is important for the TV industry to rework the generative
nucleus of the sit-com in the face of social and cultural
transformations – *Bless This House*, for example, incor-
porates and renders 'comprehensible' the late–1960s/ear-
ly–1970s theme of the 'generation gap'. It is also important for sit-coms to be generated which can engage sections
of the audience falling outside the middle ground which
the domestic sit-com seeks to address and reaffirm. Obvious examples of the latter tendency include such black
sitcoms as *No Problems*, *Sandford and Son* and *The Cosby
Show*. In the latter show, racial difference is made acceptable within the parameters of traditional family unity –
the Huxtables are an idealized family who 'just happen'

to be black. *The Cosby Show* can flaunt its 'modernity' in
its positive representation of blacks but can at the same
time hold this in place through a 'commonplace' sense of
family unity. A more obvious example of the containment
and domesticization of difference is represented by those
shows which incorporate 'supernatural' or 'otherworldly'
elements into the situation: *Bewitched*, *I Dream of Jeanie*,
My Favorite Martian, *Mork and Mindy*, *The Munsters*,
The Addams Family, and the more recent *Alf*, for example.
In each case the 'alien' elements which become incorporated within 'normal life' are, of course, detached from
the customary sinister connotations of vampires, witches,
man-made monsters, and invaders from space.

We shall conclude this general consideration of the sit-
com by looking briefly at various programmes which
attempt to broaden the sit-com through reworking or
extending the traditional areas of content (as do *The
Cosby Show* and such 'post-feminist' shows as *Kate and
Allie* and *The Golden Girls*) or through play with the self-
contained 'naturalistic' mode of the sit-com. One recent
tendency, for example – although really dating back to
Amos'n'Andy – is to break down the traditional barriers
between the series form and the serial form. *Soap* is the
most obvious example here, being a parody of the 'soap
opera' which exaggerates its characters and their problems. Other shows like *M*A*S*H* and *Cheers* also have
marked 'developmental' tendencies: in the former, not
only do individual episodes tend to intertwine three storylines but there is also a stress upon the characters' 'moral
growth' across the run of the series.[107] In *Cheers*, the
growing relationship between bar workers Sam and Diane
is developed across the boundaries of individual episodes.
This reorientation of the traditional relationship between
continuity and containment marks not only the sit-com
itself, but also other series forms like the police thriller
and the hospital drama; *Hill Street Blues* and *St Elsewhere*
represent not only hybrids between the serial and series
modes but also between genres of TV drama and comedy.

There have also, especially of late, been various attempts

to play more emphatically with the formal mechanisms of the sit-com as a televisual form. One particularly interesting example is *It's Garry Shandling's Show* (1987), which is something of a hybrid between the sit-com and the variety-show. The programme opens and closes with a monologue from the comedian, and is also reminiscent of Jack Benny's show in that the situation comprises Shandling's 'home life' and the fact that he has to present a weekly TV show from his 'home'. In its frequent self-referential gags – the theme song, for example, begins 'This is the theme to Garry's show . . .' – the programme resembles the Burns-Allen show: Shandling and other characters frequently address the camera; members of the studio audience are invited down into his living-room set; the finding of a stray collie motivates a pastiche of the credits sequence of the 'Lassie' programme; and in one episode Shandling turns the programme into a chat show while awaiting the birth of a friend's child (with the baby arriving on time to be the 'special guest'). This play with the artificiality of television and the traditional limits of the sit-com is held in place by Shandling's genial 'goofish' persona and by a conventional orientation to the plots themselves – they hinge around the obligations of friendship and the stability of the 'quasi-familial' group of regular characters.

A contrary tendency is represented by the situational comedies produced by Britain's 'alternative comedians': such shows as *The Young Ones*, *Filthy, Rich and Catflap*, *Girls on Top*, and *The New Statesman* are attempts to produce 'anti-sit-com' sit-com. In these shows there is a blatantly aggressive attack on the *decorum* of the traditional sit-com, with a tendency towards anal jokes and sexual prurience which unconsciously allies them with Benny Hill. In the process, they make a point of deliberately rupturing the sit-com's conventions of 'naturalistic' representation: with musical interruptions, extreme, repetitive physical and verbal abuse, and such 'impossible' gags as the 'post-coital' conversation between an electric plug and socket (in *The Young Ones*). The characters tend to be marked by a similar disregard for realist motivation, in favour of idiosyncratic 'alternative' performances. Rik Mayall's and Ade Edmondson's roles in *Filthy, Rich and Catflap*, for example, do not differ significantly from their 'Dangerous Brothers' stand-up routines. Such 'shock-tactics' and the destruction of situational logic also mark the *Blackadder* series starring Rowan Atkinson and co-written by 'alternative' stand-up comedian Ben Elton.

In the three series of *Blackadder* to date, the situational context is a grossly distorted representation of a period of English history which comprises the 'characters' and stereotypes which populate 'commonsense' notions of the past. The show precisely pinpoints the banality of popular conceptions of English history, making the point through the frequent use of anachronism and cliché. But unlike many of the 'alternative' sit-coms we have just referred to, the individual episodes tend, like *Fawlty Towers*, to have a tightly plotted farce narrative. The show is of further interest owing to the flexibility of its series structure: each series of six episodes is set in a different era, with the central character of each a descendant of the Blackadder line. Because the individual series are short and relatively self-contained, there is the opportunity for a few liberties to be taken with the conventions of the series form. The relations between the characters are marked by a class-based hierarchy in each series, with the Machiavellian Blackadder (Atkinson) as a frustrated figure caught in the middle between the dogsbody Baldrick (Tony Robinson) – dirty, unkempt, lacking human dignity – and a pampered, stupid, infantile ruler. The final episodes of both the second and third series disrupt the sense of maintained stability which traditionally characterizes the sit-com.

In the final episode of *Blackadder II* ('Chains'), Blackadder foils an attempt on the life of Queen Elizabeth I (Miranda Richardson) by the mad master of perverse disguise Prince Ludwig, The Indestructable (Hugh Laurie). Blackadder kills the Prince, who is disguised as the Queen's nurse, and order is conventionally restored; however, following the closing credits, the camera pans across the dead bodies of all the regular characters and finally fixes upon a standing Queen Elizabeth, who is (though in fact still played by Richardson!) Ludwig in disguise. In *Blackadder III*, the final episode ('Duel and Duality') concludes with a duel between the Duke of Wellington (Stephen Fry) and a Blackadder who is impersonating George, the Prince Regent (Hugh Laurie). His life saved by a cigarillo box – protecting him against the Duke's cannon! – Blackadder is accepted by Wellington as the rightful heir to the throne. When the real Prince Regent intervenes, Wellington shoots *him* as the imposter. This gag on the overturning of the class hierarchy is continued when the mad King George III accepts Blackadder as his true son. In each case, then, the stable situation maintained through each series can be allowed ultimately to be disrupted because each is precisely the final episode, and in the series to follow the situation will be re-established in a different historical period.

Blackadder is, like Shandling's show and those featuring the 'alternative' comics, an example of a narrative comedy programme which is structured around a recognizable comedian (outside television Atkinson is known for his one-man theatre shows). As in the cinematic genre of 'comedian comedy', the presence of the 'clown' acts as a further motivation for the comic play with the 'naturalism' and containment of the sit-com. In the final section of this chapter we shall examine *Steptoe and Son* by first considering its relationship to *Hancock's Half-Hour*, one of the most famous of British sit-coms structured around a comedian, and also an example of a show to transfer from radio to television.

The sit-com as trap

Steptoe and Son ran for four series in the 1960s and then returned from 1970 to 1974; when selected episodes were repeated in 1988 they managed consistently to make the top-ten weekly TV ratings.[108] The show began in 1962 as one of a series of ten 'comedy playlets' programmed under the title *Comedy Playhouse*. Ray Galton and Alan Simpson were commissioned to write these when their long-running partnership with Tony Hancock was terminated. Galton and Simpson first wrote for Hancock on the radio comedy-variety show *Happy Go Lucky* in 1951, and they continued to work for him both on radio and in the West End revues *London Laughs* (1952) and *The Talk Of The Town* (1954–5). With Hancock's reputation growing through the early 1950s, he was eventually offered a starring show on BBC radio, to be scripted by Galton and Simpson. *Hancock's Half-Hour* (1954) is particularly interesting for the ways in which it developed as a situational comedy structured around a comedian.

Hancock was not a conventional stand-up comedian like Bob Monkhouse or Bob Hope, but rather his act came increasingly to emphasize his *reactions* to situations. He was not a joke-teller – and was reputedly a bad ad-libber – but rather presented himself to be *laughed at*. As Freddie Hancock and David Nathan have remarked of his postwar stage performances:

> His idea of comedy was to stand in front of a microphone and work himself into a situation. He did imitations, not in the meticulous manner of an impersonator, but in the style of a clown imitating an impersonator, the funny thing being not the accuracy of the mimicry but the fact that he was doing it at all. In this way he could impersonate people his audience had never heard of . . .[109]

Hancock's Half-Hour represented an accommodation of Hancock's performance skills to the demands of repeatable situation comedy. The situation of the show was firmly centred around the persona developed by Hancock and his writers, and it deviated from the bourgeois family norm of domestic sit-com. 'Hancock' was an 'outsider': a 'belligerent, pompous, frequently childish and petulant',[110] middle-aged bachelor who was not only forever seeking to better himself but believed at the same time that he was already superior. When the show started on radio, Hancock functioned – in quite conventional fashion – as the star performer in an ensemble context, with Bill Kerr, Kenneth Williams, Sid James, and Hattie Jacques among his regular supporting players. However, in time Sid James became increasingly prominent, and the show shifted to a two-man comedy format (this becoming entrenched when the TV version started in 1956).

The early radio shows tended to include moments of fantastical exaggeration of the type particularly suited to the sound medium – for example, in 'The Television Set' (June 1955), Sid sells Hancock a build-it-yourself TV which when constructed is so large that it occupies the whole of the living room. Many of these early episodes also relied upon conventionalized plots in which Hancock is the dupe of one of Sid's elaborate swindles[111] – involving, for example, the sale of Lord's cricket ground as a farm ('Agricultural 'Ancock', February 1957). During the course of the show's run on radio and TV, Galton and Simpson moved increasingly from such devices – and such standbys as catchphrases and funny voices[112] – towards a more firmly 'naturalistic' form of situation comedy which centred upon the 'Hancock' character. 'Sunday Afternoon At Home' (April, 1958) is frequently cited to illustrate the development of the show, and is an episode from the fifth radio series in which, as Roger Wilmut has noted, 'there was no plot to speak of, and much use was made of long pauses'.[113] Indeed, Barry Took sees Galton and Simpson's distinctive contribution to broadcast comedy as 'their knack of reproducing mundane conversation and lifting it to the level of high art'.[114] The 'Sunday Afternoon' episode was deliberately 'experimental' in terms of the current context of radio comedy in that it represented a move away from tightly constructed plots and gags and towards a low-key 'naturalistic' style which capitalized upon boredom and inactivity, with Hancock and his friends sitting around at home seeking various diversions from the monotony of a Sunday. In the sixth and final radio series, Galton and Simpson developed this minimal-plot technique, and the series was also significant in replacing comedians like Kenneth Williams with straight actors.[115]

Hancock's Half-Hour, although it placed increasing emphasis upon 'Hancock' as a *character*, still incorporated moments of specialized performance (indeed, the 'Hancock' character is usually located as a professional comedian): as in 'The Economy Drive' (TV: September 1959), where he impersonates W. C. Fields; 'The Missing Page' (TV: March 1960), where he performs an intricate mime in order to explain the plot of a thriller to Sid; and in 'The Baby Sitters' (TV: April 1960),[116] where he does characteristic impersonations of Winston Churchill, George Burns, and Groucho Marx. Such routines, although frequent, are by no means the major source of the comedy. 'The Bedsitter' (June 1961), the first show of the final TV series, makes this explicit, for the whole episode is a solo performance by Hancock, an extended piece of in-character acting. As in the 'Sunday Afternoon' episode, this show hinges around nothing actually happening, upon precisely how the character reacts to a boring evening – although this time Hancock is on his own (for by the time of this series Sid James had been dropped). This is the episode of the Hancock show which most resembles a one-act play, not just in its continuity of action but also in the use of such 'dramatic' devices as the monologue and 'stage business'.

Hancock ended his partnership with Galton and Simpson before his 1963 series with ATV, but in *Steptoe and Son* the writers were able to extend many of the techniques which had interested them in *Hancock's Half-Hour*. One of the major differences, however, was that the lead roles in *Steptoe* were played by two straight actors – Harry H. Corbett as the son, Harold, and Wilfred Brambell as his father, Albert. The situation was furthermore much more rigidly defined than that of the Hancock show, which occasionally departed from its traditional setting (as in 'The Bowmans' (June 1961), where Hancock is a long-running soap-opera star). The situation in *Steptoe and Son* resembles the middle phase of *Hancock's Half-Hour* in that it centres upon a relationship between two men which – as in other two-man sitcoms like *Bootsie and Snudge*,

The Odd Couple, *Chico and the Man*, and *The Likely Lads* – oscillates between friendship and antagonism. However, unlike these other shows, the two men are united by blood rather than friendship or custom (and the situation further unites familial and working relations, for the Steptoes run a small rag-and-bone business from their home).

In *Steptoe* there is a marked non-correspondence between its *situational* 'normality' – the stable situation to which each episode returns – and the bourgeois-familial 'normality' which is the ideological touchstone of the traditional domestic sit-com. In fact, in its lack of regular female characters, its emphatic squalor, and its verbal and physical crudity (and sometimes cruelty), *Steptoe and Son* is the *inverse* of such shows: the show's situational 'inside' is the conventional 'outside', and vice versa. But at the same time, unlike many of the British 'alternative' sit-coms of the 1980s, the show was aimed at a broad family-based peak-time audience. The key to its notable success seems to be the way in which it represents a *spectacle* of inverted bourgeois decorum for a bourgeois audience: one has to know the 'rules' in order to recognize and to find funny the ways in which they are broken. As such a spectacle, the show works precisely because the Steptoes are *not* the average middle-class family (otherwise their behaviour would be problematic). They are marked out, in other words, as a special case, and the disordered, junk-cluttered setting of the Steptoe home is very much a 'world apart', isolated from the norms of middle-class existence and only occasionally and reluctantly visited by such representatives of the bourgeoisie as the vicar and his wife, a doctor, a tax officer, and Harold's short-lived bohemian acquaintances. Whereas Albert blatantly, often aggressively, rejects middle-class codes of behaviour and sensibility, Harold is continually attempting – like Hancock – to 'better' himself, to adopt bourgeois attitudes, and to impress bourgeois figures. Where Hancock's pretentions are frequently undercut by the ignorance behind his pedantry, Harold's doomed aspirations are marked particularly in his use of language: his attempts at a higher-class discourse are not only patently affected but they are also sabotaged either by Albert's crude jibes or by Harold's own lapses into his 'natural' (as the show implies) vulgarity. His high-blown, somewhat nervous rhetoric always seems to run out of steam and to run aground on such colourful 'non-U' expressions as 'I don't give a toss' and 'you little toerag'. Integral, then, to the show's situation and logic is a deterministic class ideology: Harold, despite his aspirations, cannot escape what he is – a lower-class Steptoe, like Albert.

The plots of most episodes tend to centre upon an attempt by Harold to escape from his frustrating circumstances – either directly, or through 'self-betterment' – and his inevitable failure to do so. At the end, each episode returns the situation to 'normal', at the cost of Harold's continuing frustration. This process is similar to that found in many episodes of *Hancock's Half-Hour* which, as John Fisher has noted[117] tend to contain circular plot structures, with the end representing an emphatic return to the beginning; 'The Economy Drive' and 'The Lift' (June 1961) are exemplary in this respect. Just as Hancock is perpetually frustrated in his attempt to escape from his 'character', so too is Harold, and both characters similarly are marked by a tendency to fantasize. In 'The Ladies' Man' (April 1960), an episode of his TV show, Hancock's lack of success with women motivates him to enlist in a charm school; but once there he spends most of his time daydreaming that he is a debonair, talented, and sought-after bachelor. Most often, however, the fantasies of both Hancock and Harold Steptoe are expressed through monologues. Militating against Harold's articulation of his wishes – marking them out precisely as fantasy – is the very setting itself (the squalid, cluttered home) and also the pathos-inducing comments and very presence of his father. During these monologues, Harold will often be standing in medium close-up to one side of the foreground while, in the background, Albert sits and scowls. Each of Harold's fantasies represents a potential (though often markedly unrealizable) chance to escape from the trap he finds himself in: a career as an actor ('A Star Is Born'), or a doctor ('Upstairs, Downstairs; Upstairs Downstairs'), or a writer ('Men Of Letters'), or, particularly, a chance to 'escape' through a heterosexual relationship (as in 'And So To Bed' and 'Loathe Story').

The sense of a trap is much more emphatic in *Steptoe* than in the Hancock show, and this is not solely the result of Harold's lower-class status as a rag-and-bone man but also because in his relationship with the disgusting 'dirty old man', Albert, family obligation exerts a more complex and pressurizing force than exists in the Hancock-James friendship. As we have noted above, the sit-com as a form conventionally asserts stability at the expense of change: the recurring situation is *reinstated* rather than reformed. Barry Took has suggested that 'all successful comedies have some trap in which people must exist – like marriage' and that the 'perfect situation' for a sit-com is 'a little enclosed world where you have to live by the rules'.[118] And Mick Eaton has elaborated upon the dramatic logic of the sit-com form:

> The necessity for the continuity of character and situation from week to week allows for the possibility of comedy being generated by the fact that the characters are stuck with each other. . . . It is as if the formal necessities of the series provide the existential circle from which the characters cannot escape.[119]

Whereas in the majority of sit-coms the implications of this structural necessity are played down, in *Steptoe* they are frequently made explicit – as in the following extract from one of Harold's monologues, inspired by a row over decorating:

> 'We seem to have reached our usual impasse, don't we? . . . You won't give way on anything, will you? You don't give a toss what colour we 'ave. You just try and go against me, don't you? . . . Whatever I want, you don't. . . . I mean, it's not just the decorations, it's – it's everything. I mean, every idea I have for improvement – I mean, improvements

to the house, improvements to the business – you're agin'
it. You frustrate me in everything I try to do. You are a
dyed-in-the-wool, fascist, spoiled, little know-your-place,
don't-rise-above-yourself, don't-get-out-of-your-hole, com-
placent little turd' (from 'Divided We Stand').

Harold's inability to escape from his 'trapped relationship'
with his father becomes the very principle of the comedy,
and the often overtly combative nature of the relations
between them stems from the fact that the characters are
'stuck with each other'. As the psychiatrist tells Harold of
his attempt to kill Albert in 'Loathe Story':

'It's a classical case of subconscious wish-fulfilment. These
things are quite often the result of the hyper-tension when
two people live in close proximity, in claustrophobic conditions, unable to pursue their outside interests. Happens
all the time with married couples.'

As this remark highlights, this is not the conventional
relationship between father and son, for it displaces the
more 'normal' relationship between husband and wife,
and the aggression and outright violence are marked at
all stages by the fact that women are excluded from the
situation.

The Steptoe household is devoid of women – Harold's
mother, Albert's wife, has been dead for over thirty years.
As Crowther and Pinfold have remarked:

The absence of a woman in the family was not merely a
one-off joke, it was the solid core of the piece. . . . To have
brought a woman into this all-male family would have
been not only to jeopardise the relationship between the
two principals but to cause the characters themselves to
collapse.[120]

As we have already noted, in such domestic sit-coms as
No Place Like Home and *Bless This House* women play
an integral role as the mainstay of the home, cementing
family unity. The absence of women in *Steptoe* lends to
the situation a fundamental *instability*. Women represent
a direct threat to the Harold-Albert relationship. Generally, the danger comes from Harold's attempts to secure

a girlfriend – endeavours which are always thwarted by Albert. In 'And So To Bed', for example, Harold's pursuit of the 'sex-starved' cinema usherette Marcia comes to a disastrous end after Albert accidentally punctures his son's new water-bed. And in 'Loathe Story' Harold's sexual and class aspirations are united in the figure of the upper-middle-class Bunty Kennington-Stroud (Joanna Lumley): Albert scuppers the affair in characteristic fashion through his deliberate vulgarity. In an earlier episode, 'The Step-mother' (1964), this situation is reversed in that the threat arises from Albert's plan to remarry, and it is Harold who sets in motion a scheme to break up the 'threatening' relationship. Thus women are here the 'outside' elements which have to be ejected to preserve the stability of the recurring situation. They are the object of Harold's fantasy but they tend to be held obsessively at bay. It is worth noting that in Galton and Simpson's work for Hancock women also tend to occupy a rather problematic place; according to Roger Wilmut, the team could not write particularly well for women, and female performers tended not to remain with the show very long because of the insubstantial nature of their roles.[121]

Harold and Albert remain locked within an exclusively male circuitry: the very shabbiness of their home is a testimony to its lack of a female presence (compare the *Steptoe* set with the order and cleanliness of the bourgeois home in domestic sit-coms). Under their domestic/business arrangement, Albert is supposed to do the housekeeping and prepare meals while Harold is out on the rounds. However, the old man's activities represent a parody of the maternal, nurturing role since he does as little as he possibly can get away with and is always on the lookout for his own pleasure. Another consequence of *Steptoe*'s exclusion of 'femininity' is the way in which the two men shy away from any overt acknowledgement of their emotional interdependency. There is a nervousness concerning 'sentiment', and it tends to be restricted to Harold's guilty stuttering when he articulates one of his plans to break away, or to one of Albert's pathetic, wounded looks which function as a ploy to generate such guilt. Sentiment and femininity tend, however, not to be merely *absent* but they are rather *replaced* by a comically aggressive 'masculine' conflict through which any problematic emotional and plot complications can be discharged.

The two men are continually fighting, to assert and consolidate their position within the family in regard to each other. This state of conflict, indeed, represents the 'normality' of their relations – and it is customary for the show to conclude with a violently comic chase or fight. The perpetual competition between them also tends to be marked by instances of game-playing: scrabble in 'Men Of Letters', chess in 'Cuckoo In The Nest', badminton in 'Loathe Story'. Albert is generally the winner, and in the process he affronts Harold's sense of how the game should be played (for example by the use of obscenities in scrabble). What is at stake in these games, as in the competitive 'routines' around which the show as a whole is constructed, is the position of masculine authority: Harold attempts to make Albert aware that he is dependent upon his son and should thus be grateful, whereas Albert schemingly uses various below-the-belt tactics to prevent Harold from deserting him. As David Nathan has commented:

> the old man walks a shaky path between belligerence and fear. His paternal authority is a relic of his younger and stronger days. He knows he is utterly dependent on Harold and that Harold could, if ever he took it into his head, push him into an old home or just walk out and leave him helpless. He takes refuge in a cunning pathos.[122]

This situation is strikingly similar to the *Arabian Nights* story, 'The Old Man of the Sea', where, out of pity, a young man agrees to carry on his back an elderly and infirm man, only to find that the latter is a parasite he cannot shake off. In his novel, *Beware Of Pity*, Stefan Zweig discusses this story in terms which are remarkably close to the dramatic core of *Steptoe*:

> He has become the beast of burden, the slave, of the old rascal; no matter if his knees give and his lips are parched

with thirst, he is compelled, foolish victim of his own pity, to trot on and on, is fated to drag the wicked, infamous, cunning old man for ever on his back.[123]

Whenever Harold is on the verge of leaving him, Albert will fake a heart attack or underline his infirmity by reminding his son of his war wounds. And even though Harold is aware of the old man's guile, he still finds that he is prevented from leaving because of the pressure of his emotional obligation to his father, and the feeling of guilt that this gives rise to.

What are at stake, then, in the 'serious', dramatic core of *Steptoe and Son* are familial obligation and allegiance in relation to the needs and desires of the individual. Because the situation is never allowed to be resolved, Harold's frustration is emphatically replayed. An episode entitled 'The Desperate Hours' (which is structured like a one-act play, with temporal and scenic continuity) contains what is perhaps the most markedly 'serious' treatment of these issues. The episode – which borrows and inverts the plot of the 1955 film of the same title – draws a dramatic parallel between the Steptoes and the relationship between two escaped convicts who shelter in their home: Johnny (Leonard Rossiter) and the elderly Frank (J. G. Devlin). The Steptoes are here at their most desperate, for they are destitute and hungry in the middle of winter, and the entry of the convicts establishes a comparison between their situation and the more literal trap of prison life; the convicts find the latter to be relatively luxurious! The conflict between obligation and independence which is continually articulated in the *Steptoe* series is here duplicated in the conflict of allegiances faced by Johnny, whose career in crime, imprisonment, and aborted escape attempt are all the result of his friendship with Frank. The Steptoes take sides: Harold tries to convince Johnny that he stands a better chance on his own, and Albert says that he cannot leave Frank to fend for himself. The argument becomes heated, for both Harold and Albert realize that they are in fact defending their own respective positions. Underlining the 'inevitable' resolution – Johnny returns to prison, taking Frank with him – is the familiar truth that Harold cannot escape his own prison of obligation. This episode is unusual in the degree of its dramatic seriousness: it illustrates how the situation is not *in itself* funny but rather is *made* funny.

Crowther and Pinfold have described the problematic of the *Steptoe* series as follows:

> The bonds that hold Harold to his father were those that hold children to ailing parents; that keep men and women locked in loveless marriages; that doom thousands of lives to quiet desperation from which escape is . . . impossible for the average person.[124]

It is the process of the conversion of this 'serious' situation into the terms of comedy which gives the show its particular charge. Often behind the broadest comedy in the show are actions which would ordinarily be branded disturbing or cruel: for example, in 'Loathe Story' Harold is so upset by Albert's dominating influence that while sleepwalking he attempts to cut off the old man's head with a meat cleaver.

The relations between drama and comedy are particularly clear in the episode 'Upstairs, Downstairs; Upstairs, Downstairs', in which the parallel between the *Steptoe* situation and 'The Old Man of the Sea' is most emphatic. This episode begins in a markedly serious fashion: rather than the customary extended scene between Albert and Harold there is a long sequence between Harold and a doctor. The doctor tells him that Albert is very ill and that he will be bedridden, perhaps for several months. However, Harold does not react sympathetically to the threat of this long-term disability – he is concerned overtly with how this new development represents a further imprisoning of himself to the demands of the old man. This inversion of the 'normal' reaction to such an illness is quite typical of the show. The comic effect of the scene derives from Harold's lack of decorum in front of the doctor, from his exaggerated selfishness, and from the way in which sentiment is undercut in a comically brutal fashion. Harold suggests to the doctor that Albert is only seeking attention, and that he shove the old man in hospital so that he can be off his hands:

> 'Oh look doctor – I *know* 'im. 'E's not as bad as 'e makes out. You think 'e's ill – believe me, you bung 'im in 'ospital, stretch 'im on the floor, and 'e'll make the quickest recovery known to medical science.'

The doctor, emissary of the bourgeoisie, is shocked by this competitive plea for attention: but, of course, we, the 'eavesdropping' audience who are familiar with the Steptoes' situation, know the 'true nature' of their relationship and do not share his reaction.

When the doctor leaves, Harold is called downstairs by Albert – whose nerveracking, demanding screech of ''Arold! 'Arold!' persists throughout the show – and he proceeds to 'wind up' the old man. First of all, he does an impression of a head waiter – a mockery of his service to Albert, and, like many other such moments in the series, perhaps a legacy of the writers' years with Hancock – and then he implies that Albert is on the verge of death. The old man becomes increasingly worried until he realizes what Harold is up to, and accuses him of being a 'callous little toerag'. Harold's cruelty is funny here precisely because of the way in which it makes light of the supposed seriousness of Albert's illness and the way in which it inverts bourgeois decorum (respect for the old, the infirm, human dignity, and so on). The two men then become engaged in one of their perpetual competitive rows, with the restoration to this 'normal' state of affairs serving to siphon off the serious implications of the doctor's sober announcement. Harold pretends that he will not be able to look after Albert because he is going away on holiday; however, when 'victory' is in sight, and the old man seems on the verge of tears – 'I won't be a burden to you', he pleads – Harold backs down from the 'game' and signals a truce by confessing that he was 'just muckin' about'. Such games can only go *so far* without overbalancing the comedy with its serious underpinnings: Albert further highlights the truce by delivering one of the show's recurring 'catchphrases' – 'You're a good boy, 'Arold'. But following this moment of relative quiet, Albert is once more shouting out for Harold to come and cater to his wishes, the extent of Harold's imprisoning obligation being highlighted when he has to carry him down to the outside lavatory (one of the key settings of the show).

The situation that Harold had feared comes about: when he has finished his daily round, he spends the rest of his time running and fetching for Albert. And, in the meantime, the old man makes the most of his stay in bed, inviting friends round, drinking beer, and watching the racing on TV, while Harold grows weaker and more exhausted. Whenever Harold falters, Albert produces one of his pained, sorrowful looks and laments about being a burden to him. By this stage in the show, the enslavement of Harold is on the verge of turning into a 'melodramatic' problem, but this is sidestepped by means of a markedly comic plot reversal. Twisting his back in bed, Albert finds himself suddenly cured; however, rather than informing Harold of the fact he proceeds to use the situation to his own advantage and carries on the pretence of being ill. Harold, however, noticing that the fridge has been raided in his absence, hides away in the larder and observes Albert scavenging around in the kitchen. So now a conventional comic plot of deception and counter-deception is in operation, a plot based on discrepancies of knowledge: Albert thinks that Harold is ignorant, Harold allows Albert to think he is ignorant.

Harold goes upstairs to tell Albert that he will give him a blanket bath. Albert is aghast at the prospect – being a 'dirty old man' in every way – and Harold's punishment of his father takes the form, first, of an over-vigorous flannelling, and secondly in pouring astringent surgical spirit over his groin. In a twist reminiscent of the conclusion to one of Boccaccio's stories, Albert screams 'Aaaah! Me goolies!' and leaps out of bed, with Harold proclaiming a 'miracle cure'. Harold laughs exuberantly and follows Albert about the house and yard as the old man seeks to quench the burning in his groin, eventually parking his backside in the kitchen sink. This ending is typical of the series in its combination of crudity, cruelty, and revenge, and in the physical knockabout character of its comedy. As in many other episodes, the dramatic undercurrents of the show and the concomitant emotional tensions are discharged through 'low' farce – which signifies both the restoration of 'stability' and the turning of aggression into 'masculine horseplay'. There is, in other words, no actual solution to the problems bound up within the situation itself, but rather a restoration of the competitive instability-stability of the relationship between the two men (that is, the restitution of instability *as* stability). Finally, it is worth noting that this principle of the 'discharge' of tension marks not only the way in which the plots of the individual episodes tend to be resolved, but it operates also at particular moments, whenever, in fact, the stability of the male relationship is threatened by sentiment or division.

Albert Steptoe, like Alf Garnett (Warren Mitchell), the central figure in the show *Till Death Us Do Part* (1964–74), is a 'monstrous' figure who disturbs the conventional family order and expresses opinions which run counter to accepted middle-class decorum: both characters are markedly racist, for example. However, with both shows, particularly because the family is carefully distinguished from the norm, the implications of their claustrophobic representation of family relations tend to be held in place. Although deviating in terms of their content, what is integral to these shows is a conventional use of the sit-com format – the situation is perpetually restored, and in the process it is both maintained and contained. Their very separation from the situational 'normality' of the traditional domestic sit-com localizes their deviations. As such, they function as further reminders of the ways in which institutional forms of comedy operate as vehicles for dealing with and making acceptable that which is aberrant or potentially threatening.

Notes and References

Introduction

1 Jerry Palmer, *The Logic of the Absurd*, British Film Institute, London, 1987.

1 Definitions, genres, and forms

1 On *comedia erudita*, see Marvin T. Herrick, *Italian Comedy in the Renaissance*, University of Illinois Press, Urbana, 1966, pp. 60–164. On *commedia dell'arte*, see Pierre Duchartre, *Italian Comedy*, Dover, New York, 1965. On the jig, a comic song and dance, see Michael Hattaway, *Elizabethan Popular Theatre*, Routledge & Kegan Paul, London, 1982, pp. 67–9. On the droll, a short, farcical afterpiece, see Leo Hughes, *A Century of English Farce*, Princeton University Press, Princeton, 1956, p. 214. On the afterpiece itself, see Michael R. Booth, 'Early Victorian farce, Dionysus domesticated', in Kenneth Richards and Peter Thompson (eds), *Nineteenth Century British Theatre*, Methuen, London, 1971. On pantomime, see Gerald Frow, *'Oh, Yes It Is': A History of Pantomime*, BBC, London, 1985. On flyting, a comic quarrel or debate, see David Crystal, *The Cambridge Encyclopaedia of Language*, Cambridge University Press, Cambridge, 1987, p. 60. And for farce, see Jessica Milner Davis, *Farce*, Methuen, London, 1978.

2 On the *drame* and *comédie larmoyante*, see Michael R. Booth, *English Melodrama*, Herbert Jenkins, London, 1965, Lauren Brown, *English Dramatic Form, 1660–1760*, Yale University Press, New Haven, 1981, E. J. H. Greene, *Meander to Marivaux: The History of a Comic Structure*, University of Alberta Press, Edmon-

ton, 1977, and Edna C. Frederick, *The Plot and Its Construction in Eighteenth Century Criticism of French Comedy*, Burt Franklin, New York, 1973.

3 For further confirmation of the tendency to equate comedy and drama, and to define comedies as plays, see the entries on comedy in M. H. Abrams, *A Glossary of Literary Terms*, Holt, Rinehart & Winston, New York, 1985 edn, Martin Coyle and John Peck (eds), *Literary Terms and Criticism*, Macmillan, London, 1983, and Roger Fowler (ed.), *A Modern Dictionary of Critical Terms*, Routledge & Kegan Paul, London, 1983.

4 For neoclassical reworkings of Aristotle, see Madeleine Doran, *Endeavors of Art: A Study of Form in Elizabethan Drama*, University of Wisconsin Press, Madison, 1972, Marvin T. Herrick, *Comic Theory in the Sixteenth Century*, University of Illinois Press, Urbana, 1964, and Leo Salingar, *Shakespeare and the Traditions of Comedy*, Cambridge University Press, Cambridge, 1974.

5 For further discussion of this issue, see Robert D. Hume, 'Some problems in the theory of comedy', *Journal of Aesthetics and Art Criticism*, vol. 31, no. 1, Fall 1972.

6 Linda Hutcheon, *A Theory of Parody*, Methuen, New York and London, 1985.

7 ibid., pp. 25–6.

8 Don B. Wilmeth, *The Language of American Entertainment*, Greenwood Press, Westport, 1981, p. 245.

2 Comedy and narrative

1 See Marvin T. Herrick, *Comic Theory in the Sixteenth Century*, University of Illinois Press, Urbana, 1964, pp. 106–10.

2 ibid., pp. 119–22.

3 The term 'epilogue' is being used here as defined by David Bordwell:

> in most classical Hollywood films, there is a final phase, which I shall call the epilogue (this may be quite short). . . . the epilogue functions to present the final stability achieved by the narrative: the characters' fortunes are settled. (David Bordwell, 'Happily ever after, Part Two', *The Velvet Light Trap*, no. 19, 1982, p. 4.)

4 ibid.

5 David Bordwell, Janet Staiger, and Kristin Thompson, *The Classical Hollywood Cinema*, Routledge & Kegan Paul, London, 1985, p. 175.

6 Bordwell, 'Happily ever after', p. 2.

7 On the general issues of function and motivation, see Gérard Genette, 'Vraisemblance et motivation', in *Figures II*, Editions du Seuil, Paris, 1969, pp. 71–99.

8   Translated and quoted in Herrick, op. cit., p. 119.
9   G. E. Duckworth, *The Nature of Roman Comedy*, Princeton University Press, Princeton, 1952, p. 209.
10 Brian Henderson, 'Sturges at Work', *Film Quarterly*, vol. 39, no. 2, Winter 1985–6, p. 17.
11 George Burns, *The Third Time Around*, W. H. Allen, London, 1980, p. 168.

3   Gags, jokes, wisecracks, and comic events

1   Harold Wentworth and Stuart Berg Flexner, *Dictionary of American Slang*, Harrap, London, 1967 edn, p. 563.
2   For a discussion of the work of these and other lyricists, see Caryl Brahms and Ned Sherrin, *Song by Song*, Ross Anderson, Bolton, 1984.
3   Leonard Maltin, *Of Mice and Magic: A History of American Animated Cartoons*, New American Library, New York, 1987 edn, p. 291.
4   Don B. Wilmeth, *The Language of American Entertainment*, Greenwood Press, Westport, 1981, p. 105.
5   Jean-Pierre Coursodon, *Keaton et Cie*, Editions Seghers, Paris, 1964, esp. pp. 28–50, and *Buster Keaton*, Atlas L'Herminier, Paris, 1986, pp. 243–53. On the structural features and workings of the gag, see also J.-P. Lebel, *Buster Keaton*, Zwemmer, London, 1967, esp. pp. 103–40, Francois Mars, *Le Gag*, Editions du Cerf, Paris, 1964, Jerry Palmer, *The Logic of the Absurd*, British Film Institute, London, 1987, pp. 39–58, Sylvain du Pasquier, 'Buster Keaton gags', *Journal of Modern Literature*, vol. 13, no. 2, April 1973, Jean-Pierre Simon and Daniel Percheron, 'Le Gag', in Jean Collet, Michel Marie, Daniel Percheron, Jean-Paul Simon, and Marc Vernet, *Lectures du Film*, Editions Albatross, Paris, 1976, pp. 104–7, and Jean-Paul Simon, *Le Filmique et Le Comique*, Editions Albatross, Paris, 1979, pp. 25–7.
6   Coursodon, *Keaton et Cie*, pp. 29–33 and *Buster Keaton*, pp. 243–4.
7   Coursodon, *Buster Keaton*, p. 248.
8   Charles Barr, *Laurel and Hardy*, Studio Vista, London, 1967, p. 33.
9   ibid., p. 23.
10 Brad Ashton, *How to Write Comedy*, Elm Tree Books, London, 1983, p. 85.
11 Arthur Ripley, one of Harry Langdon's gag and story writers, quoted in Raymond Durgnat, *The Crazy Mirror*, Faber, London, 1969, p. 21.
12 Walter Nash, *The Language of Humour*, Longman, London, 1985, pp. 10–11 and 33–8, and du Pasquier, op. cit., pp. 280–1.

13 Cited in Jeff Lenburg, *The Great Cartoon Directors*, MacFarland Press, Jefferson and London, 1983, p. 33.

14 Michael S. Cohen, 'Looney Tunes and Merrie Melodies', *The Velvet Light Trap*, no. 15, Fall 1975, p. 35.

15 Daniel Moews, *Buster Keaton: The Silent Features Close Up*, University of California Press, Berkeley, 1977, p. 20.

16 Frank Capra, *The Name Above the Title*, Collier Macmillan, New York, 1971, p. 123.

4 Laughter, humour, and the comic

1 Quoted in John J. Enck, *Jonson and the Comic Truth*, University of Wisconsin Press, Madison, 1957, p. 231.

2 Christopher Herbert, 'Comedy: the world of pleasure', *Genre*, vol. 18, no. 4, Winter 1984, p. 403. The works he is referring to are L. C. Knights, 'Notes on comedy', in Paul Lauter (ed.), *Theories of Comedy*, Anchor, Garden City, 1964, George Meredith, 'An essay on comedy', in Wylie Sypher (ed.), *Comedy*, Anchor, Garden City, 1956, and L. C. Potts, *Comedy*, Hutchinson, London, 1963.

3 Gerald Mast, *The Comic Mind*, Bobbs-Merrill, Indianapolis, 1973, pp. 26–7.

4 Keith Thomas, 'The place of laughter in Tudor and Stuart England', *The Times Literary Supplement*, vol. 21, January 1977, p. 80.

5 Anthony A. Ciccone, *The Language of Comedy: Four Farces by Molière*, Porrua Turanzas, Potomac, 1980, p. 5.

6 Jerry Palmer, *The Logic of the Absurd*, British Film Institute, London, 1987, p. 21.

7 On the concept and forms of the 'narrative image', see John Ellis, *Visible Fictions*, Routledge & Kegan Paul, London, 1982, pp. 30–7.

8 Palmer, op. cit., p. 29.

9 Leon Golden, *Aristotle's Poetics, A Translation and Commentary for Students of Literature*, Prentice-Hall, Englewood Cliffs, 1968, p. 9.

10 Elder Olsen, *The Theory of Comedy*, Indiana University Press, Bloomington, 1968, p. 15.

11 ibid., p. 15.

12 ibid., p. 21.

13 ibid., p. 18.

14 ibid., p. 18.

15 Palmer, op. cit., p. 40.

16 ibid., p. 40.

17 ibid., p. 42.

18 ibid., p. 43.

19 ibid., p. 45.

20   ibid., p. 64.
21   ibid., pp. 68–74.
22   Sigmund Freud, *Jokes and their Relation to the Unconscious*, Penguin, Harmondsworth, 1976.
23   Sigmund Freud, 'Humour' (1927), in volume 14 of the Pelican Freud Library, *Art and Literature*, Penguin, Harmondsworth, 1985. Freud's book on jokes was originally published in 1905.
24   ibid., p. 427.
25   ibid., p. 428.
26   Sigmund Freud, 'On narcissism: an introduction', in volume 11 of the Pelican Freud Library, *On Metapsychology: The Theory of Psychoanalysis*, Penguin, Harmondsworth, 1984, p. 84.
27   Freud, 'Humour', pp. 432–3.
28   Sandor Ferenczi, *Further Contributions to the Theory and Technique of Psychoanalysis*, Hogarth, London, 1969, p. 344.
29   J. Laplanche and J.-B. Pontalis, *The Language of Psychoanalysis*, Hogarth Press, London, 1973, pp. 250–1.
30   Jacques Lacan, *Ecrits: A Selection*, Norton, New York, 1977, p. 2.
31   Jeffrey Mehlman, 'How to read Freud on jokes: the critic as *Schadchen*', *New Literary Review*, vol. 6, no. 12, Winter 1975, p. 459.
32   See, for instance, Edith Jacobson, 'The child's laughter', *The Psychoanalytic Study of the Child*, vol. 2, 1946, and Martha Wolfenstein, 'A phase in the development of children's sense of humor', *The Psychoanalytic Study of the Child*, vol. 6, 1951. For an overview of more recent work on children's humour, see Paul E. McGhee, 'Children's humour: a review of current research' in Antony T. Chapman and Hugh Foot (eds), *It's a Funny Thing, Humour*, Pergamon, Oxford, 1977.
33   Jean Guillaumin, 'Le comique après "l'humour", une analyse inachevée', *Revue Française de Psychanalyse*, vol. 37, no. 45, July 1973, p. 638.
34   ibid., p. 638.
35   R. Howard Bloch, *The Scandal of the Fabliaux*, University of Chicago Press, Chicago, 1986.
36   ibid., pp. 127–8.

5   Verisimilitude

1   Steve Seidman, *Comedian Comedy, A Tradition in Hollywood Film*, UMI Research Press, Ann Arbor, 1981, p. 44.
2   ibid., pp. 46–7.
3   Tzvetan Todorov, *Introduction to Poetics*, Harvester, Brighton, 1981, pp. 18–19.
4   Ferrand Spence, writing in 1686, quoted in Gunnar Sorelius, '*The*

Giant Race Before the Flood': Pre-Restoration Drama on the Stage and in the Criticism of the Restoration, Almquist & Wiksells, Uppsala, 1966, p. 91.

5 Gérard Genette, 'Vraisemblance et motivation', in *Figures II*, Editions du Seuil, Paris, 1969.

6 Walter Nash, *The Language of Humour*, Longman, London, 1985, p. 116.

7 On Chaplin's use of mime as a means of transposition, see Dan Kamin, *Charlie Chaplin's One-Man Show*, Methuen, London, 1984, esp. pp. 37–55.

8 Quoted in Leonard Maltin, *Of Mice and Magic, A History of American Animated Cartoons*, New American Library, New York, 1987, p. 26.

9 See Boris Tomashevsky, 'Thematics', in Lee T. Lemon and Marion J. Reis (eds), *Russian Formalist Criticism: Four Essays*, University of Nebraska Press, Lincoln, 1965.

10 For extensive discussion of a number of other examples, see Seidman, op. cit., pp. 19–57.

11 Mick Eaton, 'Laughter in the dark', *Screen*, vol. 22, no. 2, 1981, p. 25.

12 Frank Krutnick, 'The clown prints of comedy', *Screen*, vol. 25, nos 4–5, July–October 1984, p. 58.

6 Hollywood, comedy, and the Case of the Silent Slapstick

1 See David Bordwell, Janet Staiger, and Kristin Thompson, *The Classical Hollywood Cinema*, Routledge & Kegan Paul, London, 1985.

2 On the history and structures of the American film industry, see Tino Balio (ed.), *The American Film Industry*, University of Wisconsin Press, Madison, 1985 edn, and Douglas Gomery, *The Hollywood Studio System*, Macmillan, London, 1985.

3 Bordwell, Staiger, and Thompson, op. cit., pp. 1–84.

4 Francis Patterson, writing in 1920, cit. ibid., p. 13.

5 See Steve Neale, *Genre*, British Film Institute, London, 1980.

6 See David Pirie (ed.), *Anatomy of the Movies*, Windward, London, 1981, pp. 108–9, for a ranking of stars in this period on the basis of the box-office earnings of the films in which they appeared.

7 Bordwell, Staiger, and Thompson, op. cit., p. 22.

8 Steve Seidman, *Comedian Comedy. A Tradition in Hollywood Film*, UMI Research Press, Ann Arbor, 1981.

9 ibid., pp. 2–3, 15–19.

10 ibid., pp. 19–57.

11 ibid., p. 29.

12   ibid., pp. 143–59. See also Frank Krutnik, 'The clown prints of comedy', *Screen*, vol. 25, nos 4–5, July–October 1984, pp. 53–7.

13   Seidman, op. cit., pp. 61–4.

14   On the history of the short in America prior to 1930, see Kalton C. Lahue, *World of Laughter, The Motion Picture Comedy Short, 1910–1930*, University of Oklahoma Press, Norman, 1966. On its history from the late 1920s on, see Leonard Maltin, *Selected Short Subjects, From Spanky to the Three Stooges*, Da Capo, New York, 1972. On the history of the Hollywood cartoon, see Leonard Maltin, *Of Mice and Magic: A History of American Animated Cartoons*, New American Library, New York, 1987 edn.

15   See Maltin, *Selected Short Subjects*, pp. 201–20.

16   On the economic role of the feature film immediately after the First World War, and its role in and for the oligopoly, see George Mitchell, 'The consolidation of the American film industry 1915–1920', *Cine-Tracts*, vol. 2, no. 2, Spring 1979.

17   Pirie, op. cit., p. 284.

18   Quoted in Tom Dardis, *Harold Lloyd: The Man on the Clock*, Viking, New York, 1983, p. 86.

19   Quoted in Donald McCaffrey, *Four Great Comedians: Chaplin, Lloyd, Keaton, Langdon*, Zwemmer, London, 1968, p. 92.

20   Dardis, op. cit., pp. 96–9; Lahue, op. cit., *passim*; Donald McCaffrey, *Three Classic Silent Screen Comedies Starring Harold Lloyd*, Associated University Presses, Cranbury and London, 1976, pp. 30–4 and 41–4.

21   Tom Gunning, 'The cinema of attraction: early film, its spectator and the avant-garde', *Wide Angle*, vol. 8, no. 3–4, 1986.

22   See Robert C. Allen, *Vaudeville and Film, 1895–1915*, Arno Press, New York, 1980, pp. 46–7.

23   Quoted in Brooks McNamara (ed.), *American Popular Entertainments*, Performing Arts Journal Publications, New York, 1983, p. 17.

24   On p. 29 of his book, *Movie-Made America: A Cultural History of American Movies* (Random House, New York, 1975), Robert Sklar claims that 'by 1904, comedies had become the staple of motion-picture production'. However, he offers no evidence, and precise facts and figures regarding this period of the cinema are hard to come by, in part because so many of the films have been lost.

25   Hartley Davis, 'In vaudeville' (1905) in Charles W. Stein (ed.), *American Vaudeville as Seen by its Contemporaries*, Da Capo, New York, 1984, p. 104.

26   George Speaight in *The Book of Clowns*, Sidgwick & Jackson, London, 1982, provides a description of a nineteenth-century circus routine involving a miller and chimney sweep very similar to that represented in the film:

The miller dressed in a white smock, entered with a sack of flour, and the black-coated chimney sweep carried a sack of soot. They started to argue and the chimney sweep laid a hand on the miller, leaving a black mark on the white smock. The miller retaliated, leaving a white mark on the black coat. They eventually came to blows and the white smock and the black coat were soon covered in soot and flour respectively. The climax of the fight was when the combatants emptied their sacks over each other so that the miller ended up all black, and the chimney sweep all white! (p. 50)

Owing to technical limitations on length, the film has clearly condensed an elaborate slapstick routine into a single, simple gag.

27 Michael David, *The Exploit of Pleasure*, Russell Sage Foundation, New York, 1911, quoted in Gunning, op. cit., p. 68.
28 David S. Hulfish, *The Motion Picture, Its Making and Its Theater*, Electricity Magazine Corporation, 1909, quoted in Bordwell, Staiger, and Thompson, op. cit., p. 174.
29 Thomas Gunning, *D. W. Griffith and the Narrator System: Narrative Structure and Industry Organization in Biograph Films, 1908–1909*, 2 vols, UMI, Ann Arbor, 1988, p. 404.
30 ibid., pp. 407–9.
31 ibid., p. 408.
32 ibid., pp. 408–9.
33 Cit., ibid., p. 191.
34 Quoted in Bordwell, Staiger, and Thompson, op. cit., p. 178.
35 Cit. ibid., p. 175.
36 Cit. ibid., p. 178.
37 See David Robinson, *The Great Funnies: A History of Film Comedy*, Studio Vista, London, 1969, pp. 11–27.
38 Quoted in McCaffrey, *Four Great Comedians*, p. 38.
39 Cit. ibid., pp. 38–9.
40 Dardis, op. cit., p. 88.
41 ibid., p. 142.
42 Buster Keaton (with Charles Samuels), *My Wonderful World of Slapstick*, Da Capo, New York, 1982 edn, pp. 173–4.
43 McCaffrey, *Four Great Comedians*.
44 Cit. ibid., p. 31.
45 ibid., p. 206.
46 David Bordwell and Kristin Thompson, *Film Art: An Introduction*, Knopf, New York, 1986 edn, pp. 142–6.
47 ibid., pp. 141–2.
48 ibid., p. 146.
49 ibid., p. 145.
50 Quoted in Raoul Sobel and David Francis, *Chaplin: Genesis of a Clown*, Quartet, London, 1977, p. 146.
51 Cit. ibid., p. 146.

52 Cit. ibid., p. 147.
53 ibid.
54 Cit. ibid., p. 148.
55 David Robinson, *Chaplin: His Life and Art*, Paladin, London, 1986, p. 171.
56 ibid., p. 171.
57 ibid., p. 172.

7 The comedy of the sexes

1 David Bordwell, Janet Staiger, and Kristen Thompson, *The Classical Hollywood Cinema*, Routledge & Kegan Paul, London, 1985, pp. 16–17.
2 Brian Henderson, 'Romantic comedy today: semi-tough or impossible?', *Film Quarterly*, vol. 31, no. 4, Summer 1978, p. 12.
3 For example, the various approaches collected in Christine Gledhill (ed.), *Home Is Where the Heart Is*, British Film Institute, London, 1987.
4 ibid., p. 161.
5 ibid., p. 160.
6 Steve Neale, 'Melodrama and tears', *Screen*, vol. 22, no. 6, Nov.–Dec. 1986, p. 21.
7 For further consideration of melodrama and fantasy cf. Elizabeth Cowie, 'Fantasia', *m/f*, no. 9, 1984, pp. 71–105.
8 Maria LaPlace, 'Producing and consuming the woman's film: discursive struggle in *Now Voyager*', in Gledhill, op. cit., p. 160.
9 See, for example, Ted Sennett's 'tribute' to this 'classic age', *Lunatics and Lovers*, Limelight, New York, 1985.
10 Henderson, op. cit., p. 12.
11 Steve Neale, *Genre*, British Film Institute, London, 1980, p. 19.
12 Henderson, op. cit., p. 13.
13 ibid.
14 Molly Haskell, *From Reverence to Rape: the Treatment of Women in the Movies*, New English Library, London, 1975, p. 126.
15 ibid., p. 127.
16 Sennett, op. cit., p. 53.
17 Ian Jarvie, 'In praise of romantic comedy', *Film*, no. 42, Winter 1965, p. 40.
18 Catherine Irene Johnson, *Contradiction in 1950's Comedy and Ideology*, University Microfilms, Ann Arbor, 1980, p. 74.
19 Quoted by Donald McCaffrey, *The Golden Age Of Sound Comedy*, Barnes/Tantivy, London, 1973, p. 136.
20 Sennett, op. cit., pp. 26 and 30.
21 Henderson, op. cit., p. 19.
22 Johnson, op. cit., p. 195.
23 Mick Eaton, 'Laughter in the dark', *Screen*, vol. 22, no. 2, 1981.

The strategy described here bears similarities to the 'sex scenes' in such *films noirs* as *Out of the Past* (1947) and *Double Indemnity* (1944) where intercourse is simultaneously suggested and denied; in such cases the intention is not to produce a 'gag' via such a 'discrepancy' but rather to suggest that something has indeed happened which cannot be directly represented and in so doing to testify to the transgressive power of illicit, extra-marital sexuality.

24 McCaffrey, op. cit., p. 13.

25 Sennett, op. cit., pp. 26–47 cites more than twenty 'Cinderella fantasy' films released between 1935 and 1941.

26 Wes D. Gehring, 'Screwball comedy: an overview', *Journal of Popular Film and TV*, vol. 13, no. 4, Winter 1986, p. 185.

27 ibid.

28 Frank Krutnik, 'The clown prints of comedy', *Screen*, vol. 25, nos 4–5, July–October 1984, pp. 55–7.

29 This Rodgers and Hart composition appeared in the Broadway musical *Babes in Arms*, filmed in 1939.

30 Johnson, op. cit., p. 125.

31 Another example of a subject treated to different effect in comedies and melodramas is what has been termed the 'Enoch Arden' theme – where complications ensue when a wife or husband is presumed dead and the surviving spouse remarries to be faced with the return of their first partner. Whereas melodramas like *The Man From Yesterday* (1932), *Tomorrow is Forever* (1946), and *Desire Me* (1947) deal with this problem in terms of its emotional complications, such comedies as *My Favourite Wife* (1940), *Too Many Husbands* (1940), and their remakes *Move Over Darling* (1963) and *Three for the show* (1955) are able to flirt with the situation's bigamous connotations while simultaneously disavowing any *intention* on behalf of the bigamist.

32 Stanley Cavell, *Pursuits Of Happiness: The Hollywood Comedy of Remarriage*, Harvard University Press, Cambridge, Mass., 1981, p. 57.

33 ibid.

34 ibid., p. 60.

35 Henderson, op. cit., p. 21.

36 Sigmund Freud, 'Creative writers and daydreaming' (1907), in *Art and Literature*, Pelican Freud Library, vol. 14, Harmondsworth, 1985, pp. 131–41.

37 Cf. Sigmund Freud, 'Beyond the pleasure principle' (1920), in *On Metapsychology*, Pelican Freud Library, vol. 11, Harmondsworth, 1984, pp. 286–7.

38 Cavell, op. cit., p. 18.

39 Krutnik, op. cit., p. 57.

40 Jarvie, op. cit., p. 40.

41 Richard Maltby, '*Baby Face*, or how Joe Breen made Barbara

Stanwyck atone for causing the Wall Street Crash', *Screen*, vol. 27, no. 2, March–April 1986, p. 26.

42   ibid.

43   Cf. Sumiko Higashi, *Virgins, Vamps and Flappers: The Silent Movie Heroine*, Eden Press, Montreal, 1978, p. 142.

44   Sennett, op. cit., pp. 20–1.

45   Maltby, op. cit., p. 31; Lea Jacobs, 'Censorship and the fallen woman cycle', in Gledhill, op. cit., pp. 103–9.

46   Cf. Anita Loos, *Kiss Hollywood Goodbye*, Penguin, Harmondsworth, 1979, pp. 42–50.

47   Sennett, op. cit., p. 20.

48   Cf. Jacobs, op. cit., p. 105.

49   Sennett, op. cit., p. 14.

50   Dana Polan, 'Blind insights and dark passages: the problem of placement in forties film', *The Velvet Light Trap*, no. 20, Summer 1983, p. 28.

51   Sennett, op. cit., pp. 197–224.

52   Cf. Brandon French's study of this film in her book *On the Verge of Revolt: Women in American Film of the Fifties*, Frederick Ungar, New York, 1978, pp. 73–83.

53   Quoted in Alexander Walker's *Sex In The Movies* (alt. *The Celluloid Sacrifice*), Penguin, Baltimore, 1968, p. 136.

54   Henderson, op. cit., p. 19.

55   A term also used by Richard Combs in his review of *Starting Over*, Monthly Film Bulletin, vol. 47, no. 553, February 1980, p. 28.

56   Interview with James Brooks on Barry Norman's *Film 88* programme, BBC TV, 17 February 1988.

8   Comedy, television, and variety

1   John Ellis, *Visible Fictions*, Routledge & Kegan Paul, London, 1982, pp. 127–32.

2   ibid., pp. 132–5.

3   Raymond Williams, *Television: Technology and Cultural Form*, Fontana, London, 1974.

4   Ellis, op. cit., pp. 132–4.

5   ibid., p. 112.

6   ibid.

7   On circus clowning and verbal comedy in the nineteenth century, see Peter Leslie, *A Hard Act to Follow*, Paddington Press, New York and London, 1978, p. 48; George Speaight, *the Book of Clowns*, Sidgwick & Jackson, London, 1982, p. 58, and Robert C. Toll, *On With the Show*, Oxford University Press, New York, 1976, p. 9. For examples of the stump speech and the sales pitch see Brooks McNamara (ed.), *American Popular Entertainments*,

Performing Arts Journal Publications, New York, 1983, pp. 30–53.

8 For examples of the clown and master of ceremonies banter, and minstrel show cross-talk, see Speaight, op. cit., p. 16 and McNamara, op. cit., pp. 74–6. On the history and conventions of the minstrel show in general, see Robert C. Toll, *Blacking Up: The Minstrel Show in Nineteenth-Century America*, Oxford University Press, London, 1974.

9 Extracted from 'Troubles by Joe Welch' in McNamara, op. cit., pp. 38–9.

10 Wilmut, op. cit., p. 26.

11 ibid., p. 53.

12 ibid.

13 Roger Wilmut, *From Fringe to Flying Circus*, Methuen, London, 1980.

14 ibid., p. 202.

15 ibid., p. 198.

16 ibid.

17 ibid., p. 197.

18 ibid., p. xvii.

19 On the production history of the *Python* series, and relations with the BBC, see, in particular, George Perry, *Life of Python*, Pavilion, London, 1983, esp. pp. 131–3 and 142–5.

9 Broadcast comedy and sit-com

1 John Ellis, *Visible Fictions*, Routledge & Kegan Paul, London, 1982, p. 27.

2 ibid., p. 28.

3 ibid., p. 113.

4 Arthur Wertheim, *Radio Comedy*, Oxford University Press, New York, 1979, p. 4.

5 ibid., pp. 5–8.

6 ibid., p. 16.

7 Howard Fink, 'The sponsors v. the nation's choice: North American radio drama', in Peter Lewis (ed.), *Radio Drama*, Longman, London, 1981, p. 187.

8 Jane Feuer, 'Narrative form in American network television', in Colin MacCabe (ed.) *High Theory/Low Culture: Analysing Popular Television and Film*, Manchester University Press, Manchester, 1986, p. 107.

9 Fink, op. cit., p. 188.

10 ibid.

11 Wertheim, op. cit., p. 4.

12 ibid., p. 88.

13 ibid.

14   ibid., pp. 90–1.
15   Mary Livingstone, Hilliard Marks, and Marcia Borie, *Jack Benny*, Doubleday, Garden City, New York, 1978, p. 65.
16   Wertheim, op. cit., p. 131.
17   ibid., pp. 131–56.
18   David Nathan, *The Laughtermakers*, Peter Owen, London, 1971, p. 21.
19   This show is available as an LP transcription, *The Jack Benny Show*, Radiola Records, MR–1147 (1984).
20   Livingstone, Marks, and Borie, op. cit., p. 90.
21   Wertheim, op. cit., p. 131.
22   Livingstone, Marks, and Borie, op. cit., p. 66.
23   Quoted by Wertheim, op. cit., p. 163.
24   ibid., pp. 172–9.
25   For further consideration of this area, see Richard B. Jewell, 'Hollywood and radio: competition and partnership in the 1930s', *Historical Journal of Film, Radio and Television*, vol. 4, no. 2, 1984.
26   Wertheim, op. cit., p. 266.
27   ibid., pp. 283–95.
28   ibid., p. 295.
29   ibid., p. 294.
30   ibid., pp. 268–9.
31   ibid., p. 336.
32   ibid., p. 329.
33   Roger Wilmut, *Kindly Leave the Stage! The Story of Variety 1919–1960*, Methuen, London, 1985, p. 26.
34   Asa Briggs, *The History of Broadcasting in the United Kingdom*, vol. 2, *The Golden Age of Broadcasting*, Oxford University Press, Oxford, 1965, p. 3.
35   ibid., p. 90.
36   Paul Alan Taylor, 'Theories of laughter and the production of television comedy', unpublished PhD thesis, Centre for Mass Communications Research, University of Leicester, 1985, p. 266.
37   Briggs, op. cit., p. 94.
38   ibid., p. 252.
39   Wilmut, op. cit., p. 129.
40   ibid., p. 130.
41   Taylor, op. cit., p. 233.
42   Wilmut, op. cit., p. 130.
43   Taylor, op. cit., p. 234.
44   Barry Took, *Laughter in the Air*, Robson/BBC, London, 1981, p. 18.
45   Wilmut, op. cit., p. 131.
46   Briggs, op. cit., p. 118.

47 John Fisher, *Funny Way To Be A Hero*, Muller, London, 1973, p. 124.
48 Ted Kavanagh, *Tommy Handley*, Hodder & Stoughton, London, 1949.
49 ibid., pp. 109–10.
50 ibid., p. 197.
51 Fisher, op. cit., p. 136.
52 Kavanagh, op. cit., p. 107.
53 Taylor, op. cit., p. 242.
54 ibid., p. 241.
55 Took, op. cit., pp. 39–40.
56 Wilmut, op. cit., p. 152.
57 ibid., p. 208.
58 Quoted in Nathan, op. cit., p. 30.
59 Wilmut, op. cit., p. 210.
60 ibid., p. 61.
61 Fisher, op. cit., p. 31.
62 Wilmut, op. cit., p. 213.
63 Took, op. cit., p. 122.
64 See Raymond Williams, *Television, Technology and Cultural Form*, Fontana, London, 1974, pp. 76–7.
65 Took, op. cit., p. 162.
66 As in Williams, op. cit., pp. 76–7.
67 Jack Gladden, 'Archie Bunker meets Mr Spoopendyke: nineteenth-century prototypes for domestic situation comedy', *Journal of Popular Culture*, vol. 10, no. 1, Summer 1976, pp. 167–79.
68 ibid., p. 176.
69 ibid., pp. 176–7.
70 ibid., p. 178.
71 ibid., pp. 178–9.
72 Cf. Leonard Maltin, *Selected Short Subjects, from Spanky to the Three Stooges*, Da Capo, New York, 1972, pp. 103–13.
73 Wertheim, op. cit., p. 31.
74 ibid.
75 ibid., p. 53.
76 Fink, op. cit., p. 119.
77 Wertheim, op. cit., p. 54.
78 ibid., p. 47.
79 ibid., p. 193.
80 ibid.
81 ibid., p. 208.
82 The Burns–Allen TV show is considered in more detail in Mick Eaton's article 'Television situation comedy', *Screen*, vol. 19, no. 4, Winter 1978/9, pp. 65–8.
83 Wertheim, op. cit., p. 246.
84 ibid., p. 259.

85   ibid., p. 330.

86   ibid., p. 383.

87   'The Amos'n'Andy music hall', an episode of which is available on the 2-LP set *The Amos'n'Andy Story*, Radiola Company, 2MR–2526.

88   Wertheim, op. cit., p. 384.

89   ibid., p. 393.

90   Feuer, op. cit., p. 109.

91   ibid., p. 112.

92   Philip Drummond, 'Structural and narrative constraints and strategies in *The Sweeney*', *Screen Education*, no. 20, August 1976, quoted in Eaton, op. cit., p. 69.

93   Eaton, op. cit., p. 69.

94   Bruce Crowther and Mike Pinfold, *Bring Me Laughter: Four Decades of TV Comedy*, Columbus, London, 1987, p. 120.

95   Quoted in Paul Kerr, 'The making of (the) MTM (show)', in Jane Feuer, Paul Kerr, and Tise Vahimagi (eds), *MTM, Quality Television*, British Film Institute, London, 1984, p. 88.

96   Jane Feuer, 'The MTM style', in Feuer, Kerr, and Vahimagi, op. cit., p. 37.

97   Eaton, op. cit., p. 73.

98   As Mick Eaton has put it, 'The ideology held by the institution of television as a machine for the production of meaning is that the family is a sufficiently stable situation, settled enough to be able to bear repetition and to deal with the onslaughts of the outside in a recognizable, characteristic way' (op. cit., p. 73).

99   Feuer, 'Narrative form', pp. 109–10.

100   ibid.

101   Feuer, 'The MTM style', pp. 44–5.

102   Francis Wheen, *Television*, Century, London, 1985, p. 208.

103   Gillian Swanson, 'Law and disorder', in Jim Cook (ed.) *BFI Dossier 17: Television Sitcom*, British Film Institute, London, 1984, p. 34.

104   Sigmund Freud, *Jokes and their Relation to the Unconscious*, Penguin Freud Library, vol. 6, Penguin, Harmondsworth, 1976, pp. 141–3.

105   ibid., p. 143.

106   Barry Curtis, 'Aspects of sitcom', in Cook, op. cit., p. 11.

107   Cf. Crowther and Pinfold, op. cit., p. 120.

108   Unless otherwise noted, the episodes of *Steptoe and Son* referred to here are drawn from the 1970s shows, repeated in 1988, and also available on home video releases.

109   Freddie Hancock and David Nathan, *Hancock*, Coronet, London, 1975, p. 34.

110   ibid., p. 83.

111 Roger Wilmut, *Tony Hancock, 'Artiste'*, Methuen, London, 1978, p. 64.
112 ibid., p. 45.
113 ibid., p. 72.
114 Took, op. cit., p. 130.
115 Wilmut, *Tony Hancock*, p. 73.
116 ibid., pp. 112–13.
117 Fisher, op. cit., p. 268.
118 Quoted by Wheen, op. cit., p. 205.
119 Eaton, op. cit., p. 74.
120 Crowther and Pinfold, op. cit., p. 65.
121 Wilmut, *Tony Hancock*, p. 40.
122 Nathan, op. cit., p. 129.
123 Stefan Zweig, *Beware Of Pity*, Penguin, Harmondsworth, 1986, p. 184.
124 Crowther and Pinfold, op. cit., p. 64.

Index

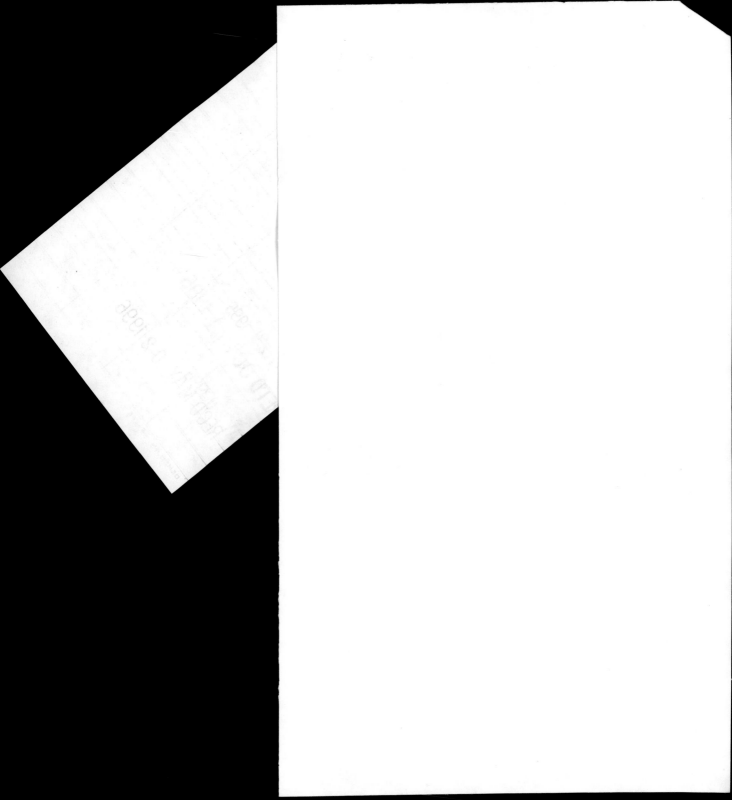

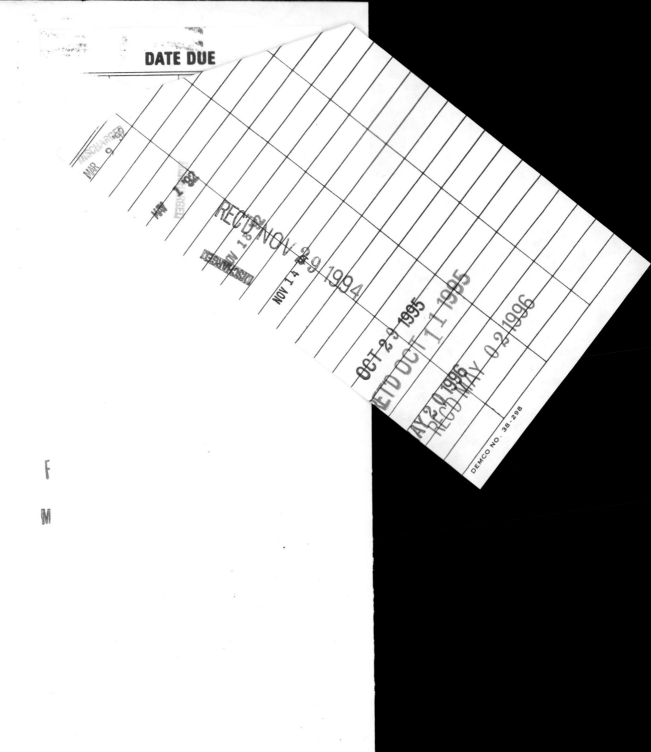